THE PROPHESIED
END-TIME

RONALD WEINLAND

the-end.com, inc., P.O. Box 551205, Dallas, TX 75355-1205
Visit our Web site at **www.the-end.com**

Library of Congress Cataloging-in-Publication Data
Weinland, Ronald.
    The Prophesied End-Time / Ronald Weinland
    ISBN: 0-9753240-0-4 (hardcover)
    ISBN: 0-9753240-1-2 (softcover)

THE PROPHESIED END-TIME

Chapter 1

THE END-TIME MESSIAH

This book will undoubtedly prove to be one of the most controversial you have ever read. Reader reaction will vary from disbelief, indignation, anger, and ridicule to eager anticipation, humility and gratitude coupled with sorrow and fear.

Reactions will also vary according to the actual time it is read. Skepticism and disbelief will fade as the events and timing of this book prove to be true.

Although this is written with strong religious content, it is not written like most religious publications: it is written to expose the glaring errors and deep-rooted hypocrisies of today's religious beliefs. People may not prefer to address religion, but religion is at the heart and core of what is currently building behind the scenes soon to explode into prophetic end-time conflict on a massive worldwide scale.

Failure to address these matters by passively ignoring the realities around us will not prevent what is coming. On the contrary, it will only exacerbate the problem.

Everything written here is timely for your life now. The impact it will have is unprecedented in all human history, and you will not have to wait long to see that these things are true.

This book is written matter-of-factly to foretell specific events that are about to come on this entire world. These events focus particularly on western Europe and the English-speaking countries referred to in specific end-time prophecies. You need to know that 9/11 will become a passing memory because far greater terror will soon strike these countries.

Much debate has followed the devastating events of 9/11 in the United States. What if...? Who is to blame? What warnings should we have looked for? What government policies could have thwarted it? What can be done to prevent such destructive terrorism in the future?

Nothing can be done, however, to prevent what is coming now. This book is written so that people might have some advance warning of what is coming. It is not written to cause panic or frighten anyone, but rather as a warning so that you can be better prepared to face these things when they happen. Not only will you need this information for yourself, but you will want to share this with others—to give help to loved ones and others you know that they too might have hope of survival.

Movies, books and religions have long-touted stories about the end of the world. Who hasn't heard of Armageddon or the four horsemen of the Apocalypse? Many are familiar with the movie *Independence Day* about an invasion of earth by beings from another world. Cartoonists, and even some who have fancied themselves prophets of God, have used signs warning "The End Is Here!" Whether it be a disaster caused by man, an asteroid from space, an invasion from another world, or some apocalyptic religious event, stories abound on library shelves and in movies that speak of the end of the world or the end of life as we know it. Sadly, because of such things, the natural reaction is to simply ridicule the whole subject.

Obviously, those who made such pronouncements were weirdos, crackpots and unsound religious zealots. However, the end-time has now come, and much of the proof has already come to pass. As the next few years pass us by, people will cease to react with scorn. Instead, they will fear what is coming next!

This book is about an "end-time" that you have never heard about before now. Many ideas about the end of the world stem from past religious interpretations of the best selling book on earth—the Bible. To confuse the issue, all of them claim to be right. However, their interpretations vary as much as do today's religious beliefs.

Individual perception is generally influenced by personal prejudices that began in childhood. This is especially true when it comes to religion (Judaism, Christianity, Islam, or any other religion). Therefore, it is logical that you could have difficulty reading this book objectively because of your prejudices. Those of traditional Christianity usually cling to specific beliefs they learned from their parents. Most Catholic homes produce Catholics. Children who are raised Baptist, Methodist, Lutheran, Church of Christ or Latter Day Saints generally grow up to continue in the same beliefs. The same is true for Jewish, Muslim and Hindu families. Such is the way of the religious world.

Events have been unfolding over the past decade that have gone unnoticed by the world. As you learn about them, you will receive help to better understand what will happen next. These events will catch the whole world off guard. They will not occur behind the scenes. These events will make the 9/11 disaster seem small by comparison.

Prophesied worldwide destruction is on the horizon. Billions are prophesied to die! You do not have another decade to prepare yourself. The urgency is now!

Religious Confusion
Religion is at the heart and core of man's deepest troubles. These troubles are about to lead into the fulfillment of end-time events. However, these events cannot be understood until we address them in their proper historical context. Today's religious confusion is at the very epicenter of what is prophesied to lead to a massive shaking of the whole world.

Initially, some of this historic review may seem a little tedious, but it is necessary. Once you begin to see what has transpired over many centuries, you will be able to more clearly grasp these deeply intriguing prophecies and their fulfillment.

Great opposition has always existed among the major faiths of Islam, Judaism and traditional Christianity. Oddly enough, all of them sprang from the same roots.

Today, as in times past, great conflict exists between Judaism and Islam even though both claim to worship the God of Abraham. Most of these people also claim Abraham as their forefather. Much conflict exists between Judaism and traditional Christianity, yet both claim to worship the same God.

Why such confusion? If there is one God, then all of them cannot be right. Who is right? As we go along, you will begin to see why there has been so much religious confusion and disagreement.

Many ironies exist in the differences among these opposing religions. One such irony that will have some impact on end-time events concerns a growing movement, in recent years, that involves a rather loosely held belief among Muslims that prophesies about an end-time leader.

Much of the Islamic world is looking for a leader to come and deliver them from the oppression of the outside world, especially the United States and her allies—Israel in particular.

A prophesied "Mahdi" is to return to restore justice to the world. This leader is to carry the name of Muhammad as part of his own, but he will not be as great as Muhammad. This Mahdi is to appear at a time of severe oppression, unite the Muslims, and bring peace and justice to the world. Some Muslims believe this Mahdi, along with the Prophet Jesus, who is also to appear at the end of time, will lead believers to victory over the infidels.

If someone claimed to be this Mahdi, at a time when many in the Muslim world increasingly believe they are being oppressed, then the idea of a great jihad (holy war) would grow in popularity. A movement is now underway that is focusing more and more upon Osama Muhammad bin Laden as being that Mahdi. Whether or not he becomes recognized as that leader, it still emphasizes the unrest that exists in much of the Islamic world.

Regardless of how a jihad becomes a reality, and it will, Islamic zealots will perpetrate far greater terrorism than 9/11. Very soon now, the loss of lives will far surpass a few thousand. It will be in the hundreds of thousands. This is difficult to accept, but it will be a reality.

Another irony, of far greater significance and interest, is one that also sheds light on this end-time. It comes from the conflicting teaching of the Jewish faith with that of traditional Christianity concerning the Biblical teaching of a Messiah.

The Jewish people have long believed that a Messiah would come to deliver their people and establish a new kingdom that will reign on this earth. Although this belief has varied through time, it has basically remained the same. Some of this will be addressed more fully as we continue.

Today, there are some differences among Jewish teachings concerning this subject.

The Reformed Jewish teaching believes in a Utopian Age, sometimes called the "Messianic Age," instead of an actual Messiah.

Conservative Jewish belief is very similar to that of the Orthodox in that the Messiah is believed to be a human being, but not divine. They believe he will restore the Jewish kingdom and extend his righteous rule over all the earth, executing judgment and righting all wrongs.

Through time, the Jewish people have longed for this prophesied Messiah to come. Today, many still look for his coming.

Judaism does not accept that the Jesus of the New Testament is that Messiah, as those in traditional Christianity profess.

Traditional Christianity believes that Jesus is the Messiah spoken of in the Old Testament but His purpose is different than that spoken of in the Old Testament concerning establishing a kingdom. Judaism and traditional Christianity believe part of the Bible story, but they can't reconcile their differences. Is there an answer?

Yes! It is quite ironic that these faiths can't put it together, for in doing so, they would learn from each other. Rather than rely on what has been handed down as a matter of traditional belief among each group from generation to generation, it is wise to focus on what the Bible has to say on the subject. The Bible tells a story that is plain and straightforward, but religious paradigms have imprisoned people in traditional teachings. As a result, their minds are closed; they are blind to the plain truth as it is written.

By looking at two prophecies in the Old Testament, regarding a Messiah, it will become clear why Jews and Christians interpret these verses differently. Both groups are in error, albeit each group has part of the story. Each group holds a vital key that the other needs.

Only when these two groups are able to acknowledge their misinterpretation will they be able to reconcile their differences. Prophecies say they will reconcile. These same prophecies tell when they will do it.

The View From Judaism

The ideas about a great deliverer (a Messiah) are drastically different from each other. Let's notice how they are different. By understanding the background (traditional thinking) of each group, we can more clearly see why they oppose each other, and we can see why they are blinded to certain prophecies they believe they understand.

A passage in Jeremiah can help you see why Judaism and Christianity are at loggerheads over these issues.

"Behold, the days come, says the LORD, that I will raise unto David a righteous Branch, and a King shall reign and prosper, and shall execute judgment and justice in the earth. In His days

Judah shall be saved, and Israel shall dwell safely: and this is His name whereby He shall be called, THE LORD OUR RIGHTEOUS-NESS. Therefore, behold, the days come, says the LORD, that they shall no more say, The LORD lives, who brought up the children of Israel out of the land of Egypt; but, The LORD lives, who brought up and led the seed of the house of Israel out of the north country, and from all countries where I had driven them; and they shall dwell in their own land." (Jeremiah 23:5-8).

If you read these verses at face value, then it should not be difficult to understand the thinking of many Jewish people through time. The history of the Jewish people is about a great struggle. They have not been well received by many peoples and nations. Their tenacity and their deep-rooted conviction surrounding their heritage and belief in God have caused them great persecution through time. Although they have seen themselves in light of this struggle, certainly the rest of the world has not.

Through time, the Jews have believed that a king would arise from among them, of the lineage of King David, and deliver them from the oppression of other peoples and nations. As these verses in Jeremiah indicate, they also believe they will be reunited, as one people in their own land, with peace and safety.

Many Jewish people believe that those things they are trying to build in Israel today are a prelude to such a time.

Perhaps the following New Testament story will make more sense to you at this point. It is the story of Jesus coming into Jerusalem, on a donkey's colt, just before his death.

"And when they drew near unto Jerusalem, and were come to Bethphage, unto the Mount of Olives, then sent Jesus two disciples, Saying unto them, Go into the village over against you, and straightway you shall find a donkey tied, and a colt with her: loose them, and bring them unto me. And if anyone says anything unto you, you shall say, The Lord has need of them, and straightway he will send them. All this was done, that it might be

fulfilled which was spoken by the prophet, saying, Tell you the daughter of Zion, Behold, your King comes unto you, meek, and sitting on a donkey, a colt, the foal of a donkey. And the disciples went, and did as Jesus commanded them, And brought the donkey and the colt, and put on them their clothes, and they set Him thereon. And a very great multitude spread their garments in the road; others cut down branches from the trees, and laid them on the road. And the multitudes that went before, and those that followed, cried, saying, Hosanna to the son of David: Blessed is He who comes in the name of the LORD; Hosanna in the highest" (Matthew 21:1-9).

What people often fail to recognize here is the sentiment of many Jewish people at that time. They were looking for a prophesied deliverer who would be their king and deliver them from the oppressive rule of the Roman Empire. They believed Jesus would fulfill those prophecies, so they greeted Him as a king, and not just any king, but the prophesied King sent from God.

It is evident, by these verses, that the Jewish people believed Jesus was a descendant of King David. They believed Jesus was the anointed one who would be their King. This news spread about Jerusalem, so much so, that even Pilate asked Jesus if He were a king. These accounts become even more meaningful, as we delve more deeply into the story.

For hundreds of years, especially during times of great oppression, the Jews have longed for these prophecies to be fulfilled. This Messiah would deliver them and bring them peace and safety. Is it any wonder that these sentiments were uppermost in the minds of Jewish people during and after the atrocities that were committed during World War II?

Here is another account of the story of Jesus coming into Jerusalem during the last few days of his life. *"On the next day many people that were come to the feast, when they heard that Jesus was coming to Jerusalem, took branches of palm trees, and went forth to meet Him, and cried, Hosanna: Blessed is the King of Israel who comes in the name of the LORD"* (John 12:12-13).

Again, those Jewish people truly believed that Jesus was the deliverer who came to them from God. The Jewish people have long believed that God would send them a king to establish a national kingdom. So, in their minds, once He had been put to death, "How could Jesus be the King of the prophecies that we have longed to see fulfilled?"

The View From Traditional Christianity

The Jewish people did not accept Jesus Christ as their Messiah because He did not deliver them or set up a national kingdom for them. On the other hand, those of traditional Christianity do accept Christ as their personal Savior, but they do not understand Him or believe the things He taught. Some in traditional Christianity have even gone so far as to say that the suffering of the Jews in the Holocaust was punishment for the murder of Jesus Christ centuries earlier. This notion is certainly perverted; it will be discussed further later in this book.

It is true that traditional Christianity embraces a number of Old Testament scriptures that have been fulfilled in Jesus Christ, but at the same time, it has overlooked vital keys that the Jewish faith embraces.

Although Jewish believers keep an annual Passover (killing and eating a lamb), they do not accept Jesus Christ as the fulfillment of that Passover lamb. Traditional Christians do accept Him, even though, as already mentioned, they do not understand the things He taught.

This understanding is clearly spoken of by the apostle Paul. *"Purge out therefore the old leaven* [In the Old Testament leaven is symbolic of sin.], *that you may be a new lump, as you are unleavened. For even Christ our Passover is sacrificed for us:"* (1 Corinthians 5:7).

The teaching of Jesus Christ coming as the Lamb of God to be sacrificed for all mankind—to die for all sin—is a basic tenet of Christian faith. Paul shows that these beliefs come from Old Testament scriptures. *"For I delivered unto you first of all that which I also received, how that Christ died for our sins according to the scriptures;"* (1 Corinthians 15:3).

The apostles quoted numerous Old Testament scriptures to show how Jesus Christ fulfilled them.

"Surely He has borne our griefs, and carried our sorrows: yet we did esteem Him stricken, smitten of God, and afflicted. But He was wounded for our transgressions, He was bruised for our iniquities: the chastisement of our peace was upon Him; and with His stripes we are healed. All we like sheep have gone astray; we have turned every one to his own way; and the LORD has laid on Him the iniquity of us all. He was oppressed and He was afflicted, yet He opened not his mouth: He is brought as a lamb to the slaughter, and as a sheep before her shearers is silent, so He opened not His mouth. He was taken from prison and from judgment: and who shall declare His generation? for He was cut off out of the land of the living [Jesus Christ was crucified.]*: for the transgression of my people He was stricken. And He made His grave with the wicked, and with the rich in His death* [A wealthy man, Joseph of Arimathea, received permission to have Jesus placed in his own new tomb (Mat. 27:57-60).]*; because He had done no violence, neither was any deceit in His mouth. Yet it pleased the LORD to bruise Him; He has put Him to grief: when you shall make His soul an offering for sin, He shall see His seed, He shall prolong His days, and the pleasure of the LORD shall prosper in His hand. He shall see the travail of His soul, and shall be satisfied: by His knowledge shall my righteous servant justify many; for He shall bear their iniquities. Therefore will I divide Him a portion with the great, and He shall divide the spoil with the strong; because He*

has poured out His soul unto death: and He was numbered with the transgressors [Jesus was crucified along with two thieves (Mark 15:27).]; *and He bore the sin of many, and made intercession for the transgressors"* (Isaiah 53:4-12).

Again, the Jewish faith does not accept that Jesus Christ fulfilled the symbolism contained in the annual observance of Passover, but the Christian faith does. This is one of two areas that are, at this time, irreconcilable between the Jewish faith and the Christian faith, yet the Old Testament clearly teaches that the Messiah would be put to death for the sins of mankind and be resurrected. The Jewish faith refuses to acknowledge this truth, yet this is a vital key that Christianity holds. Although both religious groups hold a vital key to the truth, they are unable to reconcile their differences. Therefore, they don't understand the far greater revelation concerning the role of the prophesied Messiah, as given in Old Testament scriptures.

There is an area of scripture that could help unravel the discrepancies between these two opposing faiths. If they would simply acknowledge what is stated in these verses, then they would be able to reconcile with each other.

Peter and the other apostles were gathered together to observe the annual Holy Day of Pentecost. On this occasion, soon after the death and resurrection of Jesus Christ, Peter quotes Old Testament scriptures from the Psalms about David. Neither Judaism nor traditional Christianity grasps the significance of these scriptures from the Old Testament.

"You men of Israel, hear these words; Jesus of Nazareth, a man approved by God among you by miracles and wonders and signs, which God did through Him in the midst of you, as you yourselves also know: Him, being delivered by the determined purpose and foreknowledge of God, you have taken, and by lawless hands have crucified and slain: Whom God has raised up, having loosed the pains of death: because it was not possible that He should be held

by it" (Acts 2:22-24). Peter is speaking of the Messiah who would be put to death and then resurrected, just as prophecy had declared.

Peter is quoting Psalm 16 where David writes, not about himself, but about one to come who would die and then be resurrected, whose body would not be left in sheol (Hebrew for "grave"), and thus would not have time to physically decay.

"I have set the LORD always before me: because He is at my right hand, I shall not be moved. Therefore my heart is glad, and my glory rejoices: my flesh also shall rest in hope. For you will not leave my soul in _hell_ [Hebrew – sheol, meaning "the grave"]*; neither will you allow your Holy One to see corruption. You will show me the path of life: in your presence is fullness of joy; at your right hand are pleasures for evermore"* (Psalms 16:8-11).

Peter continued by making it clear that David could not have been writing about himself.

"For David spoke concerning Him, I foresaw the LORD always before my face, for He is on my right hand, that I should not be moved: Therefore did my heart rejoice, and my tongue was glad; moreover also my flesh shall rest in hope: Because you will not leave my soul in _hell_ [This is the Greek word "hades" meaning "the grave" and corresponds to the word "sheol" in Hebrew.]*, neither will you allow your Holy One to see* _corruption_ [physical decay following death]*. You have made known to me the ways of life; you shall make me full of joy with your countenance* [In the literal presence of God.]*. Men and brethren, let me freely speak unto you of the patriarch David, that he is both dead and buried, and his tomb is with us unto this day"* (Acts 2:25-29). By quoting Psalm 16, Peter was plainly showing that David was not speaking of himself because his physical body did see corruption, as it decayed in the tomb.

David wrote in another Psalm, *"The LORD said unto my Lord, Sit you at my right hand, until I make your enemies your footstool"* (Psalm 110:1).

Peter also quotes this same Psalm to show that David was speaking of someone other than himself because these things were not fulfilled by David. *"For David is not ascended into the heavens: but he says himself, The LORD said unto my Lord, Sit you at my right hand, Until I make your foes your footstool* (Acts 2:34-35). David clearly states that the <u>LORD</u> (Yahveh, the Eternal God) said unto his (David's) Lord (Messiah the King) that He (the Messiah) would sit at His (the Eternal's) right hand.

God made promises to David regarding the future of his throne. Some of those promises would be fulfilled by successive generations that would follow David, beginning with Solomon. Many of those blessings would be dependent upon the kind of life those future generations of kings would choose to live. However, David also understood that promises were being made concerning a future time when David's own throne would be established forever, when one of David's descendants—the Messiah—would sit upon that throne.

As Peter reminded people of different Psalms written by David himself, as well as familiar prophecies from Isaiah and Jeremiah, he went on to add, *"Therefore being a prophet and knowing that God had sworn with an oath to him, that of the <u>fruit of his body</u>* [a descendant of David], *according to the flesh, He would raise up Christ to sit on his throne* [David's throne]; *He, seeing this before spoke of the resurrection of Christ, that His soul was not left in hell, neither His flesh did see corruption"* (Acts 2:30-31).

Some of the things Peter told those Jewish people were from prophecies they knew. One of those was mentioned earlier, but it needs to be repeated here.

"Behold, the days come, says the LORD, that I will raise unto David a righteous Branch, and a King shall reign and prosper, and shall execute judgment and justice in the earth. In His days Judah will be saved, and Israel shall dwell safely: and this is his name whereby He shall be called, THE LORD OUR RIGHTEOUSNESS"

(Jeremiah 23:5-6).

Peter concludes this context by saying, *"Therefore let all the house of Israel know assuredly, that God has made that same Jesus, whom you have crucified, both Lord and Christ"* (Acts 2:36).

The Two Reconciled

In this story about Pentecost two vastly irreconcilable differences between Judaism and traditional Christianity have been broached.

Traditional Christianity does believe that Jesus is the Christ and He came as the Passover lamb so mankind might be saved through His death—the ultimate sacrifice for sins. He is recognized as having died and been resurrected to sit at the right hand of God, just as the Old Testament prophecies foretold.

But traditional Christianity does not understand a vital role of the Messiah that Judaism does recognize. Most of Judaism does adhere to the belief that, at a future time, the Messiah will come and establish his throne over Judah and all Israel. Some in Judaism believe that this throne will eventually extend over all the earth. Christianity does not understand that the Messiah is indeed to reign on this earth, not in heaven. Even in this, Judaism has only partial understanding.

The dilemma is that neither faith understands the timing of events recorded in scripture. Judaism looks for a Messiah to come and sees him as coming only to accomplish what the scriptures prophesy concerning His kingdom. It does not grasp that prophecy clearly shows He was to fulfill two unique roles at two separate times on this earth. The first fulfillment was to be born of human flesh of the lineage of David, and as Peter quoted from Old Testament scriptures, the Messiah would die and be resurrected to sit at the right hand of God.

The second fulfillment is the establishment of a literal Kingdom on this earth. That time is referred to throughout the Bible as the end-time—a time at the end. You cannot understand this time of the end until you know what has been happening on the earth throughout the ages concerning God's plan and purpose for all mankind.

Judaism fails to grasp that the Messiah's role was to come in a physical life first. He would die for all mankind and be resurrected to be in heaven with the Eternal God until the time of the end. Then He would come to this earth a second time to establish God's Kingdom on the earth, not just over Judah and all Israel—but over all the earth!

Although Judaism does recognize there will be a Kingdom, they do not understand how, when and through whom it will be established.

Traditional Christianity calls Jesus the Christ, the Messiah, but they do not acknowledge His Kingdom that will come to rule this earth at the end-time. They have clouded the literal Kingdom that is to come to this earth with a type of kingdom they believe is in heaven. They believe mankind must come to "accept Jesus Christ as personal Savior," so that at death, they will be resurrected into heaven. But heaven is not the Kingdom spoken of in prophecy, over which the Messiah is to reign.

We are nearing a transition in time when many in traditional Christianity will begin to acknowledge that Jesus is indeed the Messiah who is going to come to reign in His Kingdom on this earth. We are nearing the prophetic time when many in Judaism will begin to acknowledge that the Messiah is coming, and that he is that Jesus who was on this earth 2,000 years ago as the Passover of all mankind. These people do not at this time believe these things to be true, but events are about to commence that will cause many of them to change their minds and acknowledge that Jesus Christ is coming to rule this earth.

A Kingdom On This Earth!

Traditional Christianity teaches that the Kingdom of God is in heaven or in one's heart. Heaven is described as the place one hopes to go after death. But traditional Christianity needs to carefully review some very obvious scriptures that reveal the truth about this matter, as well as other scriptures that show Christ as a King who is to reign on this earth.

We have already quoted Peter's very candid statement regarding David. He said, *"Men and brethren, let me speak freely unto you of the patriarch David, that he is both dead and buried, and his tomb is with us unto this day"* (Acts 2:29). Peter went on to say, *"For David is not ascended into the heavens..."* (Acts 2:34).

It seems difficult for most people to accept that when people die, they are indeed dead, and they stay in that state until they are resurrected. The physical body returns to the dust of the earth. That is why the prophecy concerning the Messiah's physical body not seeing corruption (physical decay) is so important. He was going to be different from others, in that after his death, his body would not decay, but be resurrected.

How can these verses be reconciled with the beliefs of traditional Christianity? How is it that David could still be in his grave, not in heaven? What kind of a man was David? God said that he was a man after His own heart. How is it then that David, who wrote so many of the Psalms, did not go to heaven?

And what about the very words of Jesus Christ? He said, *"And no man has ascended up to heaven, but He who came down from heaven, even the Son of man who is in heaven"* (John 3:13). If the words of Jesus Christ are true, then how can traditional Christianity say that people have gone to heaven when Jesus says that no one has gone there? The scriptures show that the Son of Man is the only one who has gone to heaven. Christ said these things before He died and was resurrected. Notice what is stated later in the book of John. *"Then said Jesus unto them, Yet a little while am I with you, and then I go unto Him who sent me. You shall seek me, and shall not find me: and where I am, there you cannot come"* (Jn. 7:33-34).

Traditional Christianity teaches that the soul goes to heaven or hell at death. It teaches that the soul is the essence of a person that can leave the physical body after death. This is not a biblical teaching. It is recorded twice in Ezekiel 18 that *"the soul that sins, it shall die."* "The soul" is simply a biblical expression for describing the essence of life that makes up every living creature. Even animals are described as being "living souls."

James writes about the soul that can die. *"Brethren, if any of you do err from the truth, and one converts him; Let him know, that he who turns a sinner from the error of his way shall save a soul from death, and shall hide a multitude of sins"* (James 5:19-20). If the soul automatically goes to either heaven or hell upon death, how is it possible that it could die?

The truth is that mankind does not go to heaven after death. The clear teaching of the Bible is that mankind dies and awaits a resurrection from God at God's appointed time. Understanding the role of the Messiah will also help you to understand when God will resurrect all who have ever died.

A Worldwide Government

When people read the Bible, they skim over most of it because it doesn't make sense to them. Some believe that much of the Bible is simply a mystery. That is partly true because until God reveals the meaning mankind cannot fully understand. Preachers and Bible scholars do not understand most of God's plan and purpose, therefore, they can't explain it to others.

An example of scripture that has perplexed traditional Christianity is in the twentieth chapter of Revelation. It is about a future event called the "first resurrection," but it also speaks of a "second death."

"Blessed and holy is he who has part in the first resurrection: On such the second death has no power, ..." (Revelation 20:6). What is this "first resurrection," and what is this "second death?"

Can someone actually die twice? And if they can die twice, then how is it possible that they are able to live twice, in order to die twice? This is written in the New Testament, but traditional Christianity doesn't address it—they don't understand it.

Understanding the first resurrection and the second death is only possible when you know God's overall plan for mankind. Yet, even that requires more knowledge about the role of the Messiah, who is coming, a second time, to establish a Kingdom on earth.

On Passover, when He stood before Pilate to be judged, Jesus made statements that should stand out to us. However, people pass over them, blinded to their implication. Jesus' answers to Pilate are hidden from understanding because people don't understand the Messiah's role in God's plan for mankind on this earth.

"Then Pilate entered into the judgment hall again, and called Jesus, and said unto Him, Are you <u>the King</u> of the Jews? Jesus answered him, Do you say this thing of yourself, or did others tell you this of me? Pilate answered, Am I a Jew? Your own nation and the chief priests have delivered you unto me: what have you done? Jesus answered, <u>My kingdom</u> is not of this world: if my kingdom were of this world, then would my servants fight, that I should not be delivered to the Jews: but now is <u>my kingdom</u> not from here. Pilate therefore said unto Him, Are you a king then? Jesus answered, You say that I am a king. <u>To this end was I born</u>, and for this cause came I into the world, that I should bear witness unto the truth. Every one who is of the truth hears my voice" (John 18:33-37).

One of the primary accusations brought by leading Jews at that time had to do with a movement from other Jewish people who began to look upon Jesus as the Messiah—the prophesied King of Israel. *"On the next day many people that were come to the feast, when they heard that Jesus was coming to Jerusalem, Took branches of palm trees and went forth to meet Him, and cried, Hosanna: Blessed is the King of Israel who comes in the name of the LORD"* (John 12:12-13).

If the Jewish leaders were going to get help from the Roman government to execute Jesus, then they had to have cause. They misused what others said about His being the King of Israel who had come to deliver them. If they accused Jesus of claiming to be that King, then He would have been considered subversive to the Roman government, which would then put Him to death.

In this account, Pilate asked Jesus if He were a king. What was His response? Jesus said, "My kingdom is not of this world." What does that mean? Again, the understanding of God's Kingdom and Christ's role in God's plan will give you the answer.

Although the Messiah's timing for coming to establish the Kingdom of God on the earth is evident in the New Testament, traditional Christianity does not recognize it.

If anyone believes that the New Testament is the inspired word of God, then that person should pay special attention to what John wrote at the very beginning of the Book of Revelation. *"The Revelation of Jesus Christ, which God gave unto Him, to show unto His servants things which must shortly come to pass; and He sent and signified it by His angel unto His servant John: Who bore* <u>*record*</u> *of the word of God, and of the* <u>*testimony*</u> *of Jesus Christ, and of all things that he saw. Blessed is he who reads, and they who hear the words of this prophecy, and keep those things which are written therein: for the time is at hand"* (Revelation 1:1-3).

The words "record" and "testimony" are the same Greek word. It is used much like we would use it in the context of a court of law, when witnesses give testimony. These verses are saying that record (witness) is given by these words from God to Jesus Christ and that John is the witness of the testimony given by Jesus Christ. If people believe this, then they must accept what God has given to be recorded. If someone will not receive these words as being true, then they are actually calling God and Jesus Christ liars. They are saying that their testimony is not true!

Notice the emphasis God places on these verses. At the end of this book it says, *"For I testify unto every man who hears the words of the prophecy of this book, If any man shall add unto these things, God shall add unto him the plagues that are written in this book: And if any man shall take away from the words of the book of this prophecy, God shall take away his part out of the book of life, and out of the holy city, and from the things which are written in this book. He who <u>testifies</u> these things says, Surely I come quickly. Amen. Even so, come, Lord Jesus"* (Revelation 22:18-20).

These are strong words of warning! Notice that Jesus Christ is coming quickly. If you understand the timing and fulfillment of Revelation, then these words will greatly impact your life. And, if Jesus Christ is coming quickly, why is He coming, and to what? The plea is made even stronger by the words, "Even so, come, Lord Jesus!"

The coming of Jesus Christ is described in powerful terms in Revelation. Why hasn't traditional Christianity embraced these words and tried to understand them as Judaism has, at least in part—that the Messiah is coming to reign over a literal Kingdom on this earth. Every reader needs to pause and consider this theme as it runs through the Book of Revelation—that Jesus Christ is coming to rule over the entire earth.

Let's read, once again, a sobering admonition at the beginning of Revelation. *"Blessed is he who reads, and they who hear the words of this prophecy, and keep those things which are written therein: for the time is at hand"* (Revelation 1:3). This book is written in the context of end-time events. These events lead to a time referred to as the day of the Lord's wrath—a time of judgment on the earth—a time when Jesus Christ will establish God's Kingdom on the earth. That day is described as being near when these prophecies begin to be fulfilled. When that time period begins, hold onto those things you have learned.

"And from Jesus Christ, who is the <u>faithful witness</u>, and the first

begotten of the dead, and the prince of the kings of the earth. Unto Him who loved us, and washed us from our sins in His own blood, And has made us kings and priests unto God and His Father..." (Revelation 1:5-6).

These verses reveal a related theme that also runs through this book—the resurrection that takes place when Jesus Christ comes to this earth. Those who are resurrected then will be given rulership with Jesus Christ—as priests and kings of a literal government.

At one point, these same people are described as being redeemed from different races and nationalities on the earth (physical human beings through time) through the blood of Jesus Christ. But notice what it says about their future role. *"...For You were slain, and have redeemed us to God by your blood out of every kindred, and tongue, and people, and nation; And have made us unto our God kings and priests: and we shall reign on the earth"* (Rev. 5:9-10).

These are further described as being a very specific number who have indeed been redeemed from the earth over the previous 6,000 years.

"And I looked, and, behold, a Lamb stood on the Mount Zion, and with Him one hundred and forty-four thousand, having His Father's name written in their foreheads. And I heard a voice from heaven, as the voice of many waters, and as the voice of a great thunder: and I heard the sound of harpists with their harps: And they sang as it were a new song before the throne, and before the four living creatures, and the elders: and no one could learn that song but the hundred and forty-four thousand who were redeemed from the earth" (Revelation 14:1-3).

As the story continues, these again are described as ruling with Jesus Christ. *"And I saw thrones, and they sat upon them, and judgment was given unto them: ...and they lived and reigned with Christ for a thousand years"* (Revelation 20:4). *"...but they shall be priests of God and of Christ, and shall reign with Him a thousand years"* (Verse 6).

Not only is this group referred to as reigning with Jesus Christ when He comes, but the actual period of time of this reign is also revealed—a thousand years.

Concerning this theme of the end-time that culminates in the return of Jesus Christ, we need to follow the story flow as it progresses through Revelation. End-time events begin when Jesus Christ opens the first seal of Revelation. As each seal is opened, of course the opening of the last seal—seventh seal draws nearer. The opening of the seventh seal begins a series of end-time events that culminates with the return of Jesus Christ to establish the Kingdom of God on earth. The opening of these seals will be covered in detail later in this book. At this point, it should be interesting to the reader to know that six of the seven seals have already been opened, and the seventh is very soon to follow. You live at the most climactic time of all human history.

The coming of Jesus Christ will happen on the Day of the Lord, which is at the very end of this age. It marks the beginning of a new age for mankind on the earth when the government—the Kingdom of God will reign. Once the seventh seal is opened, a series of seven trumpets is blown, revealing a sequence of events that will occur over a three and one-half year time period.

"And the seventh angel sounded: and there were great voices in heaven, saying, The kingdoms of this world have become the kingdoms of our Lord, and of His Christ; and He shall reign for ever and ever" (Revelation 11:15). This describes the coming of the Messiah and His reign over all nations of the earth. The initial reign of that Kingdom lasts for a thousand years, but events that follow will extend that reign into all time. Those events will be addressed later.

As described earlier, Judaism and traditional Christianity have always been at a great impasse concerning the role of the Messiah. Judaism understands, in a limited way, that the Messiah is to establish a Kingdom on this earth, but they believe it is a Jewish kingdom. They believe the Messiah (a human being who is not divine) will extend his righteous rule over the earth, execute judgment and right all wrongs.

Traditional Christianity sees the Messiah as the Lamb of God who came and died for everyone. Therefore, it is difficult for many to see Jesus as a King reigning over the nations with great power, yet that is how He is described. *"And I saw heaven opened, and behold a white horse; and He who sat upon him was called Faithful and True, and in righteousness He does judge and make war. His eyes were as a flame of fire, and on His head were many crowns; and He had a name written, that no man knew, but He Himself. And He was clothed with a robe dipped in blood: and His name is called The Word of God. And the armies in heaven followed Him upon white horses, clothed in fine linen, white and clean. And out of His mouth goes a sharp sword, that with it He should strike the nations: and He shall rule them with a rod of iron: and He Himself treads the winepress of the fierceness and wrath of Almighty God. And He has on His robe and on His thigh a name written, KING OF KINGS AND LORD OF LORDS"* (Revelation 19:11-16).

This story of Christ coming to rule on the earth, in the Kingdom of God, is a story referred to throughout the New Testament as the gospel (Greek for "good news"). However, much of traditional Christianity has limited the gospel to a message about the personage of Jesus Christ. Therefore, they overlook the good news that Jesus Christ brought: He is returning to establish the Kingdom of God to rule and reign on the earth!

The Gospel of the Kingdom of God

Not only have Judaism and traditional Christianity been at odds with each other over the role of the Messiah, both have misunderstood the revelation to mankind from their God. The Bible is a continuing revelation, from Genesis to Revelation, of God's plan and purpose for mankind. Over the past six thousand years of history—mankind's time on earth since Adam and Eve—God has been progressively revealing His plan and purpose.

This progressive revelation is described in scripture as the gospel—the good news.

The Book of Mark begins by announcing that someone would come to prepare the way for the coming (first coming) of Jesus Christ. This "someone" was John the Baptist. But Mark actually begins by saying, *"The <u>beginning of the gospel</u> of Jesus Christ, the Son of God; As it is written in the prophets, Behold, I send My messenger before your face, who shall prepare your way before you. The voice of one crying in the wilderness, Prepare you the way of the Lord, make His paths straight. John did baptize in the wilderness, and preach the baptism of repentance for the remission of sins"* (Mark 1:1-4).

It says that this is the beginning of the gospel of Jesus Christ. It does not say it is a gospel about the personage of Jesus Christ. Instead, it is clearly the beginning of good news being given by Jesus Christ. This good news was the message that Jesus Christ came to preach and reveal to mankind, at that time. It was a message about the very plan and purpose of God, which is being accomplished through Jesus Christ.

The "beginning" of that good news was the message He started to teach as soon as His ministry began, after John prepared the way. Let's focus on part of the message of Jesus Christ that remains clouded, due to the narrow-sightedness of traditional Christianity, concerning the fully revealed purpose of the Messiah—the Christ.

"Now after that John was put in prison, Jesus came into Galilee, preaching <u>the gospel of the kingdom of God</u>, And saying, The time is fulfilled, and <u>the kingdom of God</u> is at hand: Repent you, and <u>believe the gospel</u>" (Mark 1:14).

Jesus Christ began preaching a message of good news about the Kingdom of God. He said the time for that Kingdom was at hand. It was at hand because the One who will reign in that Kingdom was then on the earth. He was not going to establish His Kingdom then, but He was bringing good news concerning it.

Jesus brought this same good news as He went about preaching to the Jews on the Sabbath. *"And Jesus went about all Galilee, teaching in their synagogues, and preaching the gospel of the kingdom..."* (Matthew 4:23).

This was such an important message that He even included it in His instructions to the disciples on how to pray. He gave them an outline for prayer: *"After this manner therefore pray you: Our Father in heaven, Hallowed be your name. Your kingdom come..."* (Matthew 6:9-10). The outline ends with Jesus Christ again showing the importance of the Kingdom. *"And lead us not into temptation, but deliver us from evil: For yours is the kingdom, and the power, and the glory, for ever. Amen"* (Matthew 6:13). The lesson to be learned is that the Kingdom is in the power of God the Father.

Jesus Christ revealed that it is God's will that mankind look forward to the time when He would bring His world-ruling Kingdom to this earth. This was to be a central focus for mankind, so much so, that Jesus Christ said one should pray, with desire, to see that Kingdom come to this earth.

Christ admonished His followers to focus on the purpose of God's Kingdom. *"But seek you first the kingdom of God, and His righteousness..."* (Matthew 6:33). The importance of this Kingdom was emphasized by equating the desire to see that Kingdom come with that of seeking the very righteousness of God in one's life.

Jesus used numerous parables to teach about this Kingdom. On one occasion he gave the people a particular parable because they thought the Kingdom was to come right then. *"And as they heard these things, He added and spoke a parable, because He was near unto Jerusalem, and because they thought that the kingdom of God should immediately appear. He said therefore, A certain nobleman went into a far country to receive for himself a kingdom, and to return*. *And he called his ten servants, and delivered them ten pounds, and said unto them, Put it to work till I come. But his citizens hated him, and sent a message after him, saying, We will not have this man to reign over us"* (Luke 19:11-14). Jesus Christ gave this parable to describe, in part, what would prophetically happen concerning the Kingdom. He described himself as the nobleman who went into a far country (heaven). This He did after His death and resurrection. Later, in these same verses, He explained how He would return later and demand an answer from His servants concerning what they had done with what had been given them. This parable also brings out an age-old truth: mankind does not really want the Kingdom of God to reign over him.

A Kingdom is about to come to this earth to reign over God's creation, but man does not want it. Regardless of man's wishes, God's world-ruling government is coming. Whether the world believes it or wants it is not important. Jesus Christ is coming as soon as end-time events are finished!

Notice what the following scripture says concerning the commencement of end-time events:

"And Jesus went out, and departed from the temple: and His disciples came to Him to show Him the buildings of the temple. And Jesus said unto them, See you not all these things? verily I say unto you, There shall not be left here one stone upon another, that shall not be thrown down. And as He sat upon the Mount of Olives, the disciples came to Him privately, saying, Tell us, when shall these things be? and what will be the sign of Your coming, and of the end of the world [Gk.– "age"]*?"* (Matthew 24:1-3).

The disciples were admiring the buildings of the temple as they walked with Jesus. Christ told them that there would come a time when all the stones of the temple would be cast down—not one stone left upon another. Most scholars think this means the literal destruction of the temple in Jerusalem. They fail to recognize that Christ was speaking of a future event that would take place in the spiritual temple of God—the Church.

The same type of misunderstanding occurred when the Jews asked Christ for a sign, and He told them, *"destroy this temple, and in three days I will raise it up"* (John 2:19). They mocked Him because they thought He was speaking of the physical temple. In both cases, the people didn't understand the spiritual application of what Christ was telling them.

After this, the disciples wanted to know more about the specific timing of this event and the sign of His coming and the end of the age.

The word "age" is sometimes translated as "world." That is why many believe this is speaking of the very end of the world. But it is not speaking of apocalyptic events that will destroy the world. It is speaking of a "specific time" in the world—an end-time. This is in context with other Biblical prophecies that speak of an end-time. This is when apocalyptic events will happen on the earth, not to destroy it, but to bring an end to man's rulership on the earth and usher in a new era—the Kingdom of God.

That is why Pilate's question for Jesus has such significance.

"Then Pilate entered into the judgment hall again, and called Jesus, and said unto Him, Are you the King of the Jews? Jesus answered him, Are you saying this thing of yourself, or did others tell you this of me? Pilate answered, Am I a Jew? Your own nation and the chief priests have delivered you unto me: what have you done? Jesus answered, My kingdom is not of this <u>world</u>: if my kingdom were of this <u>world</u>, then would my servants fight, that I should not be delivered to the Jews: but now is <u>my kingdom</u> not from here. Pilate therefore said unto Him, Are you a king then? Jesus answered, You say that I am a king. To this end was I born, and for this cause came I into the world, that I should bear witness unto the truth. Every one who is of the truth hears my voice" (John 18:33-37).

In these verses, the word "world" has been translated from the same Greek word (kosmos) as the word "age" in Matthew 24. This word, translated as "world," is usually used in a context referring to mankind, in the world. In a well known verse, often quoted by traditional Christianity, it says, "God so loved the world that He gave His only begotten Son." Most understand this, by the context alone, to mean mankind (the people) not the physical world (the earth).

Christ was literally saying that His Kingdom was not of man's world. His Kingdom would follow this age—this time of man's rulership in the world. Mankind will no longer rule himself, but he will be ruled by the Kingdom of God—in this new age. That is the continuing revelation of the Bible, the "good news," the gospel. Jesus Christ will come at the end of man's time and finally bring true peace and prosperity for everyone in God's time!

Before the "good news" of God's Kingdom can take place, the world must go through a final three and a half years of great tribulation, which will bring an end to the governments of man. The world will resist and fight against that Kingdom. This is the final stage of end-time events spoken of throughout the Bible. These events will culminate in a final and horrific third world-war. The story will be covered thoroughly in the chapters to follow.

The Kingdom is Spiritual

One area of understanding still needs to be clarified in regard to the Kingdom of God. This Kingdom will reign on the earth, beginning at the return of Jesus Christ. However, those living on the earth will not be <u>in</u> that Kingdom. They will merely be ruled over by it.

Many in traditional Christianity do not understand this message because they teach that the Kingdom is about heaven. Much of this confusion comes from scriptures that refer to the Kingdom in the context of heaven. Therefore, they believe they must go to heaven to be in the Kingdom. They simply fail to grasp that the Kingdom comes from God. It receives its power and authority from God, but it will come to reign on the earth at the end of this age. But what is that Kingdom?

"Then Jesus said unto His disciples, verily I say unto you, That a rich man shall hardly enter into the <u>*kingdom of heaven*</u>. *And again I say unto you, It is easier for a camel to go through the eye of a needle, than for a rich man to enter into the* <u>*kingdom of God"*</u> (Matthew 19:23-24).

Jesus Christ is explaining how difficult it is for the rich to follow the way that leads into the Kingdom. Being rich physically or spiritually, in this context, represents an attitude about oneself. It is an attitude of pride—how human nature sees itself. It seeks to justify self. Human nature tends to see itself as right; it is wealthy in its own eyes. So much so, that it will not listen to instruction and correction from God. A mind of inflated self-worth cannot be changed against its will, yet God makes it clear that we must repent of our ways and receive the one and only true way of God, which will lead us into His Kingdom. But again, what is that Kingdom?

The "kingdom of heaven" spoken of here is the Kingdom of God. It shows the same origin—it must come from God out of heaven. Such expressions are speaking about the same thing.

This is easier to see when you begin to understand the role of the Messiah. He will come to this earth to rule in a literal Kingdom, as the King of kings. That Kingdom will rule the earth—rule over mankind for 1,000 years, as was previously shown. But what is difficult for people to grasp is that the Kingdom of God is spiritual.

God the Father—the God of Abraham, Isaac and Jacob—Yahweh (the Eternal God) of the Old Testament is a spirit being, composed of spirit. His power, by which He created the universe, is of the spirit. It is often called the Holy Spirit because it reveals the source as coming from God, who is Holy. The Holy Spirit is the power that proceeds from God. It is not a separate spirit being (sometimes called the holy ghost), as some believe.

God the Father is a spirit being, and He created other spirit beings, called angels. There is a spiritual realm. Angels dwell there. Some of those angels, along with Lucifer, rebelled against God and were cast to this earth. They became known as demons, foul spirits and fallen angels. Lucifer became known as Satan the Devil. Although these things are clearly in the Bible, few people really believe them.

Yet, God is spirit, and His Son, Jesus Christ, is now spirit. Jesus Christ was born into a physical world. His Father was Yahweh (the Eternal God) and His mother was the virgin Mary. He lived as a physical human being until He was killed—put to death as the Passover for all mankind.

The apostle Peter spoke of this by saying, *"For Christ also has once suffered for sins, the just for the unjust, that He might bring us to God, being put to death in the flesh, but made alive by the Spirit"* (1 Peter 3:18).

Jesus became the first person to be resurrected, as a spirit being, and born into a spiritual family—above that of the angelic realm. After His resurrection, He manifested Himself in human form to the disciples and taught them for forty days. Spirit beings can appear in human form when God gives them the power to do so. When these beings are in their spirit form, physical human beings cannot see them.

After Jesus was resurrected from the dead, He appeared to Mary the following morning and told her to go tell the disciples that He was now going to ascend to his Father and their Father. Later that same day, as evening drew near, Jesus came upon two people walking and He began to talk with them about the events of the past few days. However, they did not know that it was Jesus who spoke until He departed from them. But notice how He departed. *" And their eyes were opened, and they knew Him; and He vanished out of their sight"* (Luke 24:31). He simply disappeared before their very eyes.

Later that evening, Jesus appeared before the disciples. Notice the account.

"Then the same day at evening, being the first day of the week, when the doors were shut where the disciples were assembled for fear of the Jews, came Jesus and stood in the midst, and said unto them, Peace be unto you" (John 20:19). The doors where the disciples were gathered together were shut, yet Jesus Christ suddenly appeared in their presence and spoke to them.

Here is another account of this same occasion. *"And as they thus spoke, Jesus himself stood in the midst of them, and said unto them, Peace be unto you. But they were terrified and frightened, and supposed they had seen a spirit. And He said unto them, Why are you troubled? and why do doubts arise in your hearts? Behold my hands and my feet, that it is I myself: handle me and see; for a spirit has not flesh and bones, as you see me have"* (Luke 24:36-39). The disciples were so shaken that Jesus had to calm them down by letting them know that they couldn't see spirit and showing them that He had literally manifested Himself physically to them.

So when Jesus Christ comes in His Kingdom, as King of kings, to reign over this entire world, He will manifest Himself in physical form, just as He did to His disciples. Jesus Christ will be the King of kings in this Kingdom. But others, who are part of this Kingdom, will also come to this earth with Jesus Christ.

Over the past 6,000 years, God has been calling some to be inheritors with Jesus Christ in that Kingdom. They will return with Him, to reign on the earth, in the Kingdom of God. These were those spoken of earlier in this chapter. They came from different races and nationalities on the earth (physical human beings through time) and were redeemed through the blood of Jesus Christ. But notice what it says about their future role. *"... For you were slain, and have redeemed us to God by your blood out of every kindred, and tongue, and people, and nation; And have made us unto our God kings and priests: and we shall reign on the earth"* (Revelation 5:9-10).

These are the 144,000 spoken of in the Book of Revelation who are resurrected at Christ's return. They will reign with Him for 1,000 years in the Kingdom of God on this earth. God has made them kings and priests, and they will come with Jesus Christ when He returns. This Kingdom is a spiritual Kingdom because all the members are spirit beings—composed of spirit—in the Family of God.

The Kingdom of God is spiritual and will reign over mankind on the earth. Those who live out their physical lives during that time—during the millennial reign of Christ—are not part of that Kingdom. They are merely ruled over by it.

But it is God's purpose that everyone, in time, have the opportunity to become part of that same Kingdom, if they so choose. Those things will be covered more thoroughly in another chapter.

Now that the role of the Messiah—the Christ—has been addressed, we need to focus on the time in which we live. The time for Christ's return to this earth has come. We are at the end of 6,000 years of mankind's allotted time of self-rule. We are already in the prophesied time of the end. Most of the prophecies about the Church at the end-time have already been fulfilled. Those, too, will be addressed later, but first, you need to know what will happen next that will reveal the validity of the things written in this book.

You should begin to prepare yourself because great physical tribulation is about to burst forth on this earth. It is coming regardless of how you feel about it.

Chapter 2

THE SEVENTH SEAL

As this book is being written, only a short time remains before end-time cataclysmic events will begin to happen on this earth. On the other hand, as you read it, those events spoken of here may already be under way.

The soon-coming time of trouble and devastation is so great that God says there has never been a time like it during man's 6,000 year period on this earth. This great physical tribulation will last for three and a half years. Then, on the very last day, the greatest destruction of all will come upon mankind—thereby ending World War III. On that day, God Himself will bring judgment, death and destruction upon this world. On this same day, Jesus Christ, the prophesied Messiah, will return with 144,000 resurrected members of the Family of God—the Kingdom of God—to reign over this earth! A new world order, with a single world government, will begin ruling on the earth.

People of old (Abel, Noah, Job, Abraham, Sarah, Moses, David, Ruth, Daniel, Peter, Paul, John, and many others written about in the pages of the Bible) will be resurrected on that day. This may sound insane to you, but that is exactly what is coming, and it is coming soon.

God has foretold that most will not believe what is about to come to pass, not even as this world is plunged into the most cataclysmic times it has ever seen. The possibility of such events occurring may seem incredulous to you, perhaps so much so, that you don't want to read any farther. But just in case... if there is the slightest possibility... wouldn't it be wise for you to know what to look for, so that if indeed it does occur, exactly like this book says, then you can more wisely begin acting upon it?

The sooner you take personal action to deal with what will begin to rapidly unfold, the better equipped you will be to survive, and thereby give help to loved ones, so that they too may survive.

God has foretold not only the magnitude of these events, but also the countries and exact areas of the world that will experience specific plagues and cataclysms. God is even more specific when He describes the percentage of the population that will survive in certain countries.

The testimony that God gives is true concerning the end-time tribulation and the eruption of the last world war. The North American continent alone will experience a horrifying cataclysm beyond human belief. This prophetic record can be illustrated by using the combined populations of Canada and the United States as an example. Although it is somewhat larger, let's use the figure of 300 million in our illustration. The prophecies concerning this specific portion of end-time devastation are not recorded in specific numbers of people, but in percentages of population. If 300 million were the combined total, 200 million, or two-thirds, would die in the first several months. Of the remaining 100 million, only 10 percent, 10 million, would survive to live on into the new world at Jesus Christ's coming. The devastation and loss of life in certain areas of the world are even greater than this.

You cannot afford to ignore or reject that which is written in this book. Sadly, most of the world will ignore and reject it, just as people did in the days of Noah. Most people today don't even believe the story of Noah. But it is true, and yes, those of that time mocked Noah and his family. But the mocking stopped when the waters began to rise. They continued to rise until everyone was dead. Worldwide destruction is coming, but millions will have the opportunity to live on into a new world, not just one family as in the days of Noah. If you mock what is written here, then you too will cease to do so when these things become reality—if they haven't already.

This is not, nor will it be, a popular message. Nevertheless it is true, and it will happen exactly as described. God is not concerned or swayed by what is popular with mankind. After 6,000 years, it is finally time for man to listen as God begins to speak more directly to him.

This warning will be told with greater power during that final three and one-half years. Two individuals will come on the scene, backed by the power of God with signs and miracles, and they will speak boldly about the same things that are written here. You need to be aware of this so you can respond speedily because time will be short.

The Two End-Time Witnesses

Before the third and last world war bursts on the scene, two witnesses, sent by God, will begin to say and do great things on this earth. Their job will last three and one-half years. Notice what will happen to them when their task is complete.

"And when they shall have finished their testimony [Greek – "testimony or witness"]*, the beast that ascends out of the bottomless pit shall make war against them, and shall overcome them, and kill them"* (Revelation 11:7). The beast spoken of here is a military power that emerges out of Europe for the seventh and final time in history. Its power and purpose are moved and directed by the fallen angel Lucifer—Satan, who has power to influence the minds of men to do his bidding. That same being is the one who stirred Hitler and others to do his bidding during World War II.

People tend to disregard, ignore, ridicule, or even scorn such ideas and knowledge because they cannot deal with that which is from a spirit world—that which they have no earthly means to see or measure with physical, scientific evidence. But that does not change the reality of the spiritual influences at work in this world.

The apostle Paul addressed it accurately when he said, *"But the natural man* [the normal physical man, carnal man] *receives not the things of the Spirit of God: for they are foolishness unto him: neither can he know them, because they are spiritually discerned"* (1 Corinthians 2:14).

Concerning the two witnesses: we are being told that this European military complex is the power that is finally responsible for the death of these two people. It is not only God's purpose to allow this to happen, but it also stands as a final witness and sign to the world, that these two are exactly who God says they are—His two witnesses.

It goes on to say, *"And their dead bodies shall lie in the street of the great city, which spiritually is called Sodom and Egypt, where also our Lord was crucified"* (Revelation 11:8). These two will be killed in Jerusalem with the approval and authority of this European military might. The uncomplimentary label given to Jerusalem in this prophecy should be noted. God says that spiritually it is like Sodom and Egypt. Religious confusion, the source of so many of man's troubles, is the cause.

Even in His time, Jesus Christ chastened the religious leaders for their hypocrisy and lies concerning the ways of God, for which they claimed to be spokesmen. Those men did not represent God truthfully at that time, and since then, it has only gotten worse.

Today, Jerusalem is spiritually a place of confusion and conflicting religious beliefs. So many different religions claim to be the true representatives of God. Yet common sense reveals that this cannot be true.

Two years ago, my wife and I took a tour of the old city of Jerusalem. Our guide explained that it is divided into four drastically different religious persuasions. These four areas are Muslim, Judaism, Armenian, and traditional western Christianity. Even within that which constitutes traditional Christianity, countless division and diversity exist. But each group claims to be the true representative of God—that it alone has the truth, the way that leads to God.

God is the One who proclaims that Jerusalem is spiritually like Sodom and Egypt. Sodom is an explicit description of sexual lewdness and perverted behavior. So concerning Jerusalem, this constitutes a condemnation that the religions there are spiritually lewd and perverted. Egypt is a Biblical description of the way of sin from which all must be delivered.

Continuing on with the description of the death of these two witnesses, it says, *"And they of the people and kindreds and tongues and nations shall see their dead bodies three days and an half, and shall not allow their dead bodies to be put in graves. And they who dwell upon the earth shall rejoice over them, and make merry, and shall send gifts one to another; because these two prophets tormented those who dwelt on the earth"* (Rev. 11:9-10).

This is typical! Rather than address what these two have been saying and admitting they have been speaking the truth, most would rather see them dead because they blame them, rather than themselves, for the torment they have been experiencing. Most people have always hated what God tells them, and they have hated His messengers. So people have chosen to hate the messenger and have even killed most of them, rather than hear the message and change!

These two will be hated by most people because of the message they will bring to this world. These two not only carry dire warnings, from God to mankind, concerning these end-time events, but they will also have power to bring devastating plagues upon the earth. This is all part of the job that God has given them to do. But human nature being what it is, people will hate them and hate their message, not realizing or accepting that it actually comes from the Eternal God.

So upon the death of these two individuals, people will have suffered so much during that final three and a half years that they will celebrate because they believe that an end to their suffering is in sight. They can now question, "How could these two have come from God if they are lying dead in the streets of Jerusalem?" As a result, through the marvel of modern technology, those who have access to television will be able to see the proof of their death as it is broadcast on the news.

However, the death of these two prophets does not end the turmoil on this earth. On the contrary, as will be shown later, two great armies are closing in on each other, to engage in a final great battle—the greatest the world has ever seen. It is at this time that Jesus Christ returns to establish His Kingdom. In that one day, the greatest destruction and death of any single day will be poured out on the earth, this time from God, as He puts an end to mankind's self-destruction.

But as for the two witnesses, *"And after the three days and an half the spirit of life from God entered into them, and they stood upon their feet; and great fear fell upon those who saw them. And they heard a great voice from heaven saying unto them, Come up here. And they ascended up to heaven in a cloud; and their enemies beheld them. And the same hour was there a great earthquake, and a tenth part of the city fell, and in the earthquake were slain of men seven thousand: and the remnant were frightened, and gave glory to the God of heaven"* (Revelation 11:11-13).

It will be explained more fully later, but these two people are resurrected, raised from death to life, at the exact same time as the resurrection of the 144,000 who are to return to this earth to rule and reign, along with Jesus Christ, in His Kingdom.

Power Given the Two Witnesses

Even though these prophesied events may seem too far-fetched for you to believe at the time you read this, consider it all, because not too long from now it will become very real to you—when these things come to pass. You are now being informed and can begin preparing for what is ahead. Disregard it now if you will, but wait and watch for these two witnesses to come on the scene. Their work will not be done in a corner, but will be seen by the entire world—however, it will not be accepted as being from God.

When the two witnesses begin to tell the world that the time of the end has come, they will have great power to back up their words—what they say comes from God, for only God can perform what they prophesy. They will be informing the world that mankind has come to the end of 6,000 years of self-rule. The world will be told that 6,000 years was given to mankind to ultimately prove that man can exercise every kind of government, economic system, religious belief, family structure, educational model—and all of them would fail, as indeed all have failed. Nothing man does can produce true freedom, continuing peace, lasting happiness, prosperity, and fullness of life.

The ways of mankind are a failure because man has rejected the one and only way that will produce the positive results he has long desired—God's way. Since Adam and Eve, mankind has gone his own way, even in his religious beliefs, which he represents as being from God. Man is deceived and self-deluded—willingly so! So is it any wonder that the world will hate the message brought by these two witnesses, who will claim that their end-time message comes from the great Creator God?

Even during this last century, mankind has witnessed an age of incredible technology and an explosion of knowledge never before experienced in all the earth's history. Yet these things have not helped mankind to solve his problems or bring this world peace. The League of Nations and now the United Nations are testimony to this truth, that mankind cannot solve his own problems and cannot bring peace to this earth.

This increase in knowledge and rapid development of technology has been withheld from mankind until the very end of the 6,000 years God allotted him to rule. God restricted mankind from such technology and knowledge until this end-time because if He had not done so man would have destroyed himself from off the face of the earth long ago. We are now at a time when God must intervene, before the growth in technology leads to even more weapons of mass destruction that man will not be able to control. God has brought mankind to this point in time in order to show him that, if He did not intervene, man would indeed destroy himself.

Do you think that the discoveries in the last century were just a matter of time and chance? Or can you indeed grasp that these things where hidden from man until our time—the end-time?

We now live at the very time when God is going to bring an end to man's ways and man's governments. But before He sends His Son, the Messiah, to establish His Kingdom to reign on the earth, God is going to humble mankind so that he will not continue to resist and fight against His way. Those who continue to fight against Him will simply die.

God gave mankind "free choice," and it is that very "free moral agency" that makes him different from the animal kingdom that functions by instinct—just as it was programmed to do from creation. The animal kingdom survives by the very instinct that God programmed into it, to respond to specific matters of nature, in a specific way. Man is not so: he was not created in a robotic state—but was given a mind capable of free thought, creativity, memory, and thereby, the ability to choose his own way.

As a result of man's freedom of choice and base physical nature, he has turned inward to the way of "get" and selfishness. God is not that way! God is outward, caring for others—loving others without selfishness. God's plan was to allow man 6,000 years of self-rule to prove that he is incapable of ruling himself or others, apart from "the way" of His Creator. Man has proven exactly that in the last 6,000 years!

Now the time has come to humble mankind, so that he can admit that the destructiveness of his own ways would end in annihilation if God did not intervene. That is why the advancement of technology, in this past century, was no longer withheld from mankind—to show what man would do with it once he was allowed to have access to it. Yes, God held it back until the end-time in order to fulfill a full witness of the life of man, over 6,000 years of history.

Now the haughtiness and pride of man will be humbled by His Creator. The attitude of man will have changed once he has experienced the physical tribulation. Mankind will be ready to be delivered by God. He will be ready to receive the Kingdom of God and the worldwide rule of Jesus Christ.

God predetermined that there would be two witnesses to proclaim this end-time message to the earth. God would give them power that will work to humble man. There has never been a time like this on the earth. There was a time when God did send some plagues on the earth—on Egypt—during a time when the Israelites were in captivity there. God so humbled Egypt that they finally poured out their riches upon the Israelites because they believed that if they did not get the Israelites out of their land they would all be destroyed.

Pharaoh's attitude is indicative of the world today: pride and haughtiness fill the earth. Everyone seems to know what is best. Even in something so minor as the world of sports, people argue over what should have been done or what would have been best. Our world is full of pride! Everyone believes that their ways, their ideas, their religion, and their viewpoints are best.

It's the same in politics. All politicians proclaim that their way, their ideas and their policies are best. Nations cannot agree. With regard to the Middle East, every leader believes his ideas offer the best solution for peace. But no one can give the people of the Middle East peace. None of today's leaders has the answer! And those standing on the side lines, touting what they know, are just as ignorant as the rest—but with an added dose of pride. Most newscasters reek of this vain, pride-filled spirit. They mold and fashion events into "news"—news as they see it—after their liking. If you cannot see this, then you have much to learn.

God is going to break this vain attitude and haughty spirit of man before He establishes His Kingdom on the earth. His two witnesses will play a major role in this. But from the very beginning of their work, the overwhelming majority of man will not believe they are sent from God. Instead, they will mock, ridicule and hold them in disdain—and those who believe them.

It took time, but even the Egyptians eventually began to believe that God was working through Aaron and Moses. At one point, God sent word to Pharaoh saying, *"...Thus says the LORD God of the Hebrews, Let my people go, that they may serve me. For I will at this time send all my plagues upon your very heart, and upon your servants, and upon your people; that you may know that there is none like me in all the earth"* (Exodus 9:13-14).

God will once again send plagues upon the earth, coinciding with the very time when mankind is about to be plunged into World War III. The unrest and power at work on this earth are leading up to the emergence of two great military powers, who will come against each other to engage in the greatest battle the earth has ever witnessed.

God even identifies these two great powers. The one that emerges first upon the scene is an ancient, resurrected power from Europe. Europe will rise again, to thrust the world into a third World War. The power they unleash will result in the death of hundreds of millions of people.

This threat is the catalyst that pushes the Far East to unite more quickly than they otherwise would into stronger alliances than they could have otherwise imagined. God specifically declares that this Asiatic power alone will destroy a third of all mankind—over one billion people.

This is the world, and the time, in which we now live. No one wants to believe it. No one wants to admit it is possible. But it will happen. This is not written to convince you that it will happen, but to simply tell you that it will happen, exactly as stated. For those who will listen, the hope is that they will begin preparing for what is inevitable. This is a message that mankind will hate! And they will hate the two who bring it. Some will try to kill them before their time, but they will not succeed. That too is prophesied!

Before this book reveals more of the specifics of end-time events, culminating in world war, more about these two witnesses must first be explained, since they come on the scene first, before World War III erupts.

God declares, *"And I will give power unto my two witnesses, and they shall prophesy a thousand two hundred and sixty days, clothed in sackcloth"* (Revelation 11:3). These two will prophesy of events that are coming, and their message will be reinforced by the power of God Almighty, through signs and miracles, mostly in the form of plagues and control over weather. By this means, God will be revealing that these two are His witnesses and that it is the end-time, the end of man's 6,000 year reign on earth.

These two will be of a humble spirit (spiritually—clothed in sackcloth), unlike those in the world around them, for they know the suffering man must experience in order to become changed in spirit. They also know that what will happen is not about them but rather about what God is doing to bring His Kingdom to the earth.

"These are the two olive trees, and the two lamp stands standing before the God of the earth" (Revelation 11:4). These two do stand in an awesomely prominent position of power. They exercise power over the earth that no human beings have ever exercised before—not even remotely. Moses announced great plagues on Pharaoh and Egypt, but nothing in comparison to the magnitude of those things done by these two prophets.

"And if any man will hurt them, fire proceeds out of their

mouth, and devours their enemies: and if any man will hurt them, he must in this manner be killed" (Revelation 11:5). Many will hate these two, with great passion. Many will desire to see them killed, and some will even attempt to do so. But these have the power to inflict death upon those who attempt such a thing. This will happen often enough that it will begin to put fear in those who attempt to kill them.

"These have power [Greek—power and authority] *to shut heaven, that it rain not in the days of their prophecy: and have power over waters to turn them to blood, and to strike the earth with all plagues, as often as they will"* (Revelation 11:6). In the beginning, very few will believe these two are sent from God, but as time progresses through this three and one-half year period, people will be moved to believe it. They can then begin preparing themselves for what is yet to come—until the Kingdom of God itself comes, with the Messiah—the Christ, as King of all kings.

But when end-time events are ready to come to a close—just before Jesus Christ returns—some will finally succeed in killing these two witnesses. *"And when they have finished their testimony, the beast that ascends out of the bottomless pit shall make war against them, and shall overcome them, and kill them"* (Rev. 11:7).

The Seventh Seal of Revelation

The time for the coming of these two witnesses of God is revealed by the opening of the Seventh Seal of Revelation. The work of these two prophets of God will commence at the same time that the Seventh Seal of Revelation is opened. Six seals have already been opened at the time of this writing.

Many religious scholars believe these first six seals concern literal physical events that will occur on the earth. But the end-time will catch the world off guard because the first six seals are not about physical events—they are about spiritual ones.

The opening of those seals has gone unnoticed by the world

because they are about a small church that was prophesied to exist at the end-time. That church was to experience events on a spiritual plane, unparalleled in history. Those prophecies have been fulfilled over the past decade and will be explained in another chapter.

The opening of the seventh seal will occur at the same time the end-time witnesses begin their work. But during the time of the Sixth Seal, the end-time tribulation is held back until the final number of those who are to become a part of God's Kingdom at Christ's return is fulfilled.

Over the past 6,000 years, God has been preparing those He called, trained and refined to become a part of His Kingdom, to reign with Jesus Christ when He returns. The last of those to be added, to complete the whole count of 144,000, is determined during this period of time. God has not revealed how many during this specific time (the opening of the Sixth Seal and its duration) are yet to be added to complete the whole. It may be only a handful, or perhaps a few hundred, but it is small.

The apostle John records what he saw during the time of the Sixth Seal—a time that must be fully accomplished before the Seventh Seal can be opened. *"And after these things I saw four angels standing on the four corners of the earth, holding the four winds of the earth, that the wind should not blow on the earth, nor on the sea, nor on any tree. And I saw another angel ascending from the east, having the seal of the living God: and he cried with a loud voice to the four angels, to whom it was given to hurt the earth and the sea, Saying, Hurt not the earth, neither the sea, nor the trees, till we have sealed the servants of our God in their foreheads. And I heard the number of those who were sealed: and there were sealed one hundred forty-four thousand..."* (Rev. 7:1-4).

During the Sixth Seal, four angels are held back from what they will eventually unleash on the earth. But once the Seventh Seal is opened, specific catastrophic events begin. The opening of the Seventh Seal and the destruction that follows when these four angels are released mark the beginning of the end-time tribulation. As soon as the 144,000 are sealed and the work of 6,000 years finally completed, the Seventh Seal is opened.

"And when He had opened the seventh seal, there was silence in heaven about the space of half an hour. And I saw the seven angels who stand before God; and to them were given seven trumpets" (Revelation 8:1-2). Each angel blows a trumpet to announce specific events to be unleashed upon the earth during this three and one-half year period of great tribulation.

"And another angel came and stood at the altar, having a golden censer; and there was given unto him much incense, that he should offer it with the prayers of all the saints upon the golden altar which was before the throne. And the smoke of the incense, which came with the prayers of the saints, ascended up before God out of the angel's hand. And the angel took the censer, and filled it with fire on the altar, and cast it into the earth: and there were voices, and thunderings, and lightnings, and an earthquake. And the seven angels who had the seven trumpets prepared themselves to sound" (Revelation 8:3-6). Thus begins the prophesied end-time.

The first four angels who had been held back during the Sixth Seal now begin to sound their trumpets and great tribulation begins to be unleashed upon the earth.

The first plague upon the earth is described by the blowing of the first trumpet. *"The first angel sounded, and there followed hail and fire mingled with blood, and they were cast upon the earth: and the third part of trees was burned up, and all green grass was burned up"* (Revelation 8:7). Famine, death and destruction are thrust upon the earth in unimaginable proportions.

On its heels is the sounding of the next trumpet. *"Then the second angel sounded, and as it were a great mountain burning with fire was cast into the sea: and the third part of the sea became blood; and the third part of the living creatures which were in the sea died; and the third part of the ships were destroyed"*

(Revelation 9:8-9). The result of the first trumpet is destruction on the land masses, while the second trumpet resulted in like devastation in the seas and oceans.

"And the third angel sounded, and there fell a great star from heaven, burning as it were a lamp, and it fell upon the third part of the rivers, and upon the springs of water; And the name of the star is called Wormwood: And the third part of the waters became wormwood; and many men died of the water, because it was made bitter" (Revelation 8:10-11). It is not yet understood what these specific events entail, but it is clear that during this third trumpet blast massive resources of drinkable water are contaminated, and hundreds of thousands of people die as a result.

Then the last of these four angels blows his trumpet. *"And the fourth angel sounded, and the third part of the sun was smitten, and the third part of the moon, and the third part of the stars; so as the third part of them was darkened, and the day shined not for a third part of it, and the night likewise"* (Rev. 8:12). The result of these plagues is a darkening of the atmosphere over a third of the earth. The light of the heavens is restricted from shining on the earth. This affects weather, especially the rapid cooling of the earth, so much so, that much more death and suffering comes upon this world.

The horrifying results of this tribulation are of a magnitude that is unpleasant to contemplate and almost impossible to imagine. But all of it will happen, just as God has said.

This devastation comes primarily upon the United States, Canada, Australia, the United Kingdom and a few of the very northwestern countries of Europe. God has much to say about these modern-day nations and the intense magnitude of their devastation during this soon coming end-time. The purpose of this book is not to convince anyone of such things, but declare them, before they happen, so that when they do occur, you can recognize them and prepare yourself accordingly for what is to follow. God makes it clear that most people will not believe these things are going to happen until they actually begin to unfold—and even then, there will only be a regrettably small percentage who do. But as these prophesied events continue to come to pass, the number of those who begin to believe will increase. Those who stubbornly refuse to believe will only increase the likelihood of their own demise.

While describing these primarily English-speaking nations, it might as well be shown how vast their destruction will become over the entire period of end-time tribulation. This was covered in part at the beginning of this chapter.

The prophet Ezekiel was given prophecy concerning these nations and their end-time demise.

"Wherefore, as I live, says the Lord GOD, Surely, because you have defiled my sanctuary with all your detestable things, and with all your abominations, therefore will I also diminish you; neither shall my eye spare, neither will I have any pity. A third part of you shall die with the pestilence, and with famine shall they be consumed in the midst of you: and a third part shall fall by the sword round about you; and I will scatter a third part into all the winds, and I will draw out a sword after them. Thus shall my anger be accomplished, and I will cause my fury to rest upon them, and I will be comforted: and they shall know that I the LORD have spoken it in my zeal, <u>when</u> I have accomplished my fury in them. Moreover I will make you waste, and a reproach among the nations that are round about you, in the sight of all who pass by. So it shall be a reproach and a taunt, an instruction and an astonishment unto the nations that are round about you, when I shall execute judgments in you in anger and in fury and in furious rebukes. I the LORD, have spoken it" (Ezekiel 5:11-15).

It will be explained later how this applies to these specific nations. Through the ages, God has sent His prophets to His people. They haven't listened. Now is man's time to be shown the power and might of God. Mankind will be humbled into listening!

Even to those who consider themselves to be religious, Jesus

Christ said, *"O Jerusalem, Jerusalem, you that kill the prophets, and stone those who are sent unto you, how often would I have gathered your children together, even as a hen gathers her chicks under her wings, and you would not!"* (Matthew 23:37). People are no different today, but they think they are—especially those who consider themselves to be religious. If Jesus Christ were to come to the earth today, instead of 2,000 years ago, the religious leaders of today would ridicule Him and seek to discredit Him. The nature of man has not changed since that time. That is why the end-time witnesses will finally be killed, but they will be protected by God until they have accomplished what He has called them to do. Yes, man is still the same. Therefore God is bringing man's age to a close by bringing His Kingdom—to change the pride-filled nature of man.

The prophecies given to Ezekiel concerning these modern-day nations are grim. Nearly two-thirds of their populations will die within months of the start of great physical tribulation on the earth. The last third will experience a sifting process in the remaining time of tribulation. Pride is so great, so difficult to break, that God reveals He will deliver only ten percent of that remaining population (a tithe of the last third remaining after the first two-thirds is destroyed). That remnant of people, which consists of those who have repented of their own ways, will begin to look to the return of Jesus Christ to deliver them. Before it is all over, the other nations of the world will not fare any better than those already mentioned. Some will experience much worse!

These revelations and their systematic manifestation will only stir up derision, bitterness and hatred. Mankind will hate what is occurring, as well as hate those who believe and teach that these events are the result of God's judgment. Yet, that is exactly what two witnesses will be doing—declaring that these catastrophes are the result of God's judgment upon the world. Not only will they be explaining why these things are happening, but they will proclaim that this is the end of man's self-rule on the earth and that Jesus Christ is about to come, with a new world-ruling Kingdom.

Most people will hate this message as well as the messengers. The two witnesses will respond by calling for more plagues to come upon unrepentant mankind. Coinciding with these events will be a movement of thousands who begin crying out to God for mercy and deliverance as they begin to come to repentance, seeking to change their lives in anticipation of God's coming Kingdom.

A Revived Roman Empire

As we have seen, once the Seventh Seal is opened, seven angels sound their trumpets during the three and one-half years of end-time tribulation. The first four angels bring incredible destruction upon the earth.

"And I beheld, and heard an angel flying through the midst of heaven, saying with a loud voice, Woe, woe, woe to the inhabitants of the earth by reason of the other blasts of the trumpet of the three angels, who are yet to sound!" (Revelation 8:13). Each of the last three trumpets is called a "woe." These will bring far greater death and destruction than do the first four.

The first of these "woes" is announced when the fifth angel sounds his trumpet. This is the beginning of World War III. The people who perpetrate this war emerge from the Europe Union. Ten European nations will finally merge together, as one, to take control of a world out of control. Not all who are in the current European Union will be part of it, but when the timing is right, a final ten will achieve the goal of a powerful Federal Europe that some leaders, even now, already envision. They will justify a powerful military action as their only hope to bring order.

Although many are sincere about what they believe they must do, they are deeply deceived and deluded by their own visions of grandeur. They see the arrogance of the United States and some of her English-speaking allies and desire a change in regard to world domination.

Desire for a stronger Europe has gradually developed among many Europeans since the early fifties. The European Common Market began to exercise some strength over the years, finally evolving into the European Union. The next step is to bring about a United States of Europe or a strong Federal Europe. That next step is very close to fruition. Catastrophic events that befall the United States and other English-speaking nations will be the catalyst.

Decisions made by the United States since 9/11 have plunged other nations of the world into decisive alliances with "set" motivations of independence, as well as an increasing desire for self-determination—resistant to policies from the United States. Nations are simply "fed up" with the arrogance they see in the wealthiest nation the world has ever known. Sadly, they do not understand their own human nature. Much of their motivation is based on jealousy.

At present, France and Germany are aligned in a common spirit. It is one of bitterness, frustration and impatience with the United States and Great Britain. They seek a stronger Europe of self-determination, along with a common military that seeks to distance itself from NATO and eventually replace it—forging the way in their Eurozone with no more interference from the United States.

Indeed, the United States is filled with arrogance and seeks to force its will on other nations of the world. Yet, that kind of national arrogance only fosters jealousies, contentions, bitterness and economic tugs of war that so often end in war.

Europe is unaware of its great vulnerability in these times. People are vulnerable to self-destruction because they do not truly believe God. They do not believe the power and reality of a real spirit world. Yet that spirit world is now intensely active with its own struggles and fighting. The demonic world knows that it has only a short time left in which to bear influence upon the affairs of man.

When Jesus came upon a group of demons and commanded them to depart, they asked Jesus if He had come to torment them before their time. They knew that the time would come when they would be separated from the presence of mankind, but they also knew that they were nowhere near the end of the 6,000 years allotted to mankind. At the time this occurred, only 4,000 years of man's time on earth had passed.

Demonic spirit beings have been instrumental in stirring up conflict in the world—leading nations into wars and religions into deception. Countries war against each other, in the name of religion, with each thinking it has God on its side.

Consider the world of traditional Christianity. History is full of nations calling themselves Christian, that have gone to war with each other, each invoking the name of God. Such religious confusion and deception is stirred up by this spirit world of fallen angels (demons). Consider the civil war, between the north and the south in the United States, when those on both sides prayed in some of the same churches and held the same religious beliefs. During WW II, how did German and Italian Catholics feel as they warred against Catholics from the United States and vice-versa? Did they not seek the blessings of God for themselves as they entered into battle?

In the book of Daniel, God foretold of four great world-ruling kingdoms on the earth. The first was the Chaldean Empire (Babylonian) that emerged on the world scene in Daniel's time. In that prophecy, a fifth kingdom at the end-time would come upon the world to replace the kingdoms of man. Notice how that kingdom is described, at a time when the fourth and final earthly kingdom is brought to an end.

"And in the days of these kings [those who reign at the end in the final kingdom] *shall the God of heaven set up a kingdom* [His own Kingdom on earth], *which shall never be destroyed: and the*

kingdom shall not be left to other people [Man will not head this Kingdom, but spirit beings of the Family of God, who return with Christ, will rule.], *but it shall break in pieces and consume all these kingdoms, and it shall stand forever* [When this Kingdom comes, it will destroy the fourth and final prophesied kingdom of man that exists at its coming.]. *Forasmuch as you saw that the stone was cut out of the mountain without hands* [the Kingdom of God, made by God], *and that it broke in pieces the iron, the brass, the clay, the silver, and* the *gold; the great God has made known to the king* [to King Nebuchadnezzar] *what shall come to pass hereafter: and the dream is certain, and its interpretation thereof sure"* (Daniel 2:44-45). Yes, all this will happen exactly as God has said.

The fourth and last kingdom to reign on the earth is described by God in many prophecies. It is a kingdom that reigned during the time of Jesus Christ and continues up to the time He returns. It is the Roman Empire, which is described in great detail in scripture. It has had several revivals over the centuries, but it has not existed under a single national leadership or organized government.

The original Roman Empire lasted from 31 B.C. to 476 A.D. Although divided, the Roman Empire continued under the Vandals, the Heruli and the Ostrogoths. Then in 554 A.D. the empire experienced an "Imperial Restoration" under the leadership of Justinian.

It was at this time that the kingdom took on a religious alliance. The Roman Empire took on different forms, but involved the same peoples (European). The first religious revival of this kingdom occurred under the leadership of Justinian who was the first to recognize the religious authority of the Pope of the Roman Catholic Church. Thus began the first revival of the Roman Empire—now to become known as the Holy Roman Empire.

The Holy Roman Empire was revived in the Frankish Kingdom in 774 A.D. Charlemagne was crowned by the Pope in 800 A.D. Then in 962 A.D. there was a revival by a German head of government when the Pope crowned Otto the Great. A fourth revival occurred in 1520 A.D. when Charles the Great of the Hapsburg dynasty (an Austrian head) was crowned by the Pope. Another revival occurred when Napoleon (French head) was crowned by the Pope in 1805. Then, in 1814 the revivals of the Holy Roman Empire ceased.

In a struggle for dominance, a sixth revival of the Roman Empire began under the unifying efforts of Garibaldi (an Italian head) in 1870. This effort continued when Mussolini later united with Hitler in a great attempt to seize total control of the entire European continent as well as other parts of the world, but this was crushed in 1945.

Regardless of its name, several revivals of this empire have existed over the ages. God revealed that each subsequent revival would have a religious allegiance to the same church. Six have come and gone—only one remains.

It was during World War II, when the sixth revival was in full power, that a verse in prophecy was fulfilled. It speaks of these very revivals, showing that time was closing in and that the time for the Book of Revelation to be unveiled was very near. It says, *"And there are seven kings* [There would be seven revivals of the Roman Empire.]*: five have fallen, and one is* [Europe, although primarily under Hitler's leadership, was the "one is" during the sixth revival, which was emboldened with inspiration from Satan himself.]*, and the other is not yet come; and when he comes, he must continue a short time"* (Revelation 17:10). Thankfully the last revival will last only a short time—less than three and one-half years. It is interesting to note how those in the sixth revival saw themselves. It was to be a leadership that would establish a Reich on the earth—a thousand year reign. This one was referred to as the Third Reich.

The seventh and last revival will again be headed by someone who is moved to do what he will do by inspiration from Satan. Satan is the real live being, spoken of in the following verse, who has held sway over these revivals. *"And the beast that was* [Satan, who is the true head of each revival], *and is not* [yet he cannot continually exercise this power—only during each revival], *even he is the eighth* [counted as the eighth because he is actually over each of the seven revivals], *and is of the seven, and goes into perdition"* (Revelation 17:11).

Again, this information concerning all these matters reserved for the end-time is not given to try to persuade anyone now, but only to help give understanding, so that when it comes to pass, you can "then know" and choose how to respond.

Although the leaders of this last revival in Europe believe they are in total control of their own destiny, they are ignorant of the fact that they are being stirred up, deceived and led by a power much greater than theirs—that which exists in a spirit world.

Now we come to the time of the seventh and last revival of the old Roman Empire. *"And the fifth angel sounded, and I saw a star fall from heaven unto the earth: and to him was given the key of the bottomless pit. And he opened the <u>bottomless pit</u>* [Bible symbolism for a place of restraint]; *and there arose a smoke out of the pit, as the smoke of a great furnace; and the sun and the air were darkened by reason of the smoke of the pit. And there came out of the smoke locusts upon the earth* [Bible symbolism for a massive, destructive army]: *and unto them was given power, as the scorpions of the earth have power* [to strike quickly and paralyze]*"* (Revelation 9:1-3). During World War II this kind of action was described as blitzkrieg (lightning war). It is going to happen again!

A "star" is often used as Biblical symbolism for an angel. Here, an angel is given a key which symbolically unlocks the restraint of a being who will now be allowed to exercise great power on the earth once again. Satan has been restrained between the individual revivals of the Holy Roman Empire, but once again he is allowed to embolden the desires and intents of the hearts of men who already seek to revive the power and influence of that European

Empire of old.

As an aside, to show how people read so much of the Bible in literal physical terms, there is a story that traditional Christianity has perpetuated, but which is foolishly in error. It concerns a sign that many refer to around Christmas time that is supposedly the scene of a real star that pointed the way to the birthplace of Jesus. They do not understand that the star referred to was not a physical one in the heavens, but a spiritual one—an angel. The Bible simply states a story about wise men, out of the east, who had come to find the Messiah, the One who was reported to be born king of the Jews. These men said that they saw His star in the east. This angel had revealed to them the time and location of Jesus' birth. It was not about a star in the heavens that somehow set over the area of Bethlehem.

To perpetuate such a physical anomaly is much like the perpetuation of Santa Clause, the Easter Bunny and other similar stories that make true religion seem foolish to reasonable thinking people. Is it any wonder that religion is considered nothing but fables in the minds of so many?

This spirit being, who is being released from his restraint, is described in terms of a spiritual realm much like a person speaking of someone taking a key and unlocking a prison cell or removing shackles from someone. In this case, the story goes on to make it very clear who was being released.

The real power behind the physical leadership, of this last revival, is a spirit being. *"And they had as king over them, the angel of the bottomless pit, whose name in the Hebrew tongue is Abaddon, but in the Greek tongue has his name Apollyon"* (Revelation 9:11). These are indeed other names for Satan.

This great power, out of Europe, will be able to accomplish what they were unable to do in World War II. This time they will defeat the United Kingdom—and much more than that, they will defeat the United States, Canada and their allies.

A Defiant Response

It is appropriate at this juncture to point out the natural response most will have when they hear these pronouncements of doom and gloom. Most people will not believe these things. Ironically, this book is actually declaring the very gospel (Greek–"good news") of Jesus Christ, which is the good news about the Kingdom of God. The very thing that most will not understand is that man must first be humbled before the gospel message about the Kingdom of God can finally come to pass. After man's era has ended (6,000 years), then God's era will begin, when His Kingdom comes to rule over the earth.

So again, the natural response of people will be to either ignore or ridicule the message contained in this book. No one of notoriety is warning of such impending worldwide disaster. And great educators and leaders will not place any credibility on these words, not now, not before it actually begins to happen.

No well known religious leader is saying such things, and even if they did, most people would consider them to be "off" mentally. As a matter of fact, all religious leaders of any reputation will disregard it altogether. They will actually respond by claiming such ideas as preposterous. For if any of them acknowledged these things, they would have to repent and turn from their own long-held religious beliefs.

Will Europeans be pleased to hear these things? Some may like the idea of finally becoming the greatest power on earth, with the ability to dominate the U.S. and her allies, but most will not be pleased to hear that they are being described as the final resurrection of the Roman Empire with power that will be short-lived. They certainly will not be pleased to hear that their end—their downfall will make the aftermath of World War II seem insignificant by comparison. That downfall will be described later in this chapter.

Will the U.S., Canada, Australia, the United Kingdom and others among their allies be pleased by these pronouncements? Regardless of their response, and understandably it will be negative, their demise will be swift when it comes. These things are not a matter of whether or not we like what we hear. It is simply a matter of what God says will, very soon now, come to pass.

God is the one who declares what will come to pass in this end-time. It is not intended to be well received. It is intended to be the strongest correction and humbling that has ever been poured out upon mankind.

Naturally peoples and nations will not give any credibility to what is written here. People have too much pride to believe they are wrong concerning their ideals and religious beliefs. Yet it is for this very reason that God will give great power to His two end-time prophets, for the purpose of correction and to testify to the truth of the matters contained in this book.

As time progresses through the end-time tribulation, increasing numbers of people will respond and acknowledge what is true. They will begin to seek deliverance from God, with the hope of living into the new world that Jesus Christ is bringing.

But the overwhelming majority will not respond in this fashion, and as a result of their obstinance, arrogance and pride, they will be among those destroyed during this three and a half years of tribulation.

These are dismal forebodings, not intended to be easy to hear. Political correctness is of no importance here. It is reality, and it is about to come on the earth. You will have only one choice—to respond. How will you respond? Will it be in arrogance and defiance, as most around you? Or will you take hold of your life and acknowledge that man has not lived according to God's ways. Will you repent and receive God's rule in your life? Will you receive correction now and gladly receive the Kingdom of God in a new age for mankind? If you choose to refuse, you choose to die! If you repent, perhaps you can live into the new age.

The Second Woe!

When the fifth trumpet is blown, a powerful military might will arise from ten nations in Europe. A Third World War will become a reality at that time. The devastation and death that follows will mount into the loss of hundreds of millions of lives.

But the action of this seventh and final revival of the Holy Roman Empire stirs another part of the world into massive military action. A response from nations in Asia will generate the largest army the world has ever known.

The blowing of the fifth trumpet was described as the first of three great woes to come upon mankind. Next, God warns about the second woe that is generated by the action of the first.

"One woe is past; and, behold, there come two woes more hereafter. And the sixth angel sounded, and I heard a voice from the four horns of the golden altar which is before God, Saying to the sixth angel who had the trumpet, Release the four angels who are bound at the great river Euphrates. And the four angels were released, who were prepared for an hour, and a day, and a month, and a year, for to kill a third part of men" (Revelation 9:12-15).

The blowing of the sixth trumpet is described as the second great woe to come upon mankind. This occurs well into the final three and one-half years of great and final tribulation on earth. The power unleashed by this fierce power results in the death of a third of all mankind—well over a billion people.

God even foretold the size of this Asiatic horde that would burst forth upon the earth at this time.

"And the number of the army of the horsemen was two hundred million: and I heard the number of them. And thus I saw the horses in the vision, and those who sat on them, having breastplates of fire, and of jacinth, and brimstone: and the heads of the horses were as the heads of lions; and out of their mouths came fire and smoke and brimstone. By these three was the third part of men killed, by the fire, and by the smoke, and the brimstone which came

out of their mouths. For their power is in their mouth, and in their tails: for their tails were like unto serpents, and had heads, and with them they do hurt" (Revelation 9:16-19).

Much more could be told about the military powers that will soon appear on this earth, but that is not for this book. Such matters, and much more, are to be made known by the two prophets who are to appear once the first trumpet of the Seventh Seal is blown.

At the end of three and one-half years of great physical tribulation, one great woe is yet to occur. By this time six trumpets have already sounded, and the destruction that followed is incomprehensible. The overwhelming majority of all life has been erased from the earth.

One would think that, by this time, the remainder of mankind would have repented and turned to God. Not so! Man still remains in defiance to God even after all this devastation and after all that God's two witnesses have declared has come to pass. This indeed reveals the depth of the haughtiness and pride of man!

Although the majority of human life has been destroyed by this time, most of those who remain still hold onto their selfish ways with their selfish beliefs. Several million have repented by this time, but the majority still living has not. Most who have repented are among those already conquered by these two great armies.

In the following verses God speaks of those who yet remain defiant among the nations of these two military powers. *"And the rest of the men who were not killed by these plagues yet repented not of the works of their hands, that they should not worship demons, and idols of gold, and silver, and brass, and stone, and of wood: which neither can see, nor hear, nor walk: Neither repented they of their murders, nor of their sorceries, nor of their sexual immorality, nor of their thefts"* (Revelation 9:20-21).

These two great powers remain haughty before God, since they are able to continue exercising their power over others. They have not been defeated, so they have not yet been humbled. They remain unbelieving until the bitter end.

It is inevitable that these two armies eventually confront each other. When that happens they will not use weapons of mass destruction for fear of total self-destruction. Instead, they converge on a very specific part of the earth to confront each other by more conventional means—direct head-on combat.

The preparation for this battle is of mammoth proportions—something man has never before contemplated—beyond the wildest imagination for military confrontation.

This preparation for battle is well known in history—at least by name. That name has been used in countless stories. Movies have used it in the context of the most hideous concepts of final world war. It is "Armageddon."

The Valley of Megiddo is the location for the confrontation of the two most massive armies the world has ever witnessed—the final great battle of man's 6,000 years on earth. This final battle will last only one day!

The Last Day of Tribulation!

The Battle of Armageddon has been spoken of, but never understood, by this world. It has never even been understood by Biblical scholars. Yet, it is about a real gathering of military might such as the world has never seen. It is about a final battle on earth!

As described earlier, a European military will meet to confront an Asian military that is pushing toward Europe. It is an inevitable preparation for great war between these two powers—a gathering for a final, all-out confrontation. This gathering, of two military powers, coincides with a momentous juncture in all earth's history. It is the exact time for man's self rule to end and God's rule to begin.

On the very day these two great armies prepare to confront each other, in the valley of Megiddo, the seventh trumpet is blown. This is the third and final woe upon mankind:

"The second woe is past; and, behold, the third woe comes quickly. And the seventh angel sounded; and there were great voices in heaven, saying, The <u>kingdoms of this world</u> have become the kingdoms of our Lord, and of His Christ; and He shall reign for ever and ever" (Revelation 11:14-15).

Once the third woe is announced by the seventh angel sounding his trumpet, God reveals that man's 6,000 years of self-rule has now come to an end and it is time for the Kingdom of God to begin with the reign of Jesus Christ over all nations of the earth. It all happens on the very day these two great military powers prepare to engage each other in the Valley of Megiddo.

The first thing to occur on this day is awesome beyond belief. Notice what the next few verses have to say. *"And the twenty-four elders, who sat before God on their thrones, fell upon their faces, and worshiped God, Saying, We give you thanks, O Lord God Almighty, which art, and were, and art to come; because you have taken your great power and have reigned. And the nations were angry, and your wrath is come, and the time of the dead, that they should be judged, and that you should give reward unto your servants the prophets, and to the saints, and those who fear your name, small and great, and should destroy those who destroy the earth. And the temple of God was opened in heaven, and there was seen in His temple the ark of His testament: and there were lightnings, and voices, and thunderings, and an earthquake, and great hail"* (Revelation 11:16-19).

These events, on this last day of man's rule and the beginning of God's rule, will be the most dramatic day of all human history—far beyond human ability to fully comprehend, much less believe. But it will happen at the very end of the last three and one-half years of great physical tribulation on this earth.

The twenty-four elders that are before the throne of God declare that the time has come for God to give reward to a specific group of people who have dwelt on the earth. They also acknowledge that

God is now taking to Himself His great power to begin the reign of His government on the earth. Yes, the nations are angry and many are set to destroy one another—even to resist the coming of Jesus Christ on this day. But this is the day of God's wrath to be poured out upon the earth—to put an end to man's own self-destructiveness. As these elders declare, God will destroy those who are destroying the earth—all accomplished in this one great day of human history.

But first—a great resurrection will take place. It is the time referred to earlier in this book, when the 144,000 God called during man's 6,000 year rule will be resurrected to immortal life to become the first, after Jesus Christ, to enter the Kingdom of God.

This is the same time that God's two witnesses are resurrected. Notice this again in the context of the events that are to happen on this great day.

"And when they shall have finished their testimony, the beast that ascends out of the bottomless pit shall make war against them, and shall overcome them, and kill them. And their dead bodies shall lie in the street of the great city, which spiritually is called Sodom and Egypt, where also our Lord was crucified. And they of the people and kindreds and tongues and nations shall see their dead bodies three and a half days, and shall not allow their dead bodies to be put in graves. And those who dwell upon the earth will rejoice over them, and make merry, and shall send gifts one to another; because these two prophets tormented those who dwell on the earth. And after three and a half days the spirit of life from God entered into them, and they stood upon their feet; and great fear fell upon those who saw them. And they heard a great voice from heaven saying unto them, Come up here. And they ascended up to heaven in a cloud; and their enemies beheld them. And the same hour was there a great earthquake, and the tenth part of the city fell, and in the earthquake were killed seven thousand people, and the rest were frightened, and gave glory to the God of heaven. The

second woe is past; and, behold, the third woe comes quickly" (Rev. 11:7-14).

It is at the very beginning of this last great day that the 144,000 are resurrected to reign with Jesus Christ in the Kingdom of God. These two witnesses are among those resurrected. People will actually see these two witnesses, who have been lying dead in a street in Jerusalem for three and a half days, be given life, stand up, and begin to rise into the atmosphere, along with all the others who are being resurrected at this time. This event will cause great fear to fall upon the world when people see it on television from Jerusalem. Now no one can claim any longer that these prophets were not of God, for now they are resurrected to life, and people witness their resurrection and their ascension into the atmosphere, where they meet Jesus Christ.

There are other areas of scripture that speak of this return of Jesus Christ and the resurrection that occurs at this same time.

"For if we believe that Jesus died and rose again, even so them also who sleep in Jesus will God bring with Him. For this we say unto you by the word of the Lord, that we who are alive and remain unto the coming of the Lord [when Christ comes] *shall not precede those who are asleep. For the Lord himself shall descend from heaven with a shout, with the voice of the archangel, and with the trumpet of God* [the seventh trumpet]*: and the dead in Christ shall rise first: Then we who are alive and remain shall be caught up together with them in the clouds, to meet the Lord in the air* [The resurrection is in the very atmosphere above the earth—in the clouds—to be seen by those on earth.]*: and so shall we ever be with the Lord* [They have been resurrected to immortal life, just as Jesus Christ was when He was resurrected, and they will be in the Kingdom of God with Jesus Christ.]*"* (1 Thessalonians 4:14-17).

People will be stunned by these events because they far exceed human ability to comprehend. People will be filled with fear because everyone will see this sign in the heavens—in our very atmosphere—at the coming of Jesus Christ. They will not grasp what they see, but it will be an enormous display of power and signs in the earth and in the heavens.

"For as the lightning comes out of the east, and shines even unto the west; so shall also the coming of the Son of man be" (Matthew 24:27). Jesus Christ foretold this time in several areas of scripture and made it clear that those on earth would be able to see His coming. Christ and those resurrected will literally be visible in the atmosphere and will come on down to this earth on that great day.

"Immediately after the tribulation of those days [When all great tribulation of the earth has come to an end and it is time for the return of Jesus Christ.] *shall the sun be darkened, and the moon shall not give her light, and the stars shall fall from heaven, and the powers of the heavens shall be shaken: And then shall appear the sign of the Son of man in heaven: and then shall all the tribes of the earth mourn* [People will be afraid of what they see because they cannot understand it.]*, and they shall see the Son of man coming in the clouds of heaven with power and great glory. And He shall send His angels with a great sound of a trumpet* [This is the time when the seventh trumpet is blown, announcing the time of the return of Jesus Christ, the resurrection of the 144,000, the coming of God's Kingdom to the earth, and the destruction of those who are destroying the earth.]*, and they shall gather together His elect from the four winds, from one end of heaven to the other"* (Matthew 24:29-31).

Luke records the words of Jesus concerning this same period of time. *"And there will be signs in the sun, and in the moon, and in the stars; and upon the earth distress of nations, with perplexity; the sea and the waves roaring; Men's hearts failing them for fear, and for looking after those things which are coming on the earth: for the powers of heaven shall be shaken. And then shall they see the Son of man coming in a cloud with power and great glory. And when these things begin to come to pass, then look up, and lift up your heads; for your redemption draws near"* (Luke 21:25-28).

People have read these same words in their Bibles, but they have never understood the timing or the place they hold in the plan of God. It is an awesome plan, and it is about to unfold on the earth. It is the story contained throughout the pages of the Bible, both Old and New Testaments, of good news that will one day come to pass, when God brings His Kingdom to the earth, with His Son reigning as the King of all kings—ruling all nations of the earth. That time is about to come. It will be for the good of all mankind—good news!

As this great display is seen in the heavens, those who still refuse to repent find it impossible to believe these things are from God. It is easier for them to believe something that seems more rational—an invasion from outer space. Movies like *Independence Day* and other science fiction stories are more palatable to their reasoning.

This same kind of limited reasoning is also about to change the entire focus of these two great armies who have come together to do battle in the Valley of Megiddo.

The Seven Last Plagues

The seventh trumpet announces the return of Jesus Christ and the resurrection of the 144,000, but it also announces the time of God's great wrath upon those who have been destroying the earth. The ten nations of Europe and the nations of Asia will now meet that wrath.

An overview that describes the activities of this great day, as it leads up to the wrath of God being poured out upon these two great military powers, is best understood by the following verses. At the beginning of the day, the declaration is made that it is time for God's rule to come to this earth.

"The second woe is past; and, behold, the third woe comes quickly. And the seventh angel sounded; and there were great voices in heaven, saying, The kingdoms of this world have become

the kingdoms of our Lord, and of His Christ, and He shall reign for ever and ever" (Revelation 11:14-15). The resurrection of 144,000 occurs immediately. Next comes the declaration of those things in the third woe that will be poured out upon the earth.

"And I saw another sign in heaven, great and marvelous, seven angels having the seven last plagues; for in them is filled up the wrath of God" (Revelation 15:1). The seventh trumpet also announces a time of wrath upon the two military powers and their peoples and lands. This third woe consists of seven last plagues to be poured out upon these nations—in a single day.

"And after that I looked, and, behold, the temple of the tabernacle of the testimony in heaven was opened: And the seven angels came out of the temple, having the seven plagues, clothed in pure and white linen, and having their breasts girded with golden bands. And one of the four living creatures gave unto the seven angels seven golden vials full of the wrath of God, who lives for ever and ever. And the temple was filled with smoke from the glory of God, and from His power; and no one was able to enter into the temple, till the seven plagues of the seven angels were fulfilled" (Revelation 15:5-8).

"And I heard a great voice out of the temple saying to the seven angels, Go your ways, and pour out the vials of the wrath of God upon the earth. And the first went, and poured out his vial upon the earth; and there fell a noisome and grievous sore upon the men who had the mark of the beast, and those who worshiped his image" (Revelation 16:1-2).

A great plague is poured out upon this European military, her people, and all who have allied with her. Millions die!

"And the second angel poured out his vial upon the sea; and it became as the blood of a dead man: and every living creature died in the sea. And the third angel poured out his vial upon the rivers and springs of water; and they became blood. (Revelation 16:3-4).

"And the fourth angel poured out his vial upon the sun; and power

was given unto him to scorch men with fire. And men were scorched with great heat, and blasphemed the name of God, who has power over these plagues: and they repented not to give Him glory" (Revelation 16:8-9). Throughout this day, the plagues continue to grow worse and worse, yet these people remain haughty and defiant toward God. God continues to pour out plagues upon them. Masses of people continue to die because they refuse to repent before God!

"And the fifth angel poured out his vial upon the throne of the beast; and his kingdom was full of darkness; and they gnawed their tongues for pain, And blasphemed the God of heaven because of their pains and their sores, and repented not of their deeds" (Revelation 16:10-11).

The next few verses reveal the plan God had in bringing these two great military powers into one area of the world. God planned to deal with them with fierceness and power, the results of which will be remembered and seen for generations to come.

"And the sixth angel poured out his vial upon the great river Euphrates; and the water thereof was dried up, that the way of the kings of the east might be prepared. And I saw three unclean spirits like frogs come out of the mouth of the dragon, and out of the mouth of the beast, and out of the mouth of the false prophet. For they are the spirits of demons, working miracles, which go forth unto the kings of the earth and of the whole world, to gather them to the battle of that great day of God Almighty" (Rev. 16:12-14). These verses condense the time frame of what led up to the final events of this day, that were the result of the sixth plague, God's direct confrontation with both military powers, in the region of Armageddon. *"And he gathered them together into a place called in the Hebrew tongue Armageddon"* (Rev. 16:16). Although there is a longer period of time that has led up to these military powers being moved to come together to confront one another, it is on this day that the sixth plague is poured out and these powers are dealt

with by God in the Valley of Megiddo.

On this great day, when Jesus Christ comes to begin His reign and establish the Kingdom of God on earth, God has foretold that this European might, which is the final resurrection of the old Roman Empire, will actually turn and join with the Asian powers to try to fight against Jesus Christ.

"These shall make war with the Lamb, and the Lamb shall overcome them: for He is Lord of lords, and King of kings: and those who are with Him are called, and chosen, and faithful" (Revelation 17:14).

It is on this day that these two armies will actually unite to war against the Kingdom of God that is coming. Notice how this is addressed later in the Book of Revelation, as Christ's coming is described.

"And I heard as it were the voice of a great multitude, and as the voice of many waters, and as the voice of mighty thunderings, saying, Alleluia: for the Lord God omnipotent reigns. Let us be glad and rejoice, and give honor unto Him: for the marriage of the Lamb is come, and His wife has made herself ready. And to her was granted that she should be arrayed in fine linen, clean and white: for the fine linen is the righteousness of the saints. And he said unto me, Write, Blessed are those who are called to the marriage supper of the Lamb. And he said unto me, These are the true sayings of God" (Revelation 19:6-9). The time has come for God to reign on the earth and for those who have been called out of all earth's history, over the past 6,000 years, to be resurrected (the 144,000) as part of that Kingdom. It continues with a description of the power that Jesus Christ will now begin to exercise on the earth.

"And I saw heaven opened, and behold a white horse; and He who sat upon him was called Faithful and True, and in righteousness He does judge and makes war [The coming of Jesus Christ, this time, is not as the Lamb of God, but as a King who will first make war with those who oppose Him]. *His eyes were as a*

flame of fire, and on His head were many crowns; and He had a name written, that no man knew, but He himself. And He was clothed with a robe dipped in blood: and His name is called The Word of God. And the armies which were in heaven followed Him upon white horses, clothed in fine linen, white and clean" [Those who follow Him are the 144,000.] (Revelation 19:11-14).

"And out of His mouth goes a sharp sword, that with it He should smite the nations: and He shall rule them with a rod of iron: and He treads the winepress of the fierceness and wrath of Almighty God" (Rev. 19:15). This wrath is poured out on these military powers after the sixth plague is poured out on the earth.

Revelation goes on to describe Jesus Christ and His coming.

"And He has on his robe and on his thigh a name written: KING OF KINGS AND LORD OF LORDS. And I saw an angel standing in the sun; and he cried with a loud voice, saying to all the fowls that fly in the midst of heaven, Come and gather yourselves together unto the supper of the great God; that you may eat the flesh of kings, and the flesh of captains, and the flesh of mighty men, and the flesh of horses, and of those who sit on them, and the flesh of all men, free and bond, both small and great. And I saw the beast, and the kings of the earth, and their armies, gathered together to make war against Him who sat on the horse, and against His army" (Rev. 19:16-19). Jesus Christ confronts both armies at Armageddon and destroys all of them in a swift, single moment. Tens of millions die in this area alone, and many multiple millions more will die on this day.

"And the seventh angel poured out his vial into the air; and there came a great voice out of the temple of heaven, from the throne, saying, It is done. And there were voices, and thunderings, and lightnings; and there was a great earthquake, such as was not since men were upon the earth, so mighty an earthquake, and so great. And the great city was divided into three parts, and the cities of the nations fell: and great Babylon came into remembrance

before God, to give her the cup of the wine of the fierceness of His wrath. And every island fled away, and the mountains were not found. And there fell upon men a great hail from heaven, every hailstone about the weight of a talent: and men blasphemed God because of the plague of the hail; for the plague thereof was exceeding great" (Revelation 16:17-21).

As Jesus Christ's feet touch once more on the earth, a great earthquake shakes much of the earth. A final plague is poured out upon mankind that destroys even more who still oppose Him and His Kingdom. Those who dwell on the earth will be brought down and humbled before their God, and finally, after 6,000 years of man's own selfish rule of the earth, the good news (gospel) prophesied throughout the pages of the Bible finally becomes a reality, and the Kingdom of God, God's rule, will be established on the earth!

Chapter 3

THE END-TIME ELIJAH

The previous chapter explained that in the end-time God would send his two witnesses into the world during the last three and one-half years of great physical tribulation. They will not cease to prophesy until they are killed at the very end of this period of time. Then, in three and one-half days, they will be resurrected to immortal life and rise to meet Jesus Christ on the same day that He returns to establish His Kingdom on earth—fulfilling the gospel message (good news) of the entire Bible.

Part of the message these two will bring concerns one of the primary reasons why this end-time tribulation must now come on all the earth. They will explain that God warned the world by telling it that Jesus Christ was about to return—that this was the generation of time for this to be fulfilled. For over fifty years this world was told what was about to come—the end of man's rule and the coming rule of God over all nations. But this world rejected that message, just as it has rejected God and all He has told mankind over the past 6,000 years.

The same will be true regarding the response to this book. Although it has come from God, the world will reject it. People will not believe it, even when these things are actually being fulfilled right before their very eyes! A very small percentage of all mankind will begin to believe, repent and turn to God, but most will not!

So you might say, "I never heard such a warning" or "I have never heard about the return of Jesus Christ and that He is to reign on the earth." Nevertheless, the world was told, and they were told by the prophesied end-time Elijah, whom God said He would send before Jesus Christ would come.

The two witnesses will proclaim that the message of this end-time Elijah was rejected, that people and nations refused to repent, and therefore, all the world must suffer through the end-time tribulation. In addition, they will proclaim that man's spirit of pride must be broken before God's Kingdom comes.

Who was this man—this end-time Elijah—and what did he say? The world is going to hear his name again because they are going to be told repeatedly that they refused to take heed to what he said. He was given a great job to do toward the "end" of man's time—at the end of 6,000 years. He fulfilled several end-time prophecies through his life and his work, which was actually the manifestation of God's end-time work, through him. He was not only the end-time Elijah that was prophesied to come before Jesus Christ's coming, but he was also the only apostle that God would give to the world at the end-time.

The job of apostle relates to God's Church. In the role of apostle, God used him to revive His Church during this past century after it had nearly died out. Almost all truth from God had been lost to the people of God, the Church of God, and therefore the truth of God's ways was obviously lost to the world, since His own Church had nearly lost it.

Who was this man? You may have never even heard his name, but the world will hear it, just as they will hear much more concerning what God is about to do. This man was used by God to raise up a little flock, a small Church, but God's Church! Notice what God says about His Church.

"There is <u>one body</u> and one Spirit, even as you are called in one hope of your calling; one Lord, <u>one faith</u>, one baptism, one God and Father of all, who is above all, and through all, and in you all" (Ephesians 4:4-6). This clearly means that there is only one Body of Christ, which is the Church, and there is only one faith, which

means there is only one way to "believe" that can be true. But look at all the different doctrinal ideas and beliefs, among churches, that are at odds with one another concerning what they believe to be true.

People choose to reject these words in scripture because it would mean there is indeed only "one Church," just as God says. But most do not believe God. Thankfully, the objective of this book is not to prove these things, but only to record what is true and what is very shortly going to come to pass. Then, when everything written here does come to pass, this book will have served its purpose as a true witness of the true testimony of Jesus Christ.

Two things will be achieved by this book. First, a very small number will begin to be moved by the spirit of God to see that these things are true because God has a great purpose for those who will be called, early on, out of the confusion in the world. They will have first opportunity to turn to God and be given favor to survive what is about to come on the world and live on into a new age for mankind—under the rule of Jesus Christ on the earth. Continuing with this same point, as time progresses on, especially in the great tribulation, more and more will be drawn to God as they come to acknowledge the truth. Millions more will continue to repent and be drawn to God as they hear these same things that will be expounded upon and magnified by the two witnesses, who will come on the world scene. Those who repent and receive (turn to—desire) the Kingdom of God that is coming will comprise a new civilization in that new age.

Secondly, this book will stand as a witness—a true testimony of God against all who refuse and oppose what is written. The contents of this book do not have to be justified—not by argument, debate, science, scholarly dissertation, or any such thing. It is simply fact—truth from God—the Almighty God of all the universe, and "time" will prove its authenticity and the power of God to bring it to pass.

In January of 1986, the work of the end-time Elijah came to an end when he died. His name was Herbert W. Armstrong. God called him out of this world and gave him a most incredible job to perform. That job began very humbly in the early 1930s.

Molding the Elijah

Herbert W. Armstrong was a very successful advertising man in his early days, but God began to draw him out of this world and "call" him to a special job. God molded and fashioned the conditions and circumstances surrounding his life in order to prepare him for what lay ahead.

Mr. Armstrong's first real encounter with God began when his wife, Loma, challenged him concerning the Sabbath day. His strong Quaker background, mixed with his pride in self-accomplishment as a very successful business man, made this challenge a great personal battle. He knew his wife was in error over her new-found belief, but she had challenged him to prove her wrong.

Over the next six months he spent long hours in the public library. He began by trying to prove her wrong in order to help her get back to her strong Protestant roots. But the more he researched, the more he found there was no Biblical authority for the keeping of Sunday as the weekly Sabbath. Instead, he only found evidence that the weekly Sabbath was on the seventh day of the week—Saturday.

He found that Jesus Christ kept the weekly Sabbath—on the seventh day. He found that the apostles observed the weekly Sabbath—on the seventh day. Even Paul, who was sent to the gentiles—not to the Jews, taught gentiles on the seventh-day Sabbath.

As time continued, he began to find other startling things in the Bible—things he had never been taught in Sunday worship service. He found that other beliefs which he had learned in his youth did not come from scripture. He found that Easter was not taught in the

New Testament. In the King James Version Bible he found that the only place the word "Easter" had been used was mistranslated from Greek to English: it was actually the word for "Passover." What did all this mean?

God was opening the mind of Herbert W. Armstrong to truth that was fading out of this world, after so long a time, since the days of the early disciples. God's spirit was leading him into truth that was hidden from the world—from the religious world around him.

Such revelation concerning the seventh-day Sabbath, and now the Passover, led him into even deeper understanding and astonishment. He found that he had been lied to all his Protestant life in regard to the resurrection of Jesus Christ. He had always believed that Jesus was killed late on a Friday, toward sundown, and resurrected on Sunday morning. That could only mean Jesus was dead for a day and a half before being resurrected. Even this teaching of traditional Christianity would now lead to a startling revelation. (It should be noted that the counting of a Biblical day is from sundown to sundown, not midnight to midnight.)

The shock came when he read Jesus' own words explaining the only sign that He would leave to the Jews that He was the Messiah. Jesus said He would be in the heart of the earth for the same period of time that Jonah was in the belly of the great fish. That period of time, as described in the Hebrew in the Old Testament, is a very specific 72-hour period of three days and three nights.

If Jesus died on Friday and was placed in the tomb just before sunset, then that would mean he would have to be resurrected on Monday, just before sunset on that day, in order to fulfill His words and be proof that He was the Christ. Mr. Armstrong came to realize that what he had been taught all his life was in error—a lie! He was left with only one possible answer. Either Jesus did not fulfill his own prophecy, and is therefore not the Christ, or great error existed in what he had been taught all his life.

He believed that Jesus was the Christ. So what was the answer to all this? He found the answer through learning more about the weekly seventh-day Sabbath and the annual Sabbaths God gave His people long ago. He discovered that the time period, during the week of Jesus' death, was the beginning of a religious period, for the Jewish people, known as the Passover and the annual Holy Day period of the Feast of Unleavened Bread. These were annual convocations commanded by God for His people.

The first day of Unleavened Bread is described as an annual Sabbath, a Holy Day for religious observance, just like the seventh day is a weekly Sabbath. He learned that Jesus Christ was killed during the time known as the Passover. He learned that this had great significance in the Old Testament teaching, as well as in the New Testament, since Jesus Christ was to fulfill the role of our Passover lamb, the true Lamb of God, sacrificed in our stead. This made sense! It had great meaning! This was exciting understanding. This knowledge opened the door to understanding that Jesus Christ was indeed the Messiah, the Christ who was to come and rule the world.

Theologians read about the death of Jesus Christ, but they are blinded to the truth because of their own religious prejudice. So they willingly hold to a convoluted story that Jesus died just before the weekly seventh-day Sabbath began. They cling to the story that He was then resurrected on Sunday morning, thereby, through their thinking, giving credibility and authority to the Sabbath day being changed from the seventh day of the week to the first day of the week—Sunday.

Mr. Armstrong found this not only to be in error, but a blatant lie! Theologians choose to ignore the biblical record in order to sustain their own false belief and their chosen occupation in life. Mr. Armstrong learned that the Sabbath being spoken of, by those who wanted to hurry up and prepare Jesus for burial (before the Sabbath began), was not the weekly Sabbath, that would begin at sundown on Friday, but the annual Sabbath that followed the

Passover at sundown.

Those who wanted the body of Jesus, in order to prepare it for burial before the Sabbath, were wanting to do so on the Passover day, before the first day of Unleavened Bread was to begin (an annual Sabbath). They could do work on the Passover day since it was not a Sabbath (Holy Day). But they had to hurry because they could not work on the annual Sabbath that would begin as soon as the sun went down on the Passover day.

This annual Sabbath observance was not on Friday (by our Roman calendar), but on Thursday. Actually, it began after sundown on Wednesday and ended at sundown on Thursday. In the year of Jesus' death, Passover was on Wednesday. Sundown, on that Wednesday, marked the beginning of the first day (an annual Sabbath) of the Feast of Unleavened Bread (Leviticus 23).

As Mr. Armstrong learned these things—as God revealed them to him—he came to see what was true and what was a lie. The truth is that Jesus Christ did fulfill the sign He said would prove He was the Messiah. He did die toward the end of the Passover day, in mid-afternoon on Wednesday, was prepared for burial and placed in the tomb just before the annual Sabbath—just before sunset on that Wednesday.

Counting forward, it became obvious that Jesus was not resurrected on Sunday morning, but at the end of the weekly Sabbath, just before sunset on that day—just before the first day of the week began! The first day of the Biblical week began after sunset on the seventh day, after sunset on the Sabbath day. Jesus was not even resurrected on the first day of the week, but at the end of the weekly Sabbath day. This was an incredible revelation to Mr. Armstrong, just as it should be to you—if you have ears to hear and eyes to see. Much more concerning the specific timing of the Passover is covered in Chapter 7.

Everything began to truly make sense to Mr. Armstrong as he read the various accounts of the resurrection of Jesus Christ. Those who came to the tomb early Sunday morning were told that Jesus had already risen. They were not told that He had risen that morning. They did not go there after sunset, at the end of the weekly Sabbath, but they went there at the first light of morning, of the first day of the week. Jesus was not in the tomb since He had already been resurrected from the dead.

Mr. Armstrong learned a great deal in the beginning as God prepared him for the job that lay ahead. His life would prove to be one of continually learning truth God revealed to him. God used him to restore His truth to His Church—truth that not only the world had lost, but His own Church was losing.

Time to Decide
In a way similar to the beginning of Mr. Armstrong's calling and growth, learning the truth of God can now become part of your story. God is beginning a process of calling the world into a relationship with Him. Everyone who seeks to live through the end-time great tribulation and live on into a new world, where God's Kingdom reigns, will have to choose for themselves if they will receive God's truth or stubbornly hold onto traditional beliefs that are fables. It is a choice, but one that will not be up for debate with God.

People must repent of their wrong ways and receive God's way of life, or they will simply be erased from the earth at this time. The way of greatest hope (because there is still no guarantee to survive) is to repent of error and receive what it true. That is the right thing to do, no matter what the immediate outcome. If we do not receive such favor immediately, then it will come when we are resurrected to life once more (this will be explained toward the end of this book). However, your best hope, concerning your own life now and the lives of those that you love, is that you repent speedily and pour out yourself to God, seeking His guidance, forgiveness, favor, and every day help and intervention in life!

When you truly repent you will have to do as Mr. Armstrong did. As God revealed truth to him, he repented of his wrong ways and received the truth with gladness. The beginning, for him, concerned the weekly Sabbath. Will you accept what is true? Will you embrace the seventh-day Sabbath or will you continue to resist God and hold to false ways, like the world has done for so long a time?

The Sabbath is a sign of God's people. It is a sign of those who are willing to follow their God. It reveals the beginning of a right attitude that is willing to reject long-held beliefs in order to obey God and hold to what is true. The seventh-day Sabbath is a "test" command. It tests you to see if you will humble yourself willingly to accept the authority of God in your life.

"And the LORD spoke unto Moses, saying, Speak you also unto the children of Israel, saying, Verily my Sabbaths you shall keep: for it is a sign between me and you throughout your generations; that you may know that I am the LORD who does sanctify you" (Exodus 31:12-13). *"It is a sign between me and the children of Israel for ever: for in six days the LORD made the heaven and the earth, and on the seventh day He rested, and was refreshed"* (Exodus 31:17).

It truly is so simple, but man has fought against the ways of God for 6,000 years. Man has resisted the Sabbath and denied this sign between him and His God. Only when someone is faithful to the Sabbath can they hope to be sanctified—set apart—as God's people for His special purpose. Yes, it is so very simple, a sign that would be a perpetual covenant with man. It could never be changed from the seventh day to the first, for in doing so, it would lose all the great meaning God has for giving it—a perpetual sign that He is our Creator. In six days God made the world, and on the seventh He rested. God chose that day as holy time. It is for the convening of His people to be taught by Him.

But man has chosen other days of the week to look to their gods. Some chose Monday, others Friday and yet others Sunday. More will be given in Chapter 6 concerning some of these matters. For now, what will you choose? Will you hold to your false ways or accept God's true ways? It really is a simple choice. This is where you must begin. It will not be easy. It was not easy for all those who lived during the past 6,000 years and who chose to follow the true ways of God. It was hard because of the resistance, the mocking and oppression that came from others who hated such ideas and beliefs. It will be the same for you.

It should be noted here that the keeping of the seventh-day Sabbath of itself does not mean one is totally following God's true ways and that God is working with them. But the Sabbath is a test commandment and a mark (a sign) of the beginning of obedience.

Just as Mr. Armstrong made a choice when God showed him the truth about the Sabbath, you too must choose. He had to humble himself and tell his wife that she was right. He had to humble himself before God, repent and seek God's forgiveness in order to come into obedience and harmony with Him. Will you do the same?

This book is not trying to sway people into joining some movement or organization that seeks to become larger. However, that is what most organizations and movements seek to do—become larger, more powerful and wealthier. This is written to give you the tools and means whereby you can find answers to what is coming on this earth, so that you might have some opportunity to share in what lies just beyond the end-time tribulation. God is bringing His worldwide ruling Kingdom to the earth. All who live on into it will be able to become a part of His Church. It will be the only Church on earth. No other religion will exist that can hurt and deceive mankind any more. It will be "one Church." There is only one Church anyway, but in that new world it will be manifested throughout all the world!

Do you grasp what God may be offering you? What will it take to bring you to your knees? If death comes, your choice ends. If you live, how long will it be before you will repent and accept the truth you are reading?   ...You are about to find out, one way or the other!!!

The Elijah to Come

"Behold, I will send you Elijah the prophet before the coming of the great and dreadful day of the LORD: And he shall turn the heart of the fathers to the children, and the heart of the children to their fathers, lest I come and smite the earth with a curse" (Malachi 4:5-6).

This prophecy is one that focuses on an event that scholars and religious teachers have long debated concerning the coming of a Messiah. Some were so confused in the time of Jesus that they wondered if He might not be that Elijah spoken of in scripture. But this prophecy in the Book of Malachi speaks of someone who was to come to this earth in the spirit of Elijah, not the actual resurrected Elijah, before the great and dreadful day of the LORD—at the end-time.

Pay close attention to what this prophecy says because God already knew what the response of mankind would be. It has always been the same—man rejects God.

People are taught to go to the church of their choice. They are not taught that there is only one God, one faith, one true Church, and one Christ. Therefore they are blind to the reality that there cannot be hundreds of different faiths and teachings concerning God and His Son, Jesus Christ. They are deceived! They do not understand that they have simply chosen a religious "flavor" that is to their own personal liking.

Look at the history of man and what man has created after his own likeness. Look at the different ideas about a god that man prefers to believe, one you can worship at the time of your own choosing. Man's god can have different laws or no laws at all. Look at how widely fragmented traditional Christianity is.

What response would you receive if you told religious people that the seventh-day Sabbath was required? How would they respond if you told them that in order to obey God they must observe the annual Sabbaths just like the early disciples did from the time of Christ? How do you respond? Tell those in traditional Christianity that Easter is not biblical. Tell them it is a lie. What response would you get? Man hates the truth, therefore, he unwittingly hates God.

Tell them that the resurrection was not on Sunday morning and you will be seen as a crackpot, weird or pitifully ignorant. Tell them that the Catholics, in their own encyclopedia, explain that there is no authority, in scripture, for the Sabbath being changed to the first day of the week (Sunday). The Catholics candidly explain that the only authority for doing so is that of the Pope. A Pope changed it by decree long ago, and that doctrine has been supported by every Pope since. The Catholic faith, from which the Protestant faith emerged, believes that the only authority the Protestants have is that of the Pope. Tell all these things to people and see what happens. Do you think that religious prejudice, of deep proportions, does not exist in the hearts of men? Religious conflict of unimaginable proportions is about to be unleashed on the world.

Tell traditional Christianity that Easter is false. Tell the young children that Easter Bunnies don't lay eggs and that Santa Claus is a fable and has nothing to do with God. What response will you receive? You will find yourself in opposition to their gods. They will hate you for it. People do not take kindly to anyone who would dare tear down "their" gods. Yet, God is telling this to the world and will continue to do so with great power as time moves forward, all the way up to the time of the great and dreadful day of the LORD! Man will learn to swallow his pride and cast off his enormous arrogance that stands against God—against what is true.

This prophecy in Malachi concerning the end-time Elijah also contains prophetic judgment that will come. God knew, when He sent the Elijah, that he and his message would be rejected. God makes it clear that the time of his coming would be "before" the great and dreadful day of the LORD. God said that if the message of His Elijah did not change hearts that He would strike the earth with a curse. That curse upon mankind is everything that is prophesied to come on an unrepentant world at the end of 6,000 years of self-rule. God foreknew that mankind would reject the message of His end-time Elijah. Yet his coming was to stand as a witness of mankind, that mankind was still the same at the end as he has been throughout the previous 6,000 years—in defiance and opposition to his God.

God's desire for mankind is that he repent—that his heart be changed to receive the kind of heart that the faithful fathers of old—Abraham, Isaac and Jacob—possessed. But the history of man is that he rejects such a heart.

God has long expressed His desire for man to change and receive His ways, that he might live life to the full. It has been expressed in many ways and at many times.

"O that there were such an heart in them, that they would fear me, and keep all my commandments always, that it might be well with them, and with their children for ever" (Deuteronomy 5:29). This was spoken, after God gave His law to the Israelites, to show all mankind the true way of life to be lived. But God knew their heart—they would not obey.

Jesus Christ expressed this same sentiment in another way. *"O Jerusalem, Jerusalem, you that kill the prophets, and stone them who are sent unto you, how often would I have gathered your children together, even as a hen gathers her chicks under her wings, and you would not!"* (Matthew 23:37). Jesus Christ is showing, by this expression of desire toward those who were given the ways of God, that their heart, their nature, was to reject God and not receive His care and nurturing love. All mankind has that same heart and spirit.

"For I will take you from among the nations, and gather you out

of all countries, and will bring you into your own land. Then will I sprinkle clean water upon you, and you shall be clean: from all your filthiness, and from all your idols, will I cleanse you. A new heart also will I give you, and a new spirit will I put within you: and I will take the stony heart out of your flesh, and I will give you an heart of flesh. And I will put my Spirit within you, and cause you to walk in my statutes, and you shall keep my judgments, and do them" (Ez. 36:24-27). This prophecy is in response to the spirit and attitude that has existed in mankind for the past 6,000 years. God is going to bring down all nations. All governments of man will be brought to an end. God will gather all people into a single kingdom—His Kingdom over the whole earth. In the end-time, God will destroy all religions, idols, and false gods, including the false ways of what is called Christianity. Then God's Kingdom will begin to reign, and God will pour out His Spirit on all mankind. God must bring down all nations from their haughtiness and pride—humble them—so they can receive a new heart and spirit.

The story of man has been ugly over these 6,000 years. Mankind has continually rejected God except for those few, through time, that God has specifically called, humbled, molded, and fashioned to become a part of His Kingdom. They are the 144,000 He has worked with through time.

God knew that man would reject the message of His Kingdom. Therefore, the purpose of the Elijah's work would be a "witness" at the end of man's time of self-rule—that man still rejects God. God's final judgment then is indeed righteous and just. The work of the end-time Elijah would prove a "witness" against mankind and that God's witness is true.

Two Elijah's

Other than the actual Elijah, who was one of God's prophets, scripture reveals two that would come in the spirit of Elijah. One would come at the end-time. People confuse these scriptures and therefore miss their deep meaning and application.

Jesus Christ made it clear that the first one to come in the spirit of Elijah was John the Baptist.

"And His disciples asked Him, saying, Why then say the scribes that Elias [Elijah] *must come first? And Jesus answered and said unto them, Elias truly shall first come, and restore all things. But I say unto you, that Elias is come already, and they knew him not, but have done unto him whatsoever they desired* [Jesus explained that they did not recognize that John the Baptist was an Elijah to come. John was even put in prison and later killed.]. *Likewise shall also the Son of man suffer of them. Then the disciples understood that He spoke unto them of John the Baptist"* (Matthew 17:10-13).

Even the scribes in the time of Christ understood there were prophetic scriptures that spoke of an Elijah to come, before the Messiah would come. But no one understood the duality of prophecy in the scriptures or the purpose of the Messiah coming twice.

It is really quite simple because John was to pave the way for the first-coming of Jesus Christ—doing so in the spirit and power of Elijah. But the prophecy is dual—another person was to come in the spirit and power of Elijah, to prepare the way for the second-coming of Jesus Christ.

Part of the purpose in this duality is revealed by Gabriel as Zacharias is being told about his future son, John. *"And he shall go before Him in the spirit and power of Elias, to turn the hearts of the fathers to the children, and the disobedient to the wisdom of the just; to make ready a people prepared for the Lord"* (Luke 1:17). John the Baptist helped make a people ready for Jesus Christ's first-coming. John preached a message of repentance to prepare for the coming of the Messiah. By the time Jesus Christ began His ministry, a few thousand people had repented and were made ready to hear His message. But most in the land, and especially the leadership (government and religious), did not repent.

Again, this verse is simply showing part of the process of people turning from their own ways, through repentance, to the ways of God. Those referred to as the "fathers" are those mentioned in the Old Testament, who embraced the righteousness of God—whose hearts had been turned to God. Their lives were recorded for instruction and inspiration in the ways of God. The same spirit that worked with these men of old, "the fathers," was now working with their descendants, "the children," so that their hearts could now be turned to God and prepared for the preaching of Jesus Christ.

John preached a message (on a physical plane) that was received by some Jewish people of his day for the first-coming of Jesus Christ, as a physical human being. The second Elijah to come preached a message that was received on a spiritual plane, to prepare a people—the Church, for the second-coming of Jesus Christ. By the time Mr. Armstrong was called, the condition of the Church was one of being spiritually dead with nearly all truth dying out. If God had not stirred up Mr. Armstrong to fulfill the complete role of the Elijah to come, the Church of God would not exist today. This phase of God's work, through Mr. Armstrong, will be discussed more in another chapter.

Suffice it to say, it was at this time that God used Mr. Armstrong in the office of an end-time apostle to raise up the Church once more and call many into that Church to help share in the end-time work. And through his ministry, Herbert W. Armstrong would help prepare a people, on a spiritual plane, to be made ready for the second-coming of Jesus Christ. But the world rejected his message. Now, God will soon usher in the great and dreadful time of His judgment.

When the disciples asked about the Elijah to come, as recorded in Malachi, Jesus added an important description about his function. It is the most important thing to understand in order to identify who this person was.

Identifying the Second Elijah

Right after the transfiguration, when some of them witnessed a vision about the coming of the Messiah in the Kingdom of God, the disciples asked Jesus Christ about this prophecy in Malachi. They knew it was written that, before the Kingdom of God would come, an Elijah was to come on the scene, and that the great and dreadful day of the Lord would have to come before the Kingdom was established.

This Elijah to come would fulfill a duality with John by helping to prepare a people for the coming of Jesus Christ—in this case, the second-coming. These people would also have to come to repentance and have their hearts turned to the ways of God, just as their "fathers" of old had done.

So, in the end-time, a person would come in the spirit and power of Elijah to help prepare a people for the second-coming of Jesus Christ. The "hearts of the fathers"—that attitude of mind and spirit of righteous men of old who had a close relationship with God—was now being opened up to (turned to) those that God called in this end-time. As people responded to that calling, a calling into God's Church, their hearts were turned to receive that same spirit of the "hearts of the fathers." But this was not happening to the world, nor could it at this time because the world was not ready to receive it. Only those God worked with could be called during this period of the end-time.

What did Jesus Christ add to this old prophecy? *"Elias truly shall first come, and shall restore all things"* (Matthew 17:11). This Elijah would be involved in restoring all things. This did not apply to John the Baptist in any way. Nothing was restored through John the Baptist.

God used Mr. Armstrong to restore truth to His Church, in order to spiritually revive it. By the 1930s, the Church had nearly died out, but God promised that this would not happen to His Church. It had become very small—a handful of people. But as God continued to reveal truth to Mr. Armstrong, more and more people were added to the Body of Christ. Before God allowed Mr. Armstrong to die at age 93, God had restored all foundational truth that had by that time "worked" to fully revive His Church, grounding it deeply in His truth. The Church now had what was necessary—truth it was to "hold fast"—for what lay ahead. The prophesied end-time tribulation on the Church was coming, but only a remnant would survive and be prepared for the second-coming of Jesus Christ. This would fulfill a great part of the commission God gave to His end-time Elijah—preparing a people for Christ's coming. This book contains those truths that were restored to the Church.

The end-time Elijah had a commission to restore truth, but only to the Church. The witness of God is that the world would reject the message of this Elijah that this was the end-time and that God's Kingdom was about to come to this earth. The truth could not be restored to the world, not until God humbled it during the end-time tribulation. It is only after the world has experienced such a time of trouble that it will be in the right frame of mind to finally receive instruction from God—their Creator.

Understanding these truths will help you to understand another prophecy about Jesus Christ that is yet to be fulfilled. The apostle Peter quoted Old Testament prophecies when he preached this on the day of Pentecost in 31 A.D.

"Repent you therefore, and be converted, that your sins may be blotted out, when the times of refreshing shall come from the presence of the Lord; And He shall send Jesus Christ, who before was preached unto you: Whom heaven must receive [Jesus Christ would remain in heaven for nearly 2,000 years, until it was time for God's Kingdom to be established on earth. Then He would return.] *until the times of restoration of all things* [After He comes, all things will be restored to mankind—things man has continually rejected over the previous 6,000 years.], *which God has spoken by*

the mouth of all His holy prophets since the world began. For Moses truly said unto the fathers, A Prophet shall the LORD your God raise up unto you of your brethren, like unto me; Him shall you hear in all things whatsoever He shall say unto you. And it shall come to pass, that every soul, who will not hear that Prophet, shall be destroyed from among the people [Yes, the world will be made ready to receive and hear Jesus Christ.]. *Yes, and all the prophets from Samuel and those who follow after, as many as have spoken, have likewise foretold of these days. You are the children of the prophets, and of the covenant which God made with our fathers, saying to Abraham, And in your seed shall all the kindreds of the earth be blessed. Unto you first God, having raised up His Son Jesus, sent Him to bless you, in turning away every one of you from his iniquities"* (Acts 3:19-26). This foretells such an awesome time when mankind will finally receive what His Maker has desired for him from the very beginning. Finally, Jesus Christ will be able to restore all things to the entire world.

Herbert W. Armstrong

Mr. Herbert W. Armstrong was God's end-time apostle, just as much as the twelve disciples and Paul were apostles at the beginning of God's Church. He was also God's end-time Elijah. Mr. Armstrong understood the time in which he lived. He knew that God had called him to accomplish this commission. He often quoted a specific verse that identified the time and commission for his work—the job God had given him to do.

"And this gospel of the kingdom shall be preached in all the world for a witness unto all nations; and then shall the end come" (Matthew 24:14). Yes, God gave him a job of preaching the gospel to the world just before the "end" would come. The word gospel comes from the Greek, meaning the "good news." The gospel message has always been God's Word to mankind about the good news of His Kingdom that He would one day bring to this earth,

with the Messiah as King.

That message went out to the world, to the degree God deemed necessary, to fulfill a witness of what mankind was still like after nearly 6,000 years of human history. Notice how this gospel message was received. If you have not heard his name, at least consider some of the things that happened to him during the last ten to fifteen years of his life.

The gospel—good news of God's soon-coming Kingdom—was sent out to this world through the mass printing of a magazine called *The Plain Truth*. It was distributed in nations throughout the entire world. (It needs to be mentioned here that this same magazine, as well as other material published by the Worldwide Church of God, became fully corrupted throughout the 1990s after the leadership of that Church organization turned from the truth of God to the false teachings of traditional Christianity.)

The true gospel message also went out through extensive worldwide coverage, on radio and television. It was called *The World Tomorrow*. It had greater coverage worldwide than any other religious program at that time. Mr. Armstrong also went personally to world leaders with this same message.

It would be good for everyone to stop and consider the extent, both small and great, of this message that went out to the world "as a witness"—that witness being that mankind would reject the message! It is also good that we consider the leaders who received this witness. Although Mr. Armstrong received awards and honors from leaders of various nations, with many being drawn to him with a remarkable fondness, they rejected the gospel message he brought them about the Kingdom of God that is soon to come to this earth.

Early on, Mr. Armstrong received a very unique award from King Leopold III of Belgium. It was a watch made from a cannonball taken from a battlefield in World War I by Leopold's father, King Albert I. King Albert had the cannonball cast into four watch cases, with the desire that they would be presented to the four individuals that he felt had made the most significant contribution to world peace. The king never found anyone he felt worthy to receive the fourth watch, and so, he passed it on to his son, who was moved to give it to Mr. Armstrong in 1970. Yet today, many do not know the name of Herbert W. Armstrong, even though many world leaders were drawn to him. God is the one who gives favor to whom He will and He gave favor to Mr. Armstrong in the eyes of world leaders, yet they still did not receive the message he carried about the Kingdom of God that was soon to come.

Mr. Armstrong became known to many as an "ambassador without portfolio for world peace." He carried the gospel message to Prince Makasa and a number of the members of the Japanese Diet. Emperor Hirohito conferred on Herbert W. Armstrong the Order of the Sacred Treasure, Second Class—one of the highest decorations that can be presented to a non-Japanese. During a period that covered two decades, seven successive Japanese Prime Ministers counted Mr. Armstrong as a personal friend and counselor. Some members of the Japanese Diet referred to themselves as being Mr. Armstrong's Japanese sons. Yet none of these leaders accepted the message of the coming Kingdom of God.

Mr. Armstrong was endeared in friendship with King Hussein of Jordan, King Bhumibol Adulyadej and Queen Sirikit of Thailand, and Prime Ministers of Israel including Golda Meir and Menachem Begin. Others who counted him as a personal friend were Egyptian President Anwar Sadat, Jomo Kenyatta who was Founder and first President of Kenya, Emperor Haile Selassie of Ethiopia, Mayor Teddy Kollek of Jerusalem, and longtime friend Nagendra Singh, who was a Justice at the World Court in The Hague, Netherlands.

Mr. Armstrong also had personal meetings with leaders like Prime Minister Margaret Thatcher of the United Kingdom; Juan Carlos, the King of Spain; Egyptian President Hosni Mubarak; and Indian Prime Minister Indira Gandhi. Yet of all these world leaders, none received the message he carried of the soon-coming Kingdom of God.

President Ferdinand Marcos decorated Mr. Armstrong with the Presidential Merit Medal "for his moral presence and compelling influence in moving people toward the creation of a just and peaceful world order." He received the decoration of "Commander of Our Most Noble Order of the Crown of Thailand." Yet, neither these leaders nor their people received the message of the soon-coming Kingdom of God.

Other leaders with whom Mr. Armstrong met included President Allende of Chili, President Suharto of Indonesia, South Vietnam's President Nguyen van Thieu, and Mr. Armstrong was invited to Romania by President Nicolae Ceausescu. Mr. Armstrong also met with Deng Ziaoping of the People's Republic of China and was the first Christian leader to officially visit leaders inside China, yet this went unreported in the world. In this unprecedented visit, he addressed officials from 76 nations in the People's Great Hall in Beijing. He spoke concerning the way to real peace and why humanity fails to achieve it. Mr. Armstrong received many more honors and visited numerous other world leaders.

No one in modern history from any religious organization has ever received such recognition among so many world leaders as Herbert W. Armstrong, with the exception of the Pope. The Pope has received press coverage and people have been made very aware of his meetings and world travels, but that was never so with Herbert W. Armstrong. The world was largely unaware of this end-time Elijah, since he was ignored by the press and was insignificant in the eyes of society around him. Even though God gave him favor in the eyes of many world leaders to enable him to deliver God's message to them, he was shunned by most. The result would have been the same no matter how large an audience he could have reached, they would still reject God and His message to them.

But the gospel message that God sent throughout all the world, through Mr. Armstrong, stands as a witness in the end-time—toward the close of 6,000 years of man on this earth—that man is still the same since creation—he rejects the message of God, the good news of His Kingdom coming to this earth.

Yes, at the end of this age, a gospel message went out to world leaders, was preached for years over radio and television, and was published in numerous publications—primarily through *The Plain Truth* magazine, yet this witness that went into all the world was rejected by the world. That is the witness! Man is still the same as he was from the beginning. Only a few received that message—specifically those that God personally called into a relationship with Him, to become a part of His Church.

But in the scheme of things, Mr. Armstrong did not meet with all world leaders during his lifetime. Neither did *The Plain Truth* magazine nor *The World Tomorrow* broadcast reach the whole populations of this earth during his lifetime. In reality, only a few million *Plain Truth* magazines went out monthly, and those were mostly in the United States and English-speaking nations. But all of this worked to be a sufficient witness of mankind in the end of this age—man still rejected the gospel message from God.

Through Mr. Armstrong, God established three colleges called "Ambassador College." They were not large, each one having only a few hundred students. But through them God raised up a ministry to help teach His people, primarily on the weekly seventh-day Sabbath and on the annual Holy Days.

Through Mr. Armstrong, God revived His Church, which went by the organizational name of the Worldwide Church of God. It reached a small attendance (150,000) in the world's view, but it was what God chose to work with at the end-time. It was never meant to be a large Church. That was not God's purpose. His plan is to make it a large Church once His Kingdom comes to reign on the earth. It will be the only Church, and all the inhabitants of earth will be able to become part of it.

Today, the name Herbert W. Armstrong is not well known on the earth, but soon the world will hear it again. His name will be mentioned by the two witnesses who will tell all peoples that they rejected the message of the Elijah to come—they rejected God's message about His Kingdom that is now ready to be established on this earth.

The last part of the verse that mentioned the very commission of Mr. Armstrong also gives a dire statement concerning the timing of events for this earth. *"And this gospel of the kingdom shall be preached in all the world for a witness unto all the nations; and then shall the end come"* (Matthew 24:14). That gospel message was preached in all the world, as a witness to all nations, now, the end has come.

The end-time is revealed in the opening of the seals of Revelation. The second chapter covered the seventh seal and the events to occur when that seal is opened. As explained, at the time of this writing, we are only awaiting the opening of that seventh seal, as all six that precede it have already been opened. The opening of the first six seals is covered in Chapter 5. Indeed, the end-time has come upon the world, and six prophetic seals of revelation have already been opened! The end-time did come, once the gospel was preached into all the world, as a witness.

Chapter 4

THE END-TIME CHURCH

The history of God's true Church has been filled with opposition, persecution and tribulation. From the time of the original apostles until now, those who have been called to God's way of life have not been well received by the world around them.

At this point, this should be no surprise because mankind has continually resisted God and His way of life. Teachers and prophets of old were hated and killed by the very ones to whom they were sent to proclaim the ways and truth of God. It is no wonder that even those who claimed to believe and follow God and teach His ways were the very ones who wanted Jesus to be put to death. Today, people believe they are somehow different from those of the past. The overwhelming majority of people today who claim to follow God are the same as those at the time of Jesus Christ. So-called "religious people" have continued through the centuries to ridicule, persecute and even kill the true people of God.

It has already been covered how man has responded to the Sabbath day, yet it is the initial identifier of God's people. But not all who hold to a <u>teaching</u> of the seventh-day Sabbath are of God. Yet, all who are of God will be <u>faithful</u> to obey the seventh-day Sabbath. This knowledge becomes very important when examining the true history of God's true Church.

The history of the first seventy years of the Church is partially recorded in scripture. The early Church held to the commandments of God which includes the seventh-day Sabbath. Examples clearly show that Paul preached to the gentiles on the seventh-day Sabbath.

It is clear that Paul commanded the Corinthians in the proper way to observe the Passover and that they were to be obedient and keep the Feast of Unleavened Bread. Yet today, most people in traditional Christianity don't even know what the Passover and the Feast of Unleavened Bread are about, much less observe them as God commands.

The seventh-day Sabbath and the observance of the annual Sabbaths are of great importance when searching out the history of God's true Church. After the death of the apostle John, the history of the Church became clouded and obscure in the only preserved writings that follow the second and third centuries A.D. Nearly all of those writings began to focus on a different church than the one of the early apostles. This "new" church is one that observes a different Sabbath and one that promotes different religious observances than those of the early apostles. This new church that emerged on the scene is one that grew and became known as the Catholic Church. The religious leaders became known as priests, cardinals, fathers, and popes. Such descriptions did not exist in the time of the early Church.

Those who served God in the early Church had job descriptions such as apostle, evangelist and pastor. Such descriptions are important because they help reveal how God organized His Church and how He works through it.

The distinction of a job description is important in God's Church and it is never to be used as a religious title. The "new" Church that emerged on the scene used religious titles, but those titles did not describe the true organization of God's Church. Religious teachers and leaders of the Church of God obeyed what Jesus said.

When Jesus was describing the hypocrisy of the religious leaders of that time, he gave specific instruction concerning the use of a religious title. *"And* [they] *love the uppermost rooms at feasts, and the chief seats in the synagogues, and greetings in the markets, and to be called of men, Rabbi, Rabbi. But be not you called Rabbi: for one is your Master, even Christ; and all you are brethren. And call no man your Father upon the earth: for one is your Father, which is in heaven. Neither be you called Masters: for one is your Master, even Christ"* (Matthew 23:6-10).

Who has listened to even the most basic instruction given by Jesus Christ? Those who claim to be religious leaders seem to love religious titles—titles that should be used only of Jesus Christ and God the Father. This simple test in itself should be quite sufficient to separate those who are religious imposters from those who are true servants of God. So as it was during the time of Jesus Christ, most who claim to be religious leaders today like to have titles before their names—titles like Father, Reverend, Pastor, and yes, after nearly 2,000 years, some still like Rabbi.

In regard to titles, God's Church today is still like the Church during the time of the original apostles. It is still observing the same Sabbaths and teaching the same doctrines. It will always carry the same name and teach the same doctrines!

One of the last things Jesus prayed about before he was put to death concerned those who would be given to Jesus Christ to become a part of the Body of Christ. *"And now I am no more in the world, but these are in the world, and I come to you Holy Father, keep through your own name those whom you have given me, that they may be one, as we are"* (John 17:11). *"Neither pray I for these alone, but for them also which shall believe on me through their word; that they all may be one; as you, Father, art in me, and I in you, that they also may be one in us: that the world may believe that you have sent me"* (verses 20-21).

Jesus Christ asked his Father to keep, in His name, all that would become a part of the Church. The Church, as always, carries the Father's name. So another identifier of the Church is that it is called the Church of God. It cannot bear any other name. It does not belong to anyone else or to any organization. It is not Luther's or Wesley's. It is known neither by its structure as universal or catholic nor by its adherence to a systematic procedure (Methodist). It does not belong to a country—the Church of England. It is not named after some doctrinal viewpoint such as Pentecostal or Baptist. Even Jesus Christ, when He prayed to the Father, specifically said it was to be named after the Father and not Himself—it does not go by the name Church of Christ.

Do people gladly receive God's instruction? Do they thankfully receive the correction of God—thankful to no longer be deceived by the wrong day of worship or the incorrect name of God's own Church? Do people change quickly upon learning the truth? NO! Instead, they hate those who show what is true, just as the religious community hated Jesus Christ and all that He taught. People are no different today than they were 2,000 years ago. That is the true witness of man—he still rejects God. That is the very reason man has finally come to this time—the end-time.

The Church of God today is just like the Church during the time of the early apostles. It observes the seventh-day Sabbath and the annual Sabbaths, and it carries God's very name to identify it.

So just how great is the religious pride of today? You will now have the opportunity to see how strong yours is, and perhaps that of others. Yes, people hate what God says. Religious leaders do not like the instruction of Jesus Christ. They like to ignore it or claim that He actually meant something else by the things that He spoke so plainly.

So again, the church that arose, in recorded history, in the second and third centuries A.D. was not the Church of God, but one that became known as the Catholic Church. It grew large and stood alone for several hundred years continuing through the dark ages of man's struggle in Europe. Then, approximately five hundred years ago, something different began to emerge in the so-called religious world. It is called "traditional Christianity." However, the true Church of God continued to exist from the days of the apostles, but it remained small, persecuted and obscure from the world.

Nearly all of the teachings and beliefs in traditional Christianity have come from the original church that called itself Catholic. Even one of the greatest religious observances of traditional Christianity derived its very name from a religious observance of the Catholic Church. It concerns the mass of Christ—better known now as Christmas. Strangely, today many religious scholars admit that Jesus Christ was born nowhere around this time of year, but in the early fall of the year as scripture shows.

Even Easter was added by this "new church" as it continued to grow larger in the world. A great controversy recorded in history concerns the Nicene Council of 325 A.D. at which religious leaders of the time rejected the observance of the Passover and began leading the world into the observance of Easter. Easter was always to be observed on a Sunday, whereas Passover is always observed on the 14th day of the first Biblical month, which could fall on different days of the week. It was through this change, from Passover to Easter, with Easter being observed on a Sunday, that they began to teach Sunday (the first day of the week) as being the Christian Sabbath.

It was also in the Nicene Council of the Catholic Church that the false doctrine of a trinity was adopted which identified the Holy Spirit as a "being" rather than the power of God. God's Holy Spirit is the power that comes from Him. The Holy Spirit is not a separate being!

So where does traditional Christianity have its roots? If they believe in Sunday as the day of their worship, if they believe in Easter as an annual observance, and if they adhere to the teaching of a trinity, then where do they have their allegiance? Indeed, it is to the Catholic Church!

How many will receive such truth with gratitude and excitement? How many will be thankful to finally learn how they have been deceived for such a long time? How many will repent and quickly return to the seventh-day Sabbath? Do you think mankind loves the truth—that mankind loves what God tells them is true? NO! Again, that is precisely why the end-time has come.

It doesn't matter if anyone likes it or not, whether anyone accepts it or not or whether anyone believes it or not, we are at the end of man's selfish rule on the earth! This is the end of man's willingness to be deceived—with his cavalier acceptance of lies and fables. Sunday, Christmas, Easter, the Trinity, and all other religious fables are now going to be exposed for the lies they are and for the hurt and suffering that such nonsense has brought upon the world.

Will people gladly receive the correction of their Creator? Hardly! They will hate it, and they will fight against it. But God Almighty will win! Those who refuse to repent will hate you if you embrace what is true. But they will not be able to hate you very long because their reign is coming to an end. That is the gospel—the good news that God is now bringing to this earth. His Kingdom is now coming to restore truth throughout the earth.

The "Elijah to come," at the end-time, brought this message to the world—a message of good news that the end-time has come and that God's Kingdom was about to be ushered into the world. But the world hated him, as the world has always hated truth from God. The end-time Elijah was hated, the truth he brought was hated, and consequently, God was rejected at the end-time just as He has been for the past 6,000 years of man.

If you look up the name Herbert W. Armstrong on the internet, you will get a big dose of hatred. Many people have tried to stamp out and discredit anything that came through Herbert W. Armstrong. The facts about his life have been twisted, lied about and maligned by many because they hate what he taught. Yet in the maze of the internet, some have posted materials he wrote. Some believe that by doing this they are showing how wrong he was. They do not understand what is true. Instead, they believe lies, deceptions and fables. If you do look him up on the internet, try to get a copy of the book he wrote, *Mystery of the Ages.* That book is a compilation of over fifty years of revelation of truth that God delivered through the end-time Elijah! But do not follow those who claim they have continued with his work—for they have not!

The truth is that people will not receive this message now any more readily than at any other time God has sent His servants into the world. But it doesn't really matter whether they receive the truth gladly or not—God's Kingdom is now coming and everything will happen just as this book records it!

This truth can make a difference only to those who receive it. That difference is the beginning of any possibility of deliverance from what is about to come. Again, this book is not trying to convince or prove anything to anyone. God and time will take care of that! Your life and relationship with God is between you and your God—no one else!

Now, on with the history of God's true Church.

God's Message to His Church

We are going to turn to a condensed version of the history of God's true Church. It is contained in His own personal message to His Church throughout its existence up until the coming of Jesus Christ in His Kingdom. This personal message is contained in prophecy and this prophetic history is contained in the Book of Revelation.

John writes, *"I was in the Spirit in the Lord's Day, and I heard behind me a great voice, as of a trumpet, Saying, I am the Alpha and the Omega, the first and the last: and, What you see, write in a book and send it unto the seven churches which are in Asia; unto Ephesus, and unto Smyrna, and unto Pergamos, and unto Thyatira, and unto Sardis, and unto Philadelphia, and unto Laodicea"* (Revelation 1:10-11).

In this vision, John was thrust ahead in time, to the end-time and specifically the great day of God Almighty that is referred to here as "the Lord's Day."

Pausing here for a moment, it needs to be noted that many in traditional Christianity will say that this day of the Lord is about Sunday. Yet such a belief has no meaning for what God is revealing through the context of what is about to be recorded. It has already been pointed out that the seventh-day Sabbath is God's day for mankind. Scripture makes all this quite clear by another simple statement. *"For the Son of man is Lord even of the Sabbath day"* (Matthew 12:8). Jesus Christ is clearly the Lord of the seventh-day Sabbath, not the first day of the week (Sunday) that man likes to call the Lord's day.

Returning to what John wrote, it records that as he was thrust forward to the end-time, God told him to write a specific message that was to be given to seven churches. These churches were located in cities in Asia Minor, and John wrote about the specific characteristics of each of those seven church areas. Yet, these were not the only church areas in the world at the time of John. The Church in John's time had gone into many parts of the world. This message was a specific prophetic message to God's Church through time. It was a condensed message of the primary things that would transpire over the next 2,000 years to seven distinct eras of God's Church.

"Write the things which you have seen, and the things which are, and the things which shall be hereafter; The mystery of the seven stars which you saw in my right hand, and the seven golden lampstands. The seven stars are the angels of the seven churches: and the seven lampstands which you saw are the seven churches" (Revelation 1:19-20). God was revealing what was happening to the Church at that time, which was the Ephesian Era, and what would happen in those eras to follow.

The Church was small but continued to spread during the first three eras (Ephesus, Smyrna and Pergamos). The fourth era, Thyatira, was a long-lived era of the Church. Its message was one that would cover several hundred years of God's Church—for

God's people. It was a Church greatly persecuted during the Dark Ages as another church, calling itself Christian, continued to grow in greater power—even wielding power over nations. That church was the Catholic Church, and it exercised power over what many have called the Holy Roman Empire, which was far from being holy!

By the time the Sardis Church Era came, new religious groups had come on the world scene. Some had broken away from the Catholic Church. Still, others formed that had broken away from those original groups that earlier rejected the Catholic Church. Profuse religious confusion had been thrust upon the world. Then, the means of mass printing became available to help spread the growing plethora of religious ideas and doctrines.

The Sardis Era began to collapse under the pressure of so many in the world who called themselves Christian and were bombarding the world with their many false doctrines. The power of such religious confusion, which emerged from this growing freedom in religious expression, began to have a powerful weakening affect on God's Church.

The message to Sardis, the fifth church era, was indeed a sobering one. *"And unto the angel of the church in Sardis write; These things says He who has the seven Spirits of God, and the seven stars; I know your works, that you have a name* [Church of God] *that you live, but you are dead. Be watchful, and strengthen the things which remain, that are ready to die: for I have not found your works perfect before God"* (Revelation 3:1-2).

This era still carried the name "Church of God." But the warning from God was that the people had become so spiritually weak that He described them as being "spiritually" dead. They were admonished to be spiritually watchful by repenting and strengthening the truth they still had. God had shown that even the truth which still remained was about to completely die out.

It was at this point in time, toward the end of this era, that God had to intervene before His Church completely died out on the earth. Other so-called Christian organizations were flourishing through these times, but not the true Church of God. By the early 1900s, this spiritual body had indeed nearly died out. But Jesus Christ had given strong words concerning the future of the Church.

Jesus asked the disciples who people thought He was, and then finally He asked them if they truly knew who He was. *"He said unto them, But who do you say that I am? And Simon Peter answered and said, You are the Christ, the Son of the living God. And Jesus answered and said to him, Blessed are you, Simon Bar-jona: for flesh and blood has not revealed this unto you, but my Father who is in heaven. And I say unto you, that you are <u>Peter</u>* [Greek word "Petros" which means a small stone or rock.]*; and upon this <u>rock</u>* [Greek word "Petra" which is a large stone or great rock.] *I will build my church; and the gates of <u>hell</u>* [Greek—"grave"] *shall not prevail against it"* (Matthew 16:15-18).

Jesus Christ replied by telling Peter that his name meant a small stone or rock and that He was going to build the Church upon the rock that was "Petra," which meant a large stone or great rock. This had deep meaning to the disciples because the Old Testament scriptures contain many references to a rock (Hebrew word "cela"—pronounced sehlah) which is the same word in Hebrew for a "great rock," and it does so in context with God being our Cela or Petra. Jesus was making it clear that He would build the Church on the "Petra" that is God and not on man. He strengthened what He had to say by explaining that this Church would never die out. He said the gates of Hades, which concerns death and the grave, would never prevail against the Church.

By 1900 A.D., the Church was dying out and had nearly come to an end. To preserve the Church which God clearly prophesied would exist until the coming of Jesus Christ, God would have to revive it.

A New Church Era

God's plan for mankind is very specific as is the timing of that plan. God allotted 6,000 years for man's own selfish rule on earth. After that time expires, God reveals that His Kingdom would then be established on the earth with the Messiah reigning as King of kings. There will be no governments ruling on the earth except the one worldwide government that is administered by the Kingdom of God.

By the close of the Sardis Era of the Church of God, the Church had lost most of the truth God gave it in the beginning. The brethren had become weak because of this and they were dying spiritually. The time was the mid 1920s. It was God's time to begin reviving His Church, preparing it for the end-time and the coming of His Kingdom.

Only three foundational truths remained in the Sardis Era. They had the true name that identified who they were—the Church of God. They understood the seventh-day Sabbath and remained faithful to it. In addition, they still had the basic truth of tithing—ten percent of their increase was to be given to God—to God's true servants on earth.

God began to work with a man to fulfill this important end-time role of reviving the Church—and much more. That man was Herbert W. Armstrong—the very one who would fulfill the role of the prophetic end-time Elijah. He would become the one and only leader of a new era of the Church of God—the Philadelphia Era.

In the very first week of their marriage, in July of 1917, Herbert Armstrong's wife, Loma, received a message from an angel in a dream. She saw an angel descend from heaven and put his arms around the Armstrongs. The angel then announced that Jesus Christ would return in "this generation" and that Christ had important work for them to do in preparing for His coming.

This incident occurred long before either of them would learn about the end-time or that Jesus Christ would be coming to establish His Kingdom on the earth. Although he had a strong Quaker background, Mr. Armstrong was not very knowledgeable of the Bible, and he was not a very "religious" man. But Jesus Christ did have much work for them to do. Let's explain the message about Christ coming in "this generation." That happened in 1917, and there isn't much left of that generation. Anyone born in that year would be 87 today. Will it come true? Will Jesus Christ return while some of that generation still lives? You will have your answer very soon!

A few years later in 1924, Herbert and Loma Armstrong moved to the state of Oregon, where Loma became friends with Mrs. Runcorn, who was part of the Sardis Era of the Church of God. It was through that friendship that God introduced Loma to the truth about the seventh-day Sabbath. As a result, Loma challenged her husband concerning the correct day to observe.

This challenge led Mr. Armstrong into a six month, day-and-night study of the Bible. God began to open his mind to truth—truth that was dying out in the Church of God. In the summer of 1928, Mr. Armstrong gave his first sermon, on the subject of the Sabbath covenant, to that small group of people in the Sardis Era of the Church of God in Oregon.

After that first sermon, he was asked to begin preaching to a group of only a dozen people in Oregon City. God was preparing to raise up a new era of the Church—the Philadelphia Era. During his early ministry, many in the Sardis group resisted what God was revealing through Mr. Armstrong. Those who would receive what God was now revealing would be able to continue on in their growth and development into a new Church era. Those who refused simply died out spiritually.

After bringing him to full conversion, God trained, molded and fashioned Mr. Armstrong over a period of 3½ years, after which time he was ordained as a minister in June of 1931. God was going to revive the Church and once again send His Gospel of the

Kingdom into all the world as a witness to all nations.

God is exact in all that He does: He does everything in an orderly way, according to His plan, purpose and timing. Timing is important and God follows a precise plan. The raising up of a new era and choosing its leader was no small thing to God.

In his autobiography, Volume 1, Mr. Armstrong explained the significance of 100 time-cycles. He explained how God set the earth, sun and moon in their orbits to mark off divisions of time on the earth. One revolution of the earth is a day. One revolution of the moon around the earth is a lunar month (according to God's sacred calendar). One revolution of the earth around the sun is a solar year. But the earth, the sun and the moon come into almost exact conjunction only once in 19 years. Thus, 19 years make one complete time-cycle!

As Mr. Armstrong explained in his autobiography, the actual process of ordaining and imbuing the original apostles with power for the ministry occurred after 3½ years of intensive instruction and experience. Then, on Pentecost of 31 A.D., the Church began with the Ephesian Era and the Gospel of the Kingdom began to go out into the world.

In like manner, it was 100 time-cycles later that the Gospel of the Kingdom was revived to once again go out into all the world—this time, for a witness to all nations. It will become far more significant later, but Herbert W. Armstrong understood that he fulfilled the prophecies of the end-time Elijah to come, that he was the end-time apostle to the Philadelphian Era, and that his commission was summed up in Matthew 24:14. *"And this gospel of the kingdom shall be preached in all the world for a witness unto all the nations; and then shall the end come."*

This matter of "19-year time-cycles" and "100 time-cycles" will continue to be significant in other examples of God's timing for prophetic events to be accomplished and fulfilled. Those will be discussed as we come to them. Such information is not given to try to prove anything, but is simply a matter of revelation.

The Philadelphia Era

God's message to the end-time era of Philadelphia covers a span of some fifty-five years. It was an era of great restoration of truth and a spiritual rejuvenation for the Church. Indeed, this era was keenly focused upon its job, and all that it sought to accomplish was continually referred to as "the work of God." However, that keen focus of "God's work" later became a stumbling block for many because they could not discern the difference between what God was working to accomplish during the Philadelphia Era and what He has been working to accomplish during the last era, Laodicea.

The message to the Philadelphian Era begins by saying, *"And to the angel* [Greek– messenger] *of the church in Philadelphia write; These things says He who is holy, He who is true, He who has the key of David, He who opens and no man shuts; and shuts, and no man opens; I know your works: behold, I have set before you an open door, and no man can shut it: for you have a little strength, and have kept my word, and have not denied my name"* (Revelation 3:7-8).

The work of this era was made possible by doors that only God could open. These doors allowed the preaching of the Gospel in all the world as a witness. God would see to it that doors opened for preaching that Gospel. No one would be able to shut what He opened. Yet, many tried because they hated the message. Doors stayed open until God accomplished His purpose to the degree He desired, then the doors were closed.

The Church was small in the world's eyes and did not have the kind of financial power, prestige and influence that many large religious organizations have. The Church of God had little strength to accomplish the task before it, therefore God said He would open doors so that it could be done.

Publishing a magazine and promoting a radio and television

broadcast with a powerful message that ran contrary to popular religious belief was no small thing. Much opposition accompanied the work this era was to do, yet the work of God went forward and grew into a powerful end-time witness.

On January 7, 1934, *The World Tomorrow* radio program began to air. Then in February, 1934, *The Plain Truth* magazine began to be published. Both proved to be powerful tools to accomplish this new work of God, at the end-time. By the early 1980s, *The Plain Truth* was being read by over 20 million people, representing over 200 countries and territories. *The World Tomorrow* program had grown to being heard over 270 radio stations and 250 television stations worldwide. A powerful end-time witness did indeed go out to the world. Yet the world did not receive that message about the soon-coming Kingdom of God.

The end-time age of technology in radio, and later in television, enabled the preaching of the Gospel in a more powerful way on the earth. Exactly one 19-year time-cycle after the first *World Tomorrow* program began on radio, it began to be broadcast in Europe on one of the most powerful radio stations, Radio Luxembourg.

Exactly one 19-year time-cycle after the disciples first began to preach the Gospel of the Kingdom of God in 31 A.D., God opened a door for the apostle Paul to carry the same Gospel into Europe. It was exactly 100 time-cycles later that the Gospel message once again began to be preached in Europe.

The Philadelphian Era of the Church began with less than two dozen people. By the time it came to an end, the Church (known as the Worldwide Church of God) had grown to over 150,000 people worldwide. That is still very small compared to religious organizations in this world, yet large for those called to share in the ways and truth of God at the end-time.

In 1947 Mr. Armstrong started a college that would teach and train people to serve in the Work of God. Ambassador College in

Pasadena, California was the first of three liberal arts colleges. The ministry for the Church received its training in these colleges. Many others received their training there also to serve in different facets of that end-time "work."

Jesus Christ said of the end-time Elijah that he would restore all things. In the previous chapter, it was shown that Jesus Christ is the one spoken of in the Book of Acts who will fulfill the prophecy concerning the time of restitution of all things throughout the whole earth. At that time God will restore His truth and His government over all the earth. But in the prophecy of the end-time Elijah who would precede the coming Kingdom of God, the things that were to be restored concerned the Church. The life of Mr. Armstrong was one of restoring truth and God's government to the Church because it had nearly died out by the end of the Sardis Era.

The Philadelphia Era was a time for the restoration of truth in order to enliven God's Church. Sardis had become spiritually dead. The Church was revived as a result of God using His end-time apostle to restore truth to it. This was necessary in order to accomplish three primary end-time objectives. These are not listed as a matter of priority.

The first objective was to raise up a people who could serve in the Church and help support the preaching of the Gospel in all the world for an end-time witness to all nations. God chose to accomplish His work through His Church under the leadership of His end-time apostle.

A second objective was to call those who were yet needed to be molded and fashioned to become part of the soon-coming Kingdom—completing the number of the 144,000 that would return with Jesus Christ at His coming.

A third primary objective for restoring the truth was to help prepare the Church for the greatest time of trouble it would ever face in its entire history. It was to prepare it for the last era of Laodicea.

The job for the end-time Elijah was complete when Mr. Armstrong died in January of 1986. The Gospel of the Kingdom of God had gone out to the world, in the exact proportion necessary, to fulfill a witness concerning all nations at the end-time. The witness is that man is still the same: man still rejects God just as he has done for 6,000 years.

The Key of David
An important part of the message to Philadelphia had to do with the "key of David." *"And to the angel* [Greek– messenger] *of the church in Philadelphia write; These things says He who is holy, He who is true, He who has the key of David, He who opens and no man shuts; and shuts and no man opens;"* (Revelation 3:7).

The "key of David" was given to Mr. Armstrong, enabling him to understand many prophecies concerning the end-time. Some of the mystery surrounding the "key of David" was already known, but not as it applied to many end-time events as well as prophecies about specific nations in the end-time. This key, given in the Philadelphian Era, was essential in its timing for understanding the end-time. Only a summary of these matters will be covered. Again, it is not the purpose of this book to prove these matters—only to give what is true.

The Old Testament contains promises from God and prophecies concerning the nation of Israel that would be fulfilled in the end of man's age on earth—toward the end of 6,000 years. Many prophecies concerning the Messiah have never been understood by the Jewish people because they have not possessed the "key of David." Traditional Christianity has not understood what the Bible teaches concerning the fulfillment of prophetic events that have already happened—events that are about to be more fully accomplished on modern-day nations, as described prophetically, many hundreds of years ago.

Much of the Old Testament focuses on God working with a

specific physical family that grew into a nation of people. The story begins by focusing on God's dealings with Abraham and his wife, Sarah. As time passed, God began to make promises to him and his descendants, primarily Isaac and Jacob. God continued to add to these prophetic pronouncements and promises with Isaac and Jacob.

Eventually Jacob's name was changed to Israel. Joseph, one of his twelve sons, was sold into Egypt, and eventually the entire family moved there. Through time they became a nation of slaves in that country. Many have heard the story of the Exodus and how God raised up Moses to deliver His people.

After many years living in the promised land, these people desired to become a nation like others around them; they wanted a king. The first king of Israel was Saul, but he failed God and the people. God then raised up David. It is with David that a great mystery began—one that became hidden from the world—one that was to be revealed at the end-time.

David was king over the nation of Israel. This king was described by God as a man after His own heart. End-time prophecies concerning matters that are related to this king have become shrouded in mystery—sealed from understanding. God gave Mr. Armstrong the key to understand these mysteries.

Today, when most people hear the name Israel, they focus on a very troubled part of the world in the Middle East and they think of the Jewish people. When this happens, they cannot understand what God is saying concerning Old Testament prophecies. People today, including religious teachers and scholars, are immensely ignorant of Biblical history.

God changed Jacob's name to Israel, and that name was passed down through his sons and their descendants. Jacob had twelve sons and all twelve carried the name Israel. When David was king of Israel, that nation was composed of the descendants of the twelve sons of Jacob—the "twelve tribes of Israel."

At this point let's interject a story that will serve a dual purpose.

It will help clear up this matter of history that has become so clouded and hidden from understanding. It will also help clarify some material from the Book of Revelation that will be covered later. We have already covered part of the story about those who will come with Jesus Christ, in His Kingdom, at the resurrection. These are described in specific ways in the Book of Revelation, but let's build upon what we have already covered.

In Revelation 14 it speaks of this 144,000 *"...which were redeemed from the earth. These are they who were not defiled with women* [false churches]*; for they are virgins* [a spiritual description]*. These are they who follow the Lamb wheresoever He goes. These were redeemed from among men..."* (Verses 3-4). These that were redeemed from among men are further described in Revelation 5, *"...and have redeemed us to God by your blood out of every kindred, and tongue, and people, and nation, And have made us unto our God kings and priests: and we shall reign on the earth"* (Verses 9-10). Those that will reign with Jesus Christ are described as being redeemed from every kindred and tongue and people and nation.

This has presented somewhat of a dilemma for those who have been part of the true Church of God because they have believed that the 144,000 could only be made up of physical Israelites. That is not true! A very basic truth, revealed very early to the Church, was that God was also calling gentiles, who could now become part of the Church, which is also described as the spiritual "Israel of God." Becoming part of the Kingdom of God is open to all mankind, in God's time. The Kingdom of God is not restricted to any specific nationality of people. The same is true for His Church.

And so it is with this 144,000 who have been redeemed from different nations, kindred, tribes, and people on earth. The Church bears the <u>spiritual name</u> of the "Israel of God," and so does God's Kingdom. The structure of His Kingdom is actually divided, spiritually, into twelve specific divisions, each area carrying the name of a tribe of Israel, even as the whole of those original twelve tribes bore the name of Israel.

Revelation 7 describes this division of the 144,000 into twelve tribes. Dan's name has been omitted in this division of the spiritual Kingdom of Israel. Manasseh, one of Joseph's sons, will be used instead of Dan.

To most people this will still have no meaning, but everyone needs to take note of one of the names—Judah. As was already stated, Jacob, whose name was changed to Israel, had twelve sons who later comprised the twelve tribes of Israel. Even in His Kingdom, God is still going to use the division of twelve tribes, but God has specified the names that will continue to describe the organization (division) of His Kingdom.

Today when people hear the name Israel, they think of the Jews (Judah). But this is a big mistake! This ignorance has put the world in deep blindness concerning prophecies about Israel.

It is interesting to notice the first place in scripture where the word "Jew" is used. It is in 2 Kings 16. It describes an account where Israel is at war with Judah (the Jews). It shows that Ahaz was king of Judah and Pekah was king of Israel. It continues to tell how Israel allied itself with Syria to go up to Jerusalem to fight against Judah. Verse 6 describes how the king of Syria (the ally of Israel, fighting with Israel against Judah) drove the "Jews" (those of the tribe of Judah) from the area of Elath.

So how was it that Israel fought against the Jews (Judah)? After Solomon (David's son) died, the twelve tribes that made up the nation of Israel divided into two nations. The one in the south carried the name of Judah, with Jerusalem as its capital. This nation, located to the south, was composed primarily of the tribe of Judah (the Jews), but included part of Benjamin and Levi. The kings of Judah (south) continued to be from the lineage of King David of the tribe of Judah.

The kingdom to the north became known as Israel. It was made up of ten tribes, and the first king who reigned over it came out of the house of Joseph (1 Kings 11:31-37). The ten tribes of the house of Israel that made up this new kingdom of Israel were not Jews. They never were.

It is important to understand how this confusion began. Much of the Books of Kings and Chronicles is the story of both the kingdom of Judah and the kingdom of Israel and their kings. The story of the ten-tribed nation of Israel ends when they were taken captive by the Assyrians and moved northwest into areas of Europe. When the Assyrians took people captive, they moved them to other regions. During the time of Jesus Christ, people referred to as Samaritans lived in the area of the north where Israel once was. This region became known as Samaria, after the Assyrians had removed the people of the nation of Israel (moving them to Europe) and brought in the Samaritans to live in their place.

You need to know the reason why the whereabouts of the Old Testament nation of Israel is not known today. After their captivity, they were only known as the lost ten tribes of Israel. What ever happened to the millions that were taken captive? The Assyrians of that day are the Germanic people of today. But where are all those Israelites today? Again, they are not the Jewish people of the nation Israel today. The northern nation of Israel did not have any of the tribe of Judah in it—none of those Israelites were Jewish.

The reason this nation was taken captive is recorded in the Old Testament. Israel ceased to keep God's annual Holy Days and weekly seventh-day Sabbath. Instead of being obedient to God, they turned to other religious observances and began to worship Baal, a sun god, but they did so in the pretense of serving Jehovah—the Eternal God. Their new form of religious worship retained some of the customs of their past and still used the name of God, but it incorporated pagan ideas and concepts associated with the worship of Baal. The most incredible thing is that, since this was Baal worship, they changed from observance of the seventh-day Sabbath to worshiping on the first day of the week—Sunday—the day that the sun god, Baal, was worshiped.

Sunday worship, for traditional Christianity, does not have its origin in a Sunday resurrection. As we have already covered, Jesus Christ was resurrected just before sundown on the seventh-day of the week (equivalent to our late Saturday afternoon). When they came to the tomb on Sunday morning, he had already risen—not that morning, but near evening the previous day!

Before we continue with this remarkable story, let's look at another story to help you see how traditions and customs are literally handed down through generation after generation—over hundreds of years.

This is the story about the children of Israel, in the Old Testament, wandering in the wilderness after the Exodus. They had been rebellious before God, so He sent poisonous snakes among them. People began to die by the thousands (Numbers 21). After several thousand had died, the people went to Moses and repented for all they had done. God then told Moses and Aaron to make a metal pole and wrap a metal snake around the pole. Once this was finished, they erected it in the camp of Israel. The people were told that if they were bitten by a poisonous snake, they could come and look upon the brazen serpent, and they would live. The people did this and were healed of the snake bites. They did not die.

As a result of this experience, the people began to believe that some mystical power existed in this brazen serpent, and they began to look upon it as a symbol of healing. This became so well known among the Israelites that they duplicated this image and looked to it for healing. With carnal human nature, they found it easier to look upon a physical object for healing than to look to God, whom they could not see, to grant them healing.

So how deep rooted did this become? Notice what happened much later, at the time that Ahaz became king of Judah. It says of Ahaz, *"And he did that which was right in the sight of the LORD, according to all that David his father had done. He removed the high places, and broke the images, and cut down the groves, and broke in pieces the bronze serpent that Moses had made: for unto those days the children of Israel did burn incense to it: and he called it Nehushtan"* [Hebrew—"piece of brass."] (2 Kings 18:3-4). Ahaz destroyed the bronze serpent. This happened 700 years after it had been made, during the Exodus.

Sometimes it is hard for people to believe that strong-held beliefs (especially religious beliefs), with various traditions and customs, can be passed down from generation to generation, with little or no change. That is precisely what happened, at that time, concerning the serpent on a pole. But it didn't end there, did it? To this day that same symbol representing healing is with us—it is on nearly every ambulance you see and is often seen throughout hospitals. It isn't looked to for healing, but it is a modern-day symbol for healing that came from the time of the Exodus.

Now back to our story about the reason the northern kingdom of Israel was taken captive and why they lost their identity. God gave them over to the Assyrians to be taken captive around 725 B.C. because they turned away from obedience to His annual Sabbaths (Holy Days) and seventh-day Sabbath. Those same people are still observing Sunday! They began this tradition long ago—long before they were taken captive by the Assyrians.

And where are those people today? That is part of what the "key of David" reveals. There is much more to this subject. Mr. Armstrong wrote a book entitled *The United States and Britain in Prophecy* that covers this thoroughly. Perhaps you can find a copy on the internet. Several organizations offer this over the internet. It can be read online or downloaded. But again, a word of caution! These organizations offering his works have fallen away from the truths that God delivered to them through His end-time Elijah (although many claim to follow those same beliefs). Learn what you can from the books of Herbert W. Armstrong, but be wary of others who claim to follow his teachings! Instead, listen closely to those two witnesses that will soon come on the scene.

God purposed that the people of the northern kingdom of Israel would lose their identity until the end-time because of their disobedience concerning His Sabbaths. Will you learn from this lesson of history and begin to heal the breach by repenting and turning to obedience to God's Sabbaths?

Those ten tribes, that grew into several million in the kingdom of Israel, subsequently migrated from the place they were taken captive. There are some very specific end-time prophecies that pertain to the two tribes that descended from Joseph: Ephraim and Manasseh. The tribe of Manasseh is the United States of America. Ephraim is the United Kingdom and her commonwealth of nations. Joseph consists of the English-speaking nations of today. They are the largest constituents of the northern kingdom of Israel. These nations are more Israelite than the actual nation of Israel today. And the rest of the lost ten tribes? They are scattered throughout the western part of Western Europe.

The modern-day nation of Israel is that southern kingdom of Judah (Jewish). It was never a part of that northern Old Testament nation of Israel. Is it any wonder that there has always been a closer affinity among the brothers of Israel than with other nations? But people have not understood why. Even in modern times, who stands out as having the greatest affinity with the nations of Israel? It is the United States—the very nation that God prophesied long ago would become the single greatest nation the world has ever known—in the end-time!

The news of this ancestry was not received with excitement and gratitude, but with disdain and bitter denial. That was witnessed by the dismal response from more than 5,000,000 copies (in the English language alone) of *The United States and Britain in Prophecy* that were distributed since its first printing back in 1942. People didn't celebrate their roots then, and they still haven't. But in time <u>all</u> will! Israel is filled with pride! But God is going to humble the modern-day nations of Israel to get rid of that pride. The United States, standing haughtily and defiant before God, is proof of that pride. And, along with all the modern-day nations of Israel, God then will humble the rest of the world.

End-time prophecy and many of the things that can be learned through the "key of David" lead to understanding that the modern-day nations of Israel will begin suffering first in the time of great tribulation that is about to come on this earth. If you are part of one of these countries, then you can know that this tribulation will begin with you. Expect it! Prepare for it! Seek God to deliver you speedily.

In the story of these Old Testament nations of Judah and Israel, the southern kingdom of Judah was also taken captive, but they did not lose their identity. God allowed Babylon to take Judah captive for 70 years for their disobedience (shortly after 600 B.C.), but the house of Judah never turned from observance of the annual and weekly Sabbaths. This is the reason God let them retain their identity. The Jewish people have always known their identity, and they still hold to the Sabbath. But the house of Israel does not know who they are because they turned from God's Sabbaths—even to this very day!

Christ's Coming to an Existing Throne

More truth concerning the coming of the Messiah can be learned from the "key of David."

A prophetic pronouncement was given to Mary concerning the son she was going to give birth. Notice it. *"And, behold, you shall conceive in your womb, and bring forth a son, and shall call His name JESUS. He shall be great, and shall be called the Son of the Highest: and the Lord God shall give unto Him the throne of His father David"* (Luke 1:31-32).

The throne of David at this time was not in Judah, since it ceased to reign over the house of Judah nearly 600 years earlier, when the last king of Judah, Zedekiah, was taken captive into Babylon and all his sons were killed.

Jeconiah, another king of Judah, had previously been taken to Babylon as prisoner, yet he continued to live after Zedekiah died. However, his sons never reigned over the nation of Judah, after the nation was conquered. God foretold what would happen to this line of kings.

"As I live, says the LORD, though Coniah [Jeconiah or Jehoiachin as he was also called] *the son of Jehoiakim king of Judah were the signet upon my right hand, yet I would pluck you off; And I will give you into the hand of those who seek your life, and into the hand of those whose face you fear, even into the hand of Nebuchadnezzar king of Babylon, and into the hand of the Chaldeans"* (Jeremiah 22:24-25). God declared, concerning Jeconiah, that He was removing the crown—overturning the throne to another branch of Judah's family. *"Thus says the LORD, Write you this man childless, a man who shall not prosper in his days: for no man of his seed shall prosper, sitting upon the throne of David, and ruling any more in Judah"* (Jeremiah 22:30).

It is a long, detailed story. A great commission was given to the prophet Jeremiah. He was to have a direct part in the throne being overturned from ruling over the house of Judah to reigning over the house of Israel. Remember that at this time Israel had already been taken captive into Europe.

God proclaimed powerfully and repeatedly the importance of this throne that could never end. God began these prophetic proclamations long before Israel became a nation to the north of the nation of Judah.

"The scepter shall not depart from Judah [the Jews], *nor a lawgiver from between his feet, until Shiloh* [the Messiah] *come; and unto Him shall the gathering of the people be"* (Genesis 49:10). As Jacob, whose name had been changed to Israel, was

about to die, he called his twelve sons together and passed along to them prophecy from God. This prophecy would come to pass in their specific genealogies—in their peoples—all the way to the end-time and the coming of God's Kingdom. The birthright promises were passed down through Joseph, through his two sons, Ephraim and Manasseh, but the scepter promises came through Judah. It is through Judah (the Jews) that a ruling line of kings would come, leading up to the very King of kings. The scepter—the promise of the Messiah and of grace—was passed through the Jews! Jesus Christ was born of the tribe of Judah, was Jewish, and was a descendant of King David.

"I have made a covenant with my chosen, I have sworn unto David my servant, Your seed will I establish for ever, and build up your throne to all generations" (Psalms 89:3-4). God not only declared that the scepter would never leave Judah, but He said it would be established through David unto <u>all</u> generations. That means that if God is all powerful and His word is true, then the throne of David could never cease! Again, speaking of David, God says, *"My mercy will I keep for him for evermore, and my covenant shall stand fast with him. His seed also will I make to endure for ever, and his throne as the days of heaven"* (Psalms 89:28-29). The word "seed" concerning David is properly translated, in the Moffatt translation in modern English, as "dynasty." The Revised Standard Version translates it as "his [David's] line"—that is, a continuous line or succession of sons, generation after generation.

God even declared these things more powerfully by saying, *"Thus says the LORD; If you can break my covenant of the day, and m y covenant of the night, so that there should not be day and night in their season; Then may also my covenant be broken with David my servant, that he should not have a son to reign upon his throne..."* (Jeremiah 33:20-21).

In other words, if you can stop the earth from turning on its axis or if you can remove the sun, moon and stars from heaven, then and only then will anyone be able to prevent God from keeping His covenant to maintain continuously, through all generations, forever, a throne of rulership from the time of David to the return of Jesus Christ as King of kings.

But as we have seen, that throne ceased to reign over Judah when that tribe was taken into captivity in Babylon. What about God's promise? (The story is long and somewhat complicated, but most won't believe it anyway.) The prophet Jeremiah fled, along with some of the daughters of Zedekiah, the falling kingdom of Judah. They traveled to a part of the world that was far away from the troubles of those times—today it is called Ireland.

Though things be muddled in history, the tribe of Judah continued to reign, but not over the house of Judah. Eventually, a people migrated through Europe who were known as Saxons. This part of the world has had a long line of kings and queens throughout history. Though they have not always known it (or admitted it), those who ruled were of Judah (Jewish). This line of kings, through whom the scepter promise was given, now reigned over a people that had long before been taken into captivity by Assyria. These Saxons were none other than the sons of Isaac—Isaac's sons—since the Assyrian influence of dropping the sound of "i" left an identity of "Saac's sons" by sound.

Does this knowledge please the people of Europe? Is the United Kingdom pleased that those of the royal family are directly descended from King David through the last king of Judah, Zedekiah? You know the answer! But these same people bear a name that clearly identifies who they are. Even the word "British" declares who they are, although they have not remained true to their name—on the contrary, they deny it. They are Israelite, but not of Judah. They are one of the lost ten tribes that was taken into captivity. But those who are reigning are of Judah.

The house of Israel is the "covenant people." The Hebrew word for "covenant" (berith or b'rith) is pronounced as "brit." "Ish" in

Hebrew means "man or people."

A stone, believed to have come to Ireland long ago with a prophet, is called "lia-fail" or "stone of destiny." Many of the kings in the history of Ireland, Scotland and England have been coronated sitting over that very stone—including the present-day queen, Queen Elizabeth. Although the sign and then the stone itself have been removed in recent years, there was a stone resting within and under the coronation chair in Westminster Abbey, with a sign that once read "Jacob's pillar stone." Yes, it is that same stone "lia-fail"—the "stone of destiny" that was also identified as "Jacob's pillar stone" (Gen. 28:18).

A continuous line of royalty, of the tribe of Judah, has continued to reign from the time of King David until now. It has never ended—just as God said! It is this throne that Jesus Christ, the King of kings, will "overturn" once more when it is turned over to Him, when He comes to rule the whole world in the Kingdom of God.

As we read in Chapter 1, on the day of Pentecost in 31 A.D. Peter preached to the people from different Psalms written by David, and he also tied in familiar prophecies from Isaiah and Jeremiah. At one point he explained, *"Therefore being a prophet, and knowing that God had sworn with an oath to him, that of the fruit of his body* [a descendent of David], *according to the flesh, He would raise up Christ* [the Messiah] *to sit on his throne* [David's throne]; *He seeing this before spoke of the resurrection of Christ, that His soul was not left in hell* [Gk. word is "grave"], *neither His flesh did see corruption"* (Acts 2:30-31). It is an incredible thing to understand that God has been working over the centuries to one day give mankind a righteous Kingdom that is ruled by the Messiah—Jesus, the Christ.

More Revelation to Philadelphia
As we return to the story flow of God's message to the Philadelphia Era, we come to a verse that tells of an incredible revelation that

God made known to Mr. Armstrong—a most profound truth restored to the Church.

Traditional Christianity has no understanding whatever of why man was put on this earth. The most they seem to know is that man can live beyond this physical life, but for what purpose? They believe that the life man has is an immortal soul. This is totally contrary to all Biblical teaching. Yet man teaches such foolishness because he does not know the great purpose for which he was created.

Many of the world's religions teach that man is to attain to a higher life. Many believe this life is a kind of euphoric bliss, whether it be in heaven or some other place of eternal existence. It isn't clear what anyone will be doing, but somehow there is still going to be some kind of continuing life—perhaps drifting around with heavenly clouds, hearing angelic music, or looking on the face of some kind of god for all eternity. Does that sound exciting?

Well, it doesn't sound exciting. On the contrary, most religions have painted a picture of life after death that sounds kind of scary. It sounds more like stories of being on some hallucinogenic drug, drifting around in some kind of colorful bliss, with a numb mind, not really accomplishing anything—just drifting through time and space with no suffering or pain, surrounded by some kind of imagined beauty. That's scary! God is not like that. God has <u>great</u> things planned for mankind.

Let's notice more of that message to Philadelphia. *"Behold, I will make them of the synagogue of Satan, who say they are Jews, and are not, but do lie; behold, I will make them to come and worship before your feet, and to know that I have loved you"* (Revelation 3:9). This verse does not mean a race of people. This has nothing to do with someone claiming to be Jewish. How many people have you known who claim they are Jewish who actually are not? This verse is speaking of those who claim to be religious—a "spiritual Jew."

This is the same kind of thing that Paul was explaining to the gentiles when he said, *"For he is not a Jew, who is one outwardly; neither is circumcision which is outward in the flesh: but he is a Jew, who is one inwardly; and circumcision is that of the heart, in the spirit, not in the letter..."* (Romans 2:28-29). Paul was explaining that it is not a matter of race, but a matter of the spirit. God is concerned with the attitude and spirit of those who are in the Church. Righteousness and grace is not a matter of "right" by race, but a matter of a repentant and converted spirit (attitude and heart).

This part of the message to Philadelphia concerns the strong opposition they would receive. Those who claimed to be religious, whether they were part of traditional Christianity or claiming to be part of the true Church, were actually in opposition to the truth that God was restoring to the Church through His servant Herbert W. Armstrong. This opposition was powerful and will be discussed in more detail later.

But the main thrust of this verse involves a great truth that God revealed to Mr. Armstrong. Most people read over a verse like this, never stopping to ask an obvious question. How could anyone allow someone to come and worship before their feet? How is such a thing possible with God?

Scripture is very clear, from beginning to end, that only God can be worshiped. So how is it possible that God would record something of such magnitude about Mr. Armstrong and other faithful brethren in the Philadelphia Era? In this question is one of the most incredible truths God restored through Mr. Armstrong.

It is all about the very purpose of man's existence on earth. King David asked this question in a Psalm. *"When I consider your heavens, the work of your fingers, the moon and the stars, which you have ordained; What is man, that you are mindful of him? And the son of man that you visit him?"* (Psalms 8:3-4). This is the very question David was addressing. He goes on to answer it, but people still do not understand. David's question is also addressed by Paul in the Book of Hebrews. *"But one in a certain place testified, saying, What is man, that you are mindful of him? Or the son of man, that you visit him?"* (Hebrews 2:6).

Paul has been explaining to a Jewish audience the importance of the plan God is working out on this earth and how it focuses first and foremost on Jesus Christ. Let's go back to see the beginning of this story, as Paul is telling it.

"God, who at various times and in different manners spoke in time past unto the fathers by the prophets, has in these last days spoken unto us by a Son, whom He has appointed heir of all things, through whom also He made the worlds" (Hebrews 1:1-2).

Paul simply begins by explaining that God had spoken to their forefathers at different times and in different ways, through all the prophets, but has now chosen to speak through His own Son. Paul also said that God's Son has spoken to them in the last days. He was not referring to the end-time at the end of 6,000 years. By this time, 4,000 years of man had already passed. In God's plan, 2,000 years of man's self-rule were yet to follow. This past 2,000 years of the Church have been the "last days." Two-thirds of man's time was now past—the last third remained that would lead to the very end!

Paul said that God's Son had been appointed heir of all things, and "all things" scripturally means everything that God has created throughout the universe—everything that is of God the Father. But he also explained something else that people do not understand. He said that God made the worlds through Jesus Christ. This is speaking of "ages through time," not physical worlds. In other words, God's plan for His creation centers around His purpose being worked out in and through Jesus Christ.

It is through Jesus Christ that man can enter into a relationship with God, through the forgiveness of sins. It is through Jesus Christ that His life and that of the Father can begin to dwell in man, to bring about a complete change and transformation of heart and spirit—so that man can become at one with God. It is through Jesus

Christ that man can eventually be changed from mortal to immortal, in a resurrection. It is in the age to come that mankind can enter into the Kingdom of God, to share in the reign of Jesus Christ. These are the very things Paul is explaining.

"Who being the brightness of His glory, and the express image of His person, and upholding all things by the word of His power, when He had by Himself purged our sins, sat down at the right hand of the Majesty on high;" (Hebrews 1:3). Paul makes it clear that it is through God's own Son that our sins can be purged and that Christ now sits at the very right hand of God Almighty in heaven.

"Being made so much better than the angels, as He has by inheritance obtained a more excellent name than they. For unto which of the angels said He at any time, You are my Son, this day have I begotten you? And again, I will be to Him a Father, and He shall be to Me a Son? And again, when He brings in the first-begotten into the world, He said, And let all the angels of God worship Him" (Hebrews 1:4-6).

The story being told is that the Son of God has been made greater than the angels: the angels are to worship Him as they would worship the Father because the Son is God—of the God Family—on the God plane—of the God realm—of the God Kingdom. He is separate and distinct as the Son. He has been resurrected from the realm of physical man to the spirit realm of God, which is above the angelic realm—the angelic kingdom. Angels were created, not begotten. When a child is begotten in the womb, it grows until it can finally be born into the world, as a physical human being, just like its parents.

This is the story of God to mankind. It is a story that traditional Christianity has never understood. The Jews of Christ's time did not understand this teaching. Even Nicodemus, a leader and teacher among the Jews who had a more receptive spirit, did not understand what Jesus told him.

"Jesus answered and said to him, Verily, verily, I say unto you, except a man be born again, he cannot see the kingdom of God" (John 3:3). Today, far too many are deceived into believing that to be "born again" is some kind of religious experience and acceptance of Jesus Christ. That doesn't even come close to what Jesus Christ was saying. He was explaining to Nicodemus that a complete change would have to take place because a physical human being cannot be <u>in</u> the Kingdom of God. Nicodemus was thinking only of the physical birth and did not grasp the spiritual concept. He asked how it was that a person could be born twice. Jesus went on to explain:

"Jesus answered, Verily, verily, I say unto you, Except a man be born of water and of the Spirit, he cannot enter the kingdom of God. That which is born of the flesh is flesh; and that which is born of the Spirit is spirit" (John 3:5-6).

Again, Jesus Christ is very clearly telling Nicodemus that a physical human being can "enter" the kingdom of God—the realm of God, but not while they are still in the flesh. He makes it abundantly clear that there is a process whereby one can "enter" the Kingdom of God. The process begins with physical human beings. That which is begotten of flesh can only produce—give birth to—that which is of the flesh, a physical human being. That which is begotten of the spirit—the spirit of God—can produce that which can eventually be born a spirit being in the Kingdom of God and become part of the spiritual family of God. This is the only way a physical human being can "enter" the Kingdom of God.

A human life begins when physical life is begotten in the womb. Under normal circumstances this physical life will become a living human being. A spiritual life begins when a person is begotten of the spirit of God. Then through time, growth and development it can eventually be born into the God Family—the Kingdom of God—the God realm, as a spirit being, just as Jesus Christ became a spirit being in the God Family.

In Hebrews we are told that Jesus Christ, the Son of God, was made better than the angels because he was begotten of God as His Son. Then it says that Christ is now in the spirit realm—the God realm—Kingdom of God, which is above that of angels.

Paul explained in the first chapter of Hebrews that the angels were created as spirit beings to minister to those who were to become heirs of salvation. Notice! *"But unto the Son He says, Your throne, O God, is for ever and ever; A scepter of righteousness is the scepter of your kingdom"* (Hebrews 1:8). The resurrected Son of God, now in the Kingdom of God, is called "God!" He is not God the Father, but Jesus is now God the Christ—in the God Realm, in the God Family, in the Kingdom of God. He is the Son of the Father, a separate and distinct member of the God Family. He is the firstborn in this Family.

"For whom He did foreknew, He also did predestinate [predetermined as a part of His plan of salvation for mankind, before man was created] *to be conformed to the image of His Son, that He might be the firstborn among many brethren"* (Romans 8:29). Jesus Christ is described here as the "firstborn" of many brethren. God reveals that there are many to follow who will share in the Kingdom of God. Do you see it? Do you begin to grasp man's purpose? God has purposed that man become a part of His very Family, not of physical flesh, but of spirit with eternal life in the Kingdom of God—separate individual members of that Family. God is a family with the Almighty Eternal God as Father.

Returning to Hebrews we come to this quote of King David once more. *"For unto the angels has He not put in subjection the world to come, whereof we speak. But one in a certain place testified, saying, What is man that you are mindful of him? Or the son of man that you visit him?"* (Hebrews 2:5-6). It is revealed that God never intended that things be in subjection to the angelic realm, in the ages to come, but rather to the realm of God. That is why the question posed by King David is now stated by Paul.

Notice what Paul quoted David as saying. *"You made him a little lower than the angels; you crowned him with glory and honor, and did set him over the works of your hands: You have put all things in subjection under his feet..."* (Hebrews 2:7-8). David was asking a question concerning all mankind. The answer is that God's purpose was to eventually put all things in subjection under him. Notice the entire context of verse 8 and what Paul added in the remainder of the verse. *"You have put all things in subjection under his feet* [the completion of what was quoted from David]. *For in that He put all in subjection under him, He left nothing that is not put under him. But now we see not yet all things put under him."* Paul said that although it is God's purpose to put all things under subjection of man we do not yet see that fulfilled. Paul went on to show what they did see at that specific time.

"But we see Jesus, who was made a little lower than the angels for the suffering of death, crowned with glory and honor; that He by the grace of God should taste death for every man. For it became Him, for whom are all things, and by whom are all things, in bringing <u>many sons to glory</u>, to make the captain of their salvation perfect through sufferings" (Hebrews 2:9-10).

God revealed through Paul that part of the purpose of God for mankind had now been fulfilled in and through Jesus Christ, since Christ was now in the Kingdom of God. In God's time, all things will be brought into subjection to God—in the Kingdom of God. Jesus Christ is the first to be crowned with glory and honor in the God Family, and as it says, it is through Christ that many sons will be brought into that same glory—many sons born into the God Family.

So now we know that part of the message to Philadelphia addresses a matter that involves one of the greatest truths restored to the Church. That truth is that God's very purpose for man is to give him eternal life in His Family—the Family of God.

It is an incredible story. The mysteries of God's plan and

purpose through time are revealed in a basic and easy to follow story flow in the most important book that Herbert W. Armstrong ever wrote. It was his last book: a comprehensive writing of all the things God revealed and restored through him over the fifty plus years He worked with him. Again, that book is *Mystery of the Ages*.

Philadelphia's Final Admonition

The next part of the message to Philadelphia concerns a promise of protection and an impending warning. *"Because you have kept the word of my patience, I also will keep you from the hour of* <u>*temptation*</u> [trial] *which shall come upon the world, to try those who dwell upon the earth"* (Revelation 3:10).

Prophecy is often dual, having a physical and a spiritual fulfillment. Prophecy makes it very clear that man will go through great trial at the end-time period of great tribulation on the earth. But it needs to be remembered that the messages to the seven Churches are prophetic messages for seven specific eras of time for the Church over 2,000 years. Each is a message "to" the Church and primarily "about" the Church during its era.

The Philadelphia message included a promise to Mr. Armstrong and those who lived and faithfully served God during that period of time. God specifically said to Philadelphia, which means "during" the era of Philadelphia, that they would be kept from this hour or "time" of trial that was to come on the whole earth.

Whether it is dual or not is immaterial because some argue over this matter. From a purely physical perspective, God was making clear to them, that they, Philadelphia, would not experience this time of trial. The end-time physical tribulation, most assuredly, would not happen during the time of Philadelphia. But this is about much more than that! Prophetically, this is a matter that was to become a far greater concern for the Church—for its very survival!

The period of Philadelphia had some great trials characterized by much opposition from without and from within. But it was nothing by comparison to the magnitude and severity of trials the next era (Laodicea) would face.

Yes, God promised to spare Philadelphia from what would yet come on the Church. By the time Philadelphia ended, it had indeed fulfilled its name as the Worldwide Church of God since it had members in nations all over the world. The greatest time of trial ever in the history of God's Church would come during Laodicea. That would be the time of trial that would come upon the whole world—in all the Church.

At the end of Philadelphia a most important and, sadly, "little applied" admonition was given. *"Behold, I come quickly: hold that fast which you have, that no man take your crown"* (Rev. 3:11).

What did Philadelphia have that God told them to hold fast? It should be quite plain, if anyone had the slightest understanding of the history of this era. Many who lived on into the next era forgot their history. They did not grasp the admonition given by their elder brother, Jesus Christ, and their Father, who loved them.

The history of Philadelphia is filled with an exciting and continuous revelation of truth. The very work God did in Philadelphia was the result of what had transpired in Sardis over a period of a few hundred years. By the end of Sardis, God said, *"...I know your works, that you have a name that you live, and are dead. Be watchful, and strengthen the things which remain, that are ready to die:"* (Revelation 3:1-2). As we have previously discussed, Sardis had come to the point where people were spiritually dead and the truth they had was dying out. God told them to repent and strengthen what truth remained. A few did repent. But the Church had become so small and in such danger of completely dying out that God made a change. God started a new era—Philadelphia!

God had fully restored His truth to the Church during Philadelphia. God's last great admonition to Philadelphia was to "hold fast" what they now had.

The task of "holding fast" has proven to be a difficult one. Only a few remain at this time who "held fast" to those foundational truths God gave through Mr. Armstrong.

The Last Era

The seventh and final era of the Church is Laodicea. During this era man will come to the end of his 6,000 year self-rule on the earth. During Laodicea Jesus Christ will come to the earth in His Kingdom.

The history of the Church, in the fulfillment of the last three eras, is a great warning and witness to the world that the end-time is upon us. Actually, at this very moment, the history of the Laodicean Church is one of the greatest proofs and witnesses that the great physical tribulation is about to be unleashed on earth. Many of these matters will be covered more fully in the next chapter, but now we need to complete this last message to the Church.

"And unto the angel of the church of the Laodiceans write; These things says the Amen, the faithful and true witness, the beginning of the creation of God; I know your works, that you are neither cold nor hot: I would that you were cold or hot. So then because you are lukewarm, and neither cold nor hot, I will spue you out of my mouth" (Revelation 3:14-16).

This is very strong language, especially when you understand that God is saying this to His own Church. After only a few years into Laodicea, something of profound proportions happened. The Church was "spued out" (language used in the old King James Version), or as the New Kings James Bible says, "vomited out," of God's mouth. This means a complete separation from the presence of God—cut off from the flow of God's spirit in the lives of the members of the Church. Being "cut-off" from God is always the result of sin. And the sin would have to be repented of if any were to come back into a right relationship with God and once again be "received" by God.

This did happen! It happened exactly as God said it would. The Church came to a point in time where it was no longer zealous toward God and the truth He had restored. Instead, a watered-down, drowsy and complacent spirit began to grow in the Church.

Mr. Armstrong died in January of 1986. The last ten to twelve years of his life were filled with triumphs and successes, but they were also mixed with stress, opposition and trial. It was a powerfully eventful period of time with great highs and great lows, all happening in seemingly rapid succession.

During this time, some of Mr. Armstrong's greatest accomplishments were evident in his writing, the recognition he was receiving from world leaders, the growth of the Church, and the scope of all that was being produced to send the gospel into the world. His leadership produced a great sense of urgency within the Church and he was ever pressing for stronger unity. But under the surface, there was great unrest and a growing spirit of opposition that Mr. Armstrong was having to address and fight on a regular basis. But it was through his dynamic leadership, which was always strong, that he fought this ongoing battle with such fortitude. That example radiated throughout the Church and stimulated courage, commitment and dedication in others. This is even more amazing when you realize that he was a man in his late 80's. One had to see it to believe it. Mr. Armstrong died at 93.

Mr. Armstrong dealt with division and opposition with a strong arm. He was diligent in his quest to protect the flock and to keep the Church from harm. It was only through that kind of leadership, strengthened by God, that the Church remained so strong during Philadelphia.

In 1978 Mr. Armstrong had to disfellowship his own son, Garner Ted, as well as other ministers, because they were causing division in the Church. Ministers were increasingly becoming involved in internal politics and greed, seeking power and prestige, rather than humbly serving the brethren and God. Mr. Armstrong knew there were struggles among the leadership. Some in the leadership were positioning themselves for higher office when Mr. Armstrong died. It is obvious that such people were no longer faithful members of the Body of Christ. Perhaps they never were. But God allowed it to happen, rather than intervening and preventing it. He had a great purpose in allowing things to go their course, to fulfill yet another part of a great witness at the end of the age. God's Church has always struggled with those who have tried to destroy it from within.

Mr. Armstrong stayed on top of the battle. By the time he died, there were several groups that had either been put out of the Church or had simply left—all forming new organizations. Most of them called themselves the Church of God. Yet none of them were a part of the true Church of God. Sin had long before separated them from the presence of God.

Mr. Armstrong knew his death was near and he went through a very difficult time trying to prepare the Church for a change in leadership. He chose Joseph W. Tkach, Sr., to follow him. Mr. Tkach had served the headquarters of the Church for many years and had served Mr. Armstrong more directly in the last few years before his death.

Mr. Tkach started his leadership of the Church with humility, giving honor to his predecessor. He soon initiated some changes, but they were not doctrinal. This became a test to many as to whether they would faithfully support a new leader. Some did not because they took even the slightest change or deviation from the way Mr. Armstrong did things as a matter of doctrinal change—as some kind of heresy. To some, it was as if everything that Mr. Armstrong had done was beyond change.

Mr. Armstrong had his style of leadership and Mr. Tkach had his. Some matters in the beginning needed to be addressed, simply as a matter of maturity and spiritual growth of the Church. But some would not have it, and they began to be divisive. Some left very early—for the wrong reasons! They had unwittingly placed themselves in opposition to the government of God and were interfering with how God was leading His Church.

But something did happen to Mr. Tkach. He lost his humility: pride entered into his leadership. He began to reflect an actual jealousy of Mr. Armstrong, and he began to lend ear to younger, inexperienced men. Mr. Tkach's own son was determined at a very early stage to lead the Church away from the teachings of Mr. Armstrong, which were actually the ways of God.

By the late 80s and early 90s, change was becoming quite commonplace and accelerating in magnitude. During this period of time, the Church was growing weaker and weaker. A corresponding attitude that was growing during this time was one of "spiritual enlightenment" over the new doctrinal changes. These changes were contrary to the truth that God had restored during Philadelphia.

This came to a head on December 17, 1994. The unthinkable happened. Mr. Joseph W. Tkach, Sr. visited the Church in Atlanta, Georgia and gave a sermon that Sabbath day that reverberated throughout the Church of God. He declared a change in the most basic and foundational doctrines of the Church. Mr. Tkach declared that the seventh-day Sabbath and the annual Sabbaths (Holy Days of God) were no longer binding on God's Church. Sunday observance for worshiping God was now acceptable. He also declared that the law of tithing was no longer in force and that the Church did not need to adhere to the "clean and unclean" food laws as outlined in Leviticus 11. The truth of the weekly Sabbath and tithing were two of three major truths that the Sardis Church had when God declared the people to be spiritually dead.

Church Spued Out of God's Mouth
The result proved devastating to God's Church. But what followed

was the greatest proof yet that the return of Jesus Christ was now very near and that prophetic revelations would begin to be given. The very opening of the seals of Revelation would follow, and the end-time would be upon the world.

The Church did not know that this was the beginning of end-time events—that this was the starting point for the final fulfillment of numerous prophecies that focused squarely on the end-time. They are the very sign that it is now time for the coming of Jesus Christ.

After that infamous sermon given in Atlanta, the Church was thrust into the greatest time of upheaval in its nearly 2,000 years of existence. Everything that began to come upon the Church was not simply a matter of time and chance or something that God had not expected. On the contrary, these things had been prophesied to occur. They would occur at the very end of this age, just before Jesus Christ would return.

Within 30 days after Mr. Tkach's sermon in Atlanta, the unthinkable and unbelievable became reality. Nearly one-third of the entire membership of the Worldwide Church of God turned away from the truth God had told them to "hold fast." Of that third, many simply quit attending that organization and sought out other churches of traditional Christianity who observed the first day of the week as their sabbath—their day of worship. Others chose to stay in the organization and work to move it in the direction of other churches that observed Sunday as their day of worship. This would prove to be a simple task for them, since Mr. Tkach and the leadership that surrounded him wanted these changes. They were in control of the organization and could move in the direction they chose.

Over the next few months another third of the membership simply gave up and quit. People had become disillusioned and disheartened because they could not understand how such a thing could happen to the Church, if it was indeed God's Church. They had no answers as to how and why this could have happened. People simply lost faith. However, this revealed a much deeper problem that already existed. Such things do not happen overnight, but over a long period of time. People had already become so weak and spiritually lukewarm that the faith of many had become nonexistent. The Church had become like so much of traditional Christianity—simply going through the motions of religion, but not living by the Word of God. It is so easy to deceive ourselves that we are religious by going through the motions of what appears to be religious.

Very quickly a devastating blow had been struck, and the majority of the Church had fallen away from the truth. The truth had been abandoned by most in a very short time. A great falling away had occurred. An apostasy of enormous proportions had decimated the Church. ....But it all had been prophesied to happen at the end-time.

It was at this time that God made clear His will and His judgment in these matters. God does not control human life. God created us with free will—free moral agency. We must decide for ourselves if we want God's way of life or our way of life. That is our choice! God will not force us to choose His way. If He did, obviously it would not be our choice, from our true heart, and we would only be living a lie. God does not want compromise in those who follow Him. He does not want people who are willing to conform. As the old saying goes, a man convinced against his will is of the same opinion still.

God gave free choice to mankind. He desires that those who worship Him do so in spirit and in truth. Anything else would be a lie—conforming, going along, compromising. In God's time, God will give every human being the opportunity to choose His way, if that is what they truly want. When that choice is given it is a choice between living the "get" way of life which is motivated by selfishness or the "give" way of life, which is a matter of God's pure outgoing love.

The time for such a choice has been offered to the Church over the past 2,000 years, and as part of God's plan and His timing, that choice will soon be offered to the whole world.

By the time Mr. Tkach gave that sermon in Atlanta, the Church had grown very weak and lukewarm. God was not pleased with the choices they had made! He knew what would happen to spoiled children who had been given such great spiritual riches. Children usually become very spoiled when given great physical riches. God knew that even with His spirit His Church would become spoiled by all that was given to it during the Philadelphia era. By their own choices, people became lifted up with pride: they saw themselves as better than they were, looked down upon others, were unthankful, and were not appreciative of the sacrifices that went into giving them what they had. A great lesson was yet to be learned that would serve to teach the generations to follow. It was necessary to let those who lived in Laodicea make their own choices. Their choices led to a lukewarm condition even though they had God's spirit. Through this example, those who live in the ages to come will be able to learn some of the most important spiritual lessons that man must come to understand.

It happened just as God had forewarned so long ago. God knew what people would do after so much had been given during Philadelphia. After Mr. Armstrong's death, it didn't take long for pride, politics, greed, hunger for power, arrogance, lethargy, complacency, and spiritually-spoiled attitudes to appear throughout the environs of the Church. All of this was sin! Since God cannot dwell around sin, He separated the Church from Himself.

God did forewarn Laodicea. *"I know your works, that you are neither cold nor hot: I would that you were cold or hot. So then because you are lukewarm, and neither cold nor hot, I will spue you out of my mouth. Because you say, I am rich, and increased with goods, and have need of nothing; and know not that you are wretched, and miserable, and poor, and blind, and naked:"* (Revelation 3:15-17).

The first third of the Church accepted the apostasy and separated itself from God. Their choices cut them off from their God. The next third, which simply gave up and quit, was also separated from any more relationship with God. They too had now been cut off. The last third of the Church became scattered. People scrambled to some of the organizations that had previously separated from the Worldwide Church of God. Others went out to start a group or join some newly forming group. It was chaos! By this point the entirety of the Church had, in one way or another, been vomited—spued out of God's mouth—cast out of His presence.

There is only one way for anyone to come back into a relationship with God once you have been cut off. The answer should be quite obvious, but sadly it wasn't to most of the Church. When anyone is separated from the presence of God, there is only one reason for it. That reason is sin! Sin must always be repented of if someone wants to have a relationship with God—if they desire to continue in a relationship with God.

That is exactly what God told Laodicea. *"I counsel you to buy of me gold tried in the fire, that you may be rich; and white raiment, that you may be clothed, and that the shame of your nakedness do not appear; and anoint your eyes with eyesalve, that you may see. As many as I love, I rebuke and chasten: be zealous therefore, and repent"* (Revelation 3:18-19).

After being separated from God's presence, if anyone had wanted to come back into a relationship with God, they would have needed to go through a process of repentance. They would have had to ask what it was that had led to their lukewarm condition. Why did this happen to God's Church? Why had they been scattered and spued out? How could this have happened to God's Church? The answers to these questions reveal the Church's sins.

Asking God to be like gold tried in the fire is to ask to go through trials and hardships in order to see the impurities that need to be repented of before God. When gold is heated (trials), the impurities (sin) rise to the surface, and once they can be seen, then they can be skimmed off (repented of). Once people have become so weak that God says they are spiritually blind, then they need to seek help to "see" what is true and what is false in their lives because they are, of themselves, incapable of seeing it. God has to reveal it. That is what is meant by anointing one's eyes with eye salve, so they can begin to see. Many initially began to go through this process, but they did not complete it.

If people are spiritually naked, but they see themselves clothed, then a big spiritual problem exists. Can such people humble themselves and accept what God is telling them? That is the message to Laodicea. They are to seek white garments so that the shame of their nakedness is not revealed. They must repent of the sins in their lives. Laodicea's battle is one of whether or not they will accept what God tells them. Will people be zealous for God's words and repent? Will people seek to be zealous once more? Being lukewarm is not hot—not zealous toward God.

The history of Laodicea at this time is just as God had said it would be. The haughtiness is so great within the environs of the Church that ministers and brethren cannot humble themselves to admit they are wrong—that they have sinned. Most of them deny that the Church is scattered. Most deny they are Laodiceans: they still claim to be Philadelphians. They see others and believe they are Loadicean, but they see themselves as "better than that" (rich and increased with goods)—they see themselves as Philadelphians, which they believe to be better than Laodiceans. Even though they were taught about the eras of the Church, many hold to a belief that Philadelphia and Laodicea are moving along side-by-side, that somehow two different eras share the same time period. Yet, an era of time is an era of time! When one ends, another begins. But pride will not allow many to accept that truth.

The Book of Revelation declares that the words it contains are the witness of Jesus Christ and that His testimony is true. Christ's message to the last Church era has come to pass exactly as He said. The Church was separated from God—vomited from His mouth. But most are so weak (lukewarm) spiritually that they have become lifted up with pride and see themselves better than what God says they are. Few are repenting—and even that is prophesied. God has foretold how many will come through this, but each one has to be awakened out of spiritual sleep and sluggishness. It is a spiritual condition. Only God can awaken each one from that spiritually blinded condition. God has foretold how many He will awaken to be a final remnant of the whole. This too, about the Church, is for a witness, just as there is a witness of what the world is like after 6,000 years of man's self-rule.

Everyone reading this should be sobered because some of the most important prophecies about the end-time are about God's own Church. If you can begin to grasp that there are Church eras, then know that we are near the end of Laodicea, the last era—then Jesus Christ returns.

More about this era and end-time prophecies that have been fulfilled is going to be covered in the next chapter. When you begin to see the number of end-time prophecies that have already been fulfilled, then you should be sobered to the core of your being to understand that the next great prophecy to be fulfilled is the great physical tribulation upon this earth!

Chapter 5

OPENING THE SEALS OF REVELATION

The time setting for this chapter is personally most profound. This chapter covers the opening of the first six seals of Revelation. As will be explained, those six seals have already been opened at the time of this writing. The last one, the seventh, is yet to be opened. That is when the great physical tribulation will begin.

The best place to begin this chapter is in the verse that makes the writing of this chapter so personally profound.

"I John, who also am your brother, and companion in tribulation, and in the kingdom and patience of Jesus Christ, was on the isle that is called Patmos, for the word of God, and for the testimony of Jesus Christ. I was in the Spirit in the Lord's day, and heard behind me a great voice, as of a trumpet, saying, I am the Alpha and the Omega, the first and the last: and, What you see, write in a book, and send it unto the seven churches which are in Asia; unto Ephesus, and unto Smyrna, and unto Pergamos, and unto Thyatira, and unto Sardis, and unto Philadelphia, and unto Laodicea" (Revelation 1:9-11).

More about these verses will be explained later, but first it needs to be noted that John was on the Isle of Patmos, in the Aegean Sea, when God gave him this vision of those things that were to be recorded in the Book of Revelation. John was given a vision of those things that would happen in the end-time and lead up to the very return of Jesus Christ and the establishment of the Kingdom of God on the earth.

My wife and I are, at this time, on a cruise. We are visiting some of the areas where John and Paul traveled. As I write, I am able to look out my cabin window at the Isle of Patmos. Today, being a weekly Sabbath, we had opportunity to visit Patmos. It is indeed very moving personally to know what God gave to John 1907 years ago.

During the past seven years, God has been revealing to me the very meaning of the vision He gave to John. One hundred, nineteen-year time-cycles have passed from the time John wrote about his vision to the time God began to reveal the meaning and timing for the opening of the Seals of Revelation. Now, seven years later, this book is being written to declare that revelation and give witness that the first six seals have already been opened. There is but a short time before the seventh and last one will be opened.

This has much personal meaning. It reminds me of Herbert W. Armstrong's personal experience. He was personally moved to know that he was directly instrumental (used by God) to begin sending the gospel message once again into all the world after 1900 years (100, 19-year time-cycles) of its suppression.

The very proof of this book—that it is the revelation of God—will be evident a short time from now, when the Seventh Seal is opened and the two end-time witnesses come on the scene. If the things written in the book do not shortly come to pass, then what is written here is false, and I am false.

Seals Opened at the End-Time

The Book of Revelation begins and ends with strong words that record direct authority given by God, concerning what is written. It begins by saying, *"The Revelation of Jesus Christ, which God gave unto Him, to show unto His servants things which must shortly come to pass; and He sent and signified it by His angel unto His servant John:"* (Revelation 1:1).

It says that this is a revelation of Jesus Christ, not of John. It also states that it was given by God to Jesus Christ to show those things which would shortly take place. These things were not to take place in John's time or in the generations immediately to follow. The significance of these words is in the short amount of time required for these things to be fulfilled once the end-time events, spoken of in Revelation, began to be "revealed," both prophetically and literally.

"The Revelation of Jesus Christ, which God gave unto Him, to show unto His servants things which must shortly come to pass; and He sent and signified it by His angel unto His servant John: who bare record of the word of God, and of the testimony of Jesus Christ, and of all things that he saw" (Revelation 1:1-2).

Verse two goes on to clarify that what John was to record was witness (testimony) that this was the word of God and that it was the witness (testimony) of Jesus Christ. No other book in scripture begins with such a stamp of authority stating that what was given was a direct witness (testimony) from God and Jesus Christ. What is written in Revelation is of profound importance in the revelation of God's plan and work over the past 6,000 years, as well as in the transition into a new world order that will follow in the 1,000 years that His Kingdom rules the earth.

The last chapter repeats the importance of those things given in this revelation. *"And he said unto me, These sayings are faithful and true: and the Lord God of the holy prophets sent His angel to show unto His servants the things which must <u>shortly be done</u>. Behold, <u>I come quickly</u>: blessed is he who keeps the sayings of the prophecy of this book"* (Revelation 22:6-7).

When these things begin to come to pass, as the seals of Revelation begin to be opened, it will not be long before Jesus Christ comes. God has recorded that this is so by His testimony and that His words are "faithful and true."

"'I Jesus have sent my angel to testify unto you these things in the churches. I am the root and the offspring of David, and the

bright and morning star. And the Spirit and the bride say, Come. And let him who hears say, Come. And let him who is thirsty come. And whosoever will, let him take the water of life freely. For I testify to every man who hears the words of the prophecy of this book, If any man shall add unto these things, God shall add to him the plagues that are written in this book: and if any man shall take away from the words of the book of this prophecy, God shall take away his part out of the book of life, and out of the holy city, and from the things which are written in this book" (Revelation 22:16-19).

All these words bear strong record concerning the authority and power of God Almighty and His Son, Jesus Christ. When their words begin to be revealed, then those who receive them, and the truth contained in them, can hold fast to their message, and they can begin taking part in their chorus—for Jesus Christ to "Come!"

As stated, the first chapter of Revelation sets the stage for what is about to be given to John, by establishing the power and authority of what he writes as coming directly from God. Chapters two and three are messages to each of the seven Church eras that would exist from the beginning of the Church until the very return of Jesus Christ.

The first Church era covers the time of the early Church and the lifetime of the disciples. John, who wrote Revelation, was the last living disciple in that first era. Then, what John wrote was to be revealed and made manifest (to become a reality) in the last era of the Church—Laodicea.

End-time prophecies would come to pass during Laodicea. This era would last until the very return of Jesus Christ. The Book of Revelation is also revealed during this last era because it is at this time that those things written for the end-time will be fulfilled. Laodicea is indeed the end-time Church era and that era is, even now, nearly over.

After instruction, prophetic revelation and admonition were

given to each Church era, the book moves into the revelation of those things that would unfold in the end-time.

In Chapter 4, John moves ahead in his vision to those things that focus directly on the end-time. *"After this I looked, and, behold, a door was opened in heaven: and the first voice which I heard was as it were a trumpet talking with me; which said, Come up here, and I will show you things which must be hereafter"* (Revelation 4:1). When the Church reaches the time of the last era (six eras having passed), it is time for the end-time to unfold—become reality.

John then records what will become manifest on the earth at the end. But he only sees in vision what will actually transpire. *"And I saw in the right hand of Him who sat on the throne a book written within and on the backside, sealed with seven seals. And I saw a strong angel proclaiming with a loud voice, Who is worthy to open the book, and to loose the seals thereof? And no one in heaven, nor in earth, neither under the earth, was able to open the book, neither to look thereon. And I wept much, because no one was found worthy to open and to read the book, neither to look thereon. And one of the elders said unto me, Weep not: behold, the Lion of the tribe of Judah, the Root of David, has prevailed to open the book, and to loose the seven seals thereof"* (Revelation 5:1-5). It records that Jesus Christ will open the seals. They have remained sealed up until this time. That means no one can know what they are or what they mean until they are unsealed by Jesus Christ. This also means that these things cannot occur until Christ unseals them. When they are unsealed, then they come to pass—actually take place.

All that is recorded throughout these chapters about the end-time is very much like a story in Daniel. Whether it be prophecies about the end-time from the Old Testament or the numerous prophecies recorded throughout the New Testament, people throughout the ages have wanted to know what these things mean. Even the prophets of old had great desire to know more about the very prophecies that they were responsible for recording.

In the Book of Daniel we find such a story. It was toward the end of those prophecies that were being given to Daniel concerning the end-time that he expressed to God that he did not understand what was being given to him. *"And I heard, but I understood not: then I said, O my lord, what shall be the end of these things? And he said, Go your way, Daniel: for the words are closed and sealed till the time of the end"* (Daniel 12:8-9). Although the Bible is filled with prophetic writings concerning the end-time, the understanding and revelation of those things have remained hidden, sealed and closed until the time for their unveiling and fulfillment. This is that time!

So Revelation 5 records that it is Jesus Christ who will open the seals and reveal the meaning of these prophecies as well as the time for their fulfillment. Some misunderstand the name given to the book of Revelation. Since it is declared to be a "revelation" from God to man, some have taken this to mean that God told man what was to come to pass and what these prophecies mean. Not true! It is a revelation from God to man of what would come to pass at the end-time, but understanding has remained sealed until now—until the time for the revealing of the actual events—the time for the prophecies to be revealed and fulfilled.

The First Seal Opened
As we delve into the meaning of the first seal, it should sober any reader to realize, if they can come to see it, that this seal has already been opened. This knowledge should sober anyone reading it. The fact that this seal has been opened is one of the first and greatest proofs that we have already entered the age for end-time prophecies to be fulfilled. You should be even more deeply sobered in knowing that five more seals have already been opened. These six seals take us far into end-time prophetic fulfillment. Only a short time remains before great physical tribulation begins.

"And I saw when the Lamb opened one of the seals, and I heard, as it were the noise of thunder, one of the four living creatures saying, Come and see. And I saw, and behold a white horse: and he who sat on him had a bow; and a crown was given unto him: and he went forth conquering, and to conquer" (Revelation 6:1-2).

Some Bible scholars confuse what is said in these two verses with what is said later concerning the second-coming of Jesus Christ in Revelation 19. *"And I saw heaven opened, and behold a white horse; and He who sat on him was called Faithful and True, and in righteousness He does judge and makes war"* (Revelation 19:11).

Indeed, Revelation 19:11 is speaking of the second-coming of Jesus Christ, as the context shows, but this first seal is not speaking of Jesus Christ when it speaks of one who is coming and sitting on a white horse.

This seal is speaking of a counterfeit! It reveals a time when great religious deception is unleashed on earth. But as already covered in this book, great religious deception has always existed on this earth. So what can this mean? If the world has always been deceived, then who can become deceived? Only those who have had the truth revealed to them can become deceived! This is about the Church! It isn't a prophecy about the world. It is not something that happens on a physical level, but on a spiritual one: it's about the Church.

In order to better understand all this, we need to go back to the story of God's Church in this end-time. Mr. Armstrong, the end-time Elijah, was used by God to restore truth in the Church, truth that had nearly died out by the time the Sardis Era was coming to a close. Then God raised up the Philadelphia Era. Although truth was restored to the Church through Mr. Armstrong, God only revealed a basic foundational understanding concerning end-time prophetic events.

One of the most foundational truths revealed to Mr. Armstrong was the identity of the modern-day nations of Old Testament Israel. This story is long and involved, and we have only touched upon it in part in the previous chapter. But it was through the knowledge of this truth that Mr. Armstrong learned much about what would occur to specific nations during the great physical tribulation at the end, just before the coming of Jesus Christ. However, none of the seals were opened during his lifetime and therefore it was not time for many of the specifics to be revealed. Those things are reserved for the time the actual events are to be fulfilled—when they are to become a reality.

God did give Mr. Armstrong a very specific prophetic key concerning the first four seals of Revelation. He understood that the Olivet prophecies were the key to understanding these seals. Although this key was given to Mr. Armstrong, God did not fully reveal these prophecies to him. God's apostle was given this key, but he was not given the ability to use the "key" because it was not yet time for the seals to be opened. So Mr. Armstrong was limited to seeing these seals as only a physical fulfillment. He was not given to see that it was a prophetic matter concerning the very Church of God and not the physical "religious" world.

Matthew 24 and the other accounts of the Olivet prophecy parallel this account of the seals found in Revelation 6. Even within the Church, the first four seals of Revelation 6 have only been able to be seen in light of a physical fulfillment. So it is no wonder that even within the world these things have been viewed as having a physical fulfillment. The first four seals have even been referred to often as the time of the Four Horsemen of the Apocalypse because they have been viewed as being "apocalyptic" in their destructive power over the earth. Yes, apocalyptic destruction will come on this world during the great physical tribulation when the Seventh Seal is opened, but these earlier seals are about destructive power in the very Church of God. They are of an apocalyptic nature spiritually.

Let's consider the key to the seals in the Olivet prophecy. The disciples were walking with Jesus around the area of the Temple, and as they discussed its beauty, the conversation moved to questions and answers concerning the end-time.

"And Jesus went out, and departed from the temple: and His disciples came to Him for to show Him the buildings of the temple. And Jesus said unto them, See you not all these things? verily I say unto you, There shall not be left here one stone upon another, that shall not be thrown down" (Matthew 24:1-2).

Those things that Jesus began to describe to his disciples are understood by most people to be purely physical. That was a very common response to the teachings of Jesus Christ, and it is the normal human reaction because mankind, by nature, deals with the "physical" that surrounds him because he can't see or understand the "spiritual."

The Book of John is filled with such examples. In Chapter 3, Jesus spoke to Nicodemus, a great leader of the Jews. He could not understand what Jesus was talking about when He spoke of a need to be "born again" of spirit. Nicodemus asked how one could be born again once he is old. He knew he could not enter again into his mother's womb and be born a second time. Even traditional Christianity embraces a physical interpretation of this. They believe that being born again is some kind of "spiritual experience" while still in this physical body. But Jesus was explaining a literal change that has to take place in human life. That change is part of God's purpose for man. Man has the opportunity to be born of spirit essence into the Family of God as an eternal living, spirit being.

Chapter 4 of John records the account of a Samaritan woman who met Jesus at a well. Jesus explained to her that she could drink from the water in that well, but she would become thirsty again. He said He had living water to give, and if a person drank of it they would never thirst again. She asked for that water so she would never thirst again or have to return to the well to draw water. She didn't understand that he wasn't speaking of physical water, but of the spiritual water of the Word of God.

Then, in John 6, Jesus explained some of the future symbolism of the observance of Passover, which Paul later explained in 1 Corinthians 11. Jesus told His disciples they would have to eat of His flesh and drink of His blood. Verse 66 records that many of his disciples (not the twelve) quit following him after that because they were abhorred by what He had said. The Jewish people have always accepted the laws of clean and unclean foods. If they were told that they would literally be required to eat human flesh or drink human blood, then they knew that would be a flagrant and obvious breaking of God's law. But Jesus wasn't speaking of a literal physical interpretation. He was teaching His disciples about the future observance of the Passover when wine would be part of a ceremony reminding us of the spilled blood of our Passover and the eating of a piece of unleavened bread would symbolize His flesh—His physical life, sacrificed for the sins of man, as our Passover.

The Book of John continues with more stories that were interpreted on a physical plane, but were intended to be interpreted spiritually. It is the same as we return to the story of Jesus Christ talking to his disciples concerning the stones of the temple being cast down. This was not a physical interpretation, but a spiritual one. Many in the Church of God that was scattered, as well as those of traditional Christianity, foolishly believe that this is to be interpreted physically. Although the temple was destroyed by the Romans, during the first church era (Ephesus), Christ was not referring to that event. This prophecy was about the Church for a future time—the end-time.

The stones of the temple are spiritual. They are about God's own Church. *"Now therefore you are no more strangers and foreigners, but fellow citizens with the saints, and of the household of God; and are built upon the foundation of the apostles and prophets, Jesus Christ Himself being the chief corner stone; in whom the whole* *building fitly framed together grows unto <u>an holy temple</u> in the Lord: in whom you also are being built together for an habitation of God through the Spirit"* (Ephesians 2:19-22). Paul explained here that those God has called into His Church are described as being part of a spiritual temple—a holy temple in the Lord.

The apostle Peter explained this in a similar fashion. *"To whom coming, as unto <u>a living stone</u>, rejected indeed of men, but chosen of God, and precious, you also, <u>as lively stones</u>, are being built up <u>a spiritual house</u>, a holy priesthood, to offer up spiritual sacrifices, acceptable to God through Jesus Christ"* (1 Peter 2:4-5). Members of the Church of God are being described as being like "living stones" (spiritual) that are being built into a spiritual house. That spiritual house is the temple of God.

In the Olivet prophecy, as Christ explained that the stones of the temple would be cast down, He was speaking of a future time for the Church. He was speaking similarly when He told the Jews, "destroy this temple and in three days I will raise it up." On that occasion, He was speaking of Himself and foretelling His death and resurrection to follow.

Let's continue in this Olivet prophecy. *"And as He sat on the Mount of Olives, the disciples came unto Him privately, saying, Tell us, when shall these things be? And what shall be the sign of your coming, and of the end of the world* [age]*?"* (Matthew 24:3). Do you see the context of this prophecy? It not only involves the Church, but here it makes clear the timing for these things to occur. The disciples asked Jesus about the timing of events surrounding the stones of the temple being cast down. By their very question, it is clear that they knew He was speaking of the time for His coming (in His Kingdom) and the end of the age. The Olivet prophecy is about those things that would happen to the Church at the end-time, just prior to the return of Jesus Christ to establish His Kingdom.

Notice how Mark described this same account. *"Tell us, when shall these things be? And what shall be the sign when all these things shall be fulfilled?"* (Mark 13:4).

The context of all that Jesus told His disciples concerned the timing for His coming as King of kings in the Kingdom of God, and the very sign that would lead up to that time. The sign He gave involved the Church—events and signs that would occur in the Church of God—not signs in this world.

Jesus Christ began by telling the disciples about a warning. This would be valuable instruction for the Church throughout time but, more importantly, it would be a very specific warning for the Church at the end-time. *"And Jesus answered and said unto them, Take heed that no man deceive you. For many shall come in my name, saying, I am the Christ; and shall deceive many"* (Matthew 24:4-5).

Remember, this is about the Church. It is not about the world. The warning isn't to the world. Jesus is giving a warning about not becoming deceived. The world has always been deceived; only those in the Church can <u>become</u> deceived. Who could deceive the Church? He was warning about deception that would come from within, not from without. He warned that "many" would come in His name. Who can come to the Church in the name of Jesus Christ? It is the ministry of the Church! Jesus was foretelling a time when the Church would need to take warning not to become deceived. Many in the ministry would come claiming that they are teaching the truth, and pointing people to Jesus Christ, but they would deceive "many." These ministers would talk about truth that the Church knew as well as speak many true things about Jesus Christ, but they would have the ability to deceive others. This deception is only possible when someone begins to teach false doctrines mixed with the true.

This sign Jesus Christ gave the disciples would reveal when the end-time would come. This false ministry would be part of the destructive events that would come upon the Church at the end. This end-time prophecy would stand out as being unique and horribly destructive—not to the world, but to the Church. That is why prophetic end-time events that have already been fulfilled have gone unnoticed by the world. The world has not known God's Church—His small Church throughout the seven eras of its existence. Yet this is the very sign Jesus Christ gave for His coming in the Kingdom of God.

As the Olivet prophecy continues to unfold, it zeros in on events that will occur in the Church as the end-time draws near. *"And you shall hear of wars and rumors of wars: see that you be not troubled: for all these things must come to pass, but the end is not yet. For nation shall rise against nation, and kingdom against kingdom: and there shall be famines, and pestilences, and earthquakes, in different places. All these are the beginning of sorrows"* (Matthew 24:6-7).

In the last ten to fifteen years of Mr. Armstrong's life, the Church experienced great upheaval at different times and in different places. Some of the ministry began to turn from the truth they had been given. That is the time referred to in these verses. These verses are not speaking of rumors of war in the world. When war happens in the world, everyone will know it. Again, these verses aren't about the physical, but the spiritual.

Spirit beings exist who fight against God, His angels and His Church. These beings include Satan and those angels who followed him in rebellion against God—those who became known as demons. They are real spirit beings who still dwell on this earth.

The consequences for any of God's people who let down spiritually, including ministers, is that they become prey for Satan and demons. They become susceptible to their ideas and spiritual perversion. When that happens, trouble follows. As some ministers in the 1970s and early 1980s began to rebel against God, they began to teach things that were false. They became spiritually defiled. As a result of this process, which occurred over time, brethren be-came weak and spiritually starved (famine). The devastation was enormous by the time the rebellion was manifest.

So trouble did pop up in unexpected places, often preceded by rumors of unrest, disagreement and divisiveness—spiritual wars and rumors of wars. Battles of a spiritual nature would be thrust upon some congregations in different parts of this world. These things would always send a shockwave throughout the Church. The word "earthquake," as it is translated into English, is from a Greek word that can have the actual meaning of earthquake, but it can also be translated as "commotion or shaking."

These things that Jesus told his disciples were prophecies pertaining to conditions that would exist in the environs of the Church, leading up to even more specific prophecies that would occur at the very end-time.

During this time of growing unrest, the Church was actually going through the beginning phase of a transition that would later become a full reality. This transition was beginning to affect the spiritual lives of brethren—a growing Laodicean spirit and attitude. The change from one era to another was not an instant change, as one day to another, but a gradual one. Throughout the early 80s, Mr. Armstrong recognized this changing spiritual condition in the Church. As a result, he gave sermons to warn brethren against a lukewarm spiritual condition that was coming into the Church. Before his death in 1986 he preached the warning that Laodicea was coming upon the Church. He believed at least fifty percent had that spirit already working in them. The time was rapidly approaching the end of another era of the Church—Philadelphia. The last era of the Church was on the horizon—Laodicea.

This transition from Philadelphia to Laodicea was the "beginning of sorrows," just as Christ told His disciples

Then Jesus explained that this time of sorrow would actually lead into far greater sorrow within the Church because these prophecies were exclusively about the Church. We will come back to those verses, but for the sake of understanding the order of events, we need to focus on a very specific verse that Mr. Armstrong understood as being the commission God had given him. He quoted this verse often as he continued to remind the Church of the work he had been given to do, "the work" the Church had been called to support.

"And this gospel of the kingdom shall be preached in all the world for a witness unto all nations; and then shall the end come" (Matthew 24:14). Mr. Armstrong knew that this was his job, his commission—preaching the gospel, the good news of the Kingdom of God, to the world. Even though he knew what his job was as the end-time Elijah, most end-time prophecy concerning the Church was never revealed to him. The gospel message did go out into all the world to fulfill a "witness unto all nations." That witness was that mankind was still the same after 6,000 years—man continues to reject God's word and His good news for them. Multiple millions of people over several decades heard Mr. Armstrong over radio and television. They read his words in the pages of *The Plain Truth* magazine. But they rejected that message. That was the witness to all nations! However, God called a few thousand to become a part of that work He had called Mr. Armstrong to accomplish.

The Last Era Begins
Then the time for a complete transition from one era to another came in January of 1986 when Mr. Armstrong died. He knew he was about to die and would not see those end-time events that would lead up to the coming of God's Kingdom to this earth—events he had proclaimed for over fifty years. The Philadelphia Era came to a close and the Laodicea Era began.

When Mr. Armstrong believed his death was imminent, he transferred the responsibility of leadership to Joseph W. Tkach, Sr. Mr. Tkach began that task in faithfulness, upholding the truths that had been delivered to the Church and to him. Indeed, just as Jesus Christ told his disciples, the gospel would be preached in all the world for a witness to all nations, and then the end would come. At Mr. Armstrong's death, the sixth era of the Church came to a close and the last one began—the seventh one—the one at the end! It would be in this seventh era that all end-time events would be unveiled and the final end-time tribulation would come upon the whole world.

The sign of His coming is centered around all the "individual signs" of specific events that would occur in the environs of the Church at the end-time. The sign concerned the Church! Yet, the world and even many in the Church of God that was scattered have been looking to conditions in the world as being the sign of Christ's coming.

The Church began to take on a new air and attitude because of those Mr. Tkach placed in positions of leadership, including his own son. It was an air of self-importance, of spiritual arrogance and pride, of being spiritually "rich and increased with goods." This was coupled with an already weakened condition within the Church of spiritual lukewarmness and complacency. The mixture was disastrous for the Church.

Slowly but surely, through the late 80s and very early 90s, constant changes were made in various traditions, administrations, and then, even doctrines.

During this period of time, the words of Jesus took on even more significance for the end-time Church. After Jesus had told His disciples of those things that were "the beginning of sorrows," He went on to describe those things that would take place, through the early stages of Laodicea, as sorrows continued to grow.

"Then shall they deliver you up to be afflicted [Gk.– tribulation] *and shall kill you: and you shall be hated of all nations for my name's sake. And then shall many be offended, and shall betray one another, and shall hate one another. And many false prophets shall rise, and shall deceive many. And because iniquity* [Gk.– lawlessness] *shall abound, the love of many shall grow cold"*

(Matthew 24:9-12).

These verses describe a growing condition that would plague the era of Laodicea. As brethren became weaker spiritually due to a lukewarm condition, they began to fall asleep spiritually and were no longer able to stay spiritually alert, as God commanded His Church to be. This weakened condition led to a waning of the power of God's spirit in the lives of brethren. This, in turn, led to "lawlessness"—sin taking root within the Church—sin not repented of. As that condition continued to grow, God could not give His spirit or His love to the brethren. Therefore, they were cut off from a right relationship with God and with one another.

And what was the result of all this? More and more ministers joined the ranks of a false ministry. These ministers had to rely on their own knowledge because they were no longer led by God.

As doctrinal differences emerged from such a weakened condition, brother began to betray brother as brethren became offended at one another, as well as at the truth itself. As the ministry continued to become weaker, so did the Church. All this worked to place the Church in deep spiritual tribulation, resulting in more spiritual death. Through these actions the ministers and brethren were guilty of killing one another—spiritually.

As a result of this period of growing spiritual tribulation and unrest in the Church, some ministers and brethren began to leave the Worldwide Church of God. Some began to form other organizations using the name Church of God.

This sickening spiritual condition continued to grow in the Church until it finally came to a major breaking point on December 17, 1994. It was on this Sabbath day in Atlanta, Georgia that Mr. Tkach gave a sermon to a large assembly of brethren from that area of the country. In that sermon he announced major doctrinal changes that were the diametrical opposite of the truth he had received when God first called him into His Church.

He announced the most hideous heresy to which a minister of

God could possibly succumb: he declared that the seventh-day Sabbath and annual Sabbaths (Holy Days) were no longer binding on God's people and were not a sign of God's people. This was the greatest act of betrayal toward God by any of His servants in all man's 6,000-year history. But it also proved to be the primary sign to God's Church that the end-time was here and the countdown for Christ's return had begun. This event was the fulfillment of several prophecies and marked the beginning for the opening of the seals of Revelation.

Jesus Christ told his disciples that the gospel of the Kingdom would first be preached in all the world, as a witness to all nations—then the end would come. After Mr. Armstrong completed the job God had given him to do, he died, and the Philadelphia Era came to a close. Indeed, the end did come, with the beginning of the last era of the Church—Laodicea. In less than ten years, Laodicea was thrust into prophesied end-time events. Those very events would be fulfilled within a specific time frame that God predetermined long ago.

The Abomination of Desolation

Look closely at what Jesus Christ said would follow after Mr. Armstrong finished his work. *"And this gospel of the kingdom shall be preached in all the world for a witness unto all nations; and then shall the end come. When you therefore shall see the abomination of desolation, spoken of by Daniel the prophet, stand in the holy place (whoso reads, let him understand:) then let them who are in Judea flee into the mountains:"* (Matthew 24:14-16).

Many prophecies have a "physical type" of fulfillment and a "spiritual type." There was a "physical type" of fulfillment, of the desecration of the physical temple of God, in the days of Antiochus Epiphanes. He committed an "abomination of desolation" upon the physical temple by robbing its treasures and by offering swine upon its altar. Nothing could be more hideously profane, within the temple of God, than a non-Levite (priestly tribe given charge of the duties of the temple) offering an unclean animal sacrifice upon the altar.

This account in Matthew concerns a "spiritual type." But many who read it, including many who were scattered in the true Church of God, believe that a second temple must be built or that at least an altar must be erected on the Temple Mount for this prophecy to be fulfilled. They do not grasp that this is not about a physical temple, but a spiritual one—the Church of God.

So who could defile the temple of God and then proceed to work to destroy it? Could it be someone outside the Church? Hardly! Only someone from within the Church could commit such a treacherous act. That is a story recorded in a prophecy from the apostle Paul, found in 2 Thessalonians 2.

"Now we beseech you brethren, by the coming of our Lord Jesus Christ, and by our gathering together unto Him, that you be not soon shaken in mind, or be troubled, neither by spirit, nor by word, nor by letter as from us, as though the day of Christ is at hand. Let no man deceive you by any means: for that day shall not come, except there come a falling away first, and that man of sin be revealed, the son of perdition;" (2 Thessalonians 2:1-3).

The context of Paul's prophecy is very clear since he specifically referred to the timing of its fulfillment four distinct times. Notice the phrases: 1) *"the coming of our Lord Jesus Christ,"* 2) *"our gathering together unto Him"* [The gathering of the Church—the 144,000—at the coming of Christ], 3) *"as though the day of Christ is at hand,"* and 4) *"for that day shall not come, except."* The prophecy given through Paul is incredibly specific as to its timing.

Paul is explaining to the Church that very specific events must occur within the Church before the end-time comes—before the coming of Jesus Christ can occur—just before the Kingdom of God is established ("our gathering together unto Him").

This warning to the Church is the same one that Jesus Christ gave in the Olivet Prophecy concerning the time for His coming and the fulfillment of end-time events. *"And Jesus answered and said unto them, Take heed that no man deceive you. For many shall come in my name, saying, I am the Christ; and shall deceive many"* (Matthew 24:4-5). This condition grew in magnitude over time, until the prophetic event described by Paul was fulfilled. It was to be the pinnacle of deception in the Church.

The countdown for the coming of Jesus Christ and the final fulfillment of end-time events would not begin until two very specific things occurred in the Church. Paul mentioned that the end cannot come "unless the falling away comes first."

Brethren had long known that a "falling away" or "an apostasy" (in the Greek) would take place in the Church at the end-time, but the magnitude of this event was never imagined. Oftentimes over the past two thousand years brethren have fallen away from the truth. It always happened when they left those truths that God had earlier revealed to them through the power of His spirit. But this "falling away" would be different from those of the past, and it would result in the worst time of trouble (spiritual tribulation) that the Church had ever experienced.

This "falling away" would be coupled with the revealing of the "man of sin"—the son of perdition. The individual who would fulfill this verse is specific, and it would occur at a very specific time. There is only one other account of anyone ever being called a "son of perdition." That was Judas Iscariot, who was called this because he directly betrayed Jesus. He had been chosen to be one of the twelve disciples, yet he gave into his own selfish carnal nature and betrayed the Son of God.

Paul tells us more about this "man of sin" who would be revealed at the end-time. *"Who opposes and exalts himself above all that is called God, or that is worshiped; so that he as God sits in the temple of God, showing himself that he is God"* (2 Thessalonians 2:4).

In what kind of circumstance could someone be described as one who sits in the temple of God? Are they to sit in a physical temple that is yet to be built? By now you should know the answer. It is about someone in the spiritual temple!

No one could be in the spiritual temple of God unless they are a part of the Body of Christ, the Church of God. This verse is not talking about someone who sits down, as to relax in a chair, but someone in authority who is set in the Church bearing authority. This word in the Greek actually means to "cause to set" as in "to set, appoint, or to confer a kingdom on one."

Notice six examples of how this same word is used in the following verses.

1) *"And Jesus said to them, Verily I say unto you, That you who have followed me, in the regeneration when the Son of man shall sit on the throne of His glory, you also shall sit on twelve thrones, judging the twelve tribes of Israel"* (Matthew 19:28).

2) *"And He said unto her, What do you desire? She said unto Him, Grant that these my two sons may sit, the one on your right hand, and the other on the left, in your kingdom"* (Matthew 20:21).

3) *"Then spoke Jesus to the multitude, and to His disciples, saying, The scribes and the Pharisees sit in Moses' seat:"* (Matthew 23:1-2).

4) *"When Pilate therefore heard that saying, he brought Jesus forth, and sat down in the judgment seat in a place that is called the Pavement, but in Hebrew, Gabbatha"* (John 19:13).

5) *"If then you have judgments of things pertaining to this life, set them to judge who are least esteemed in the church"* (1 Corinthians 6:4).

6) *"To him who overcomes will I grant to sit with me on my throne, even as I also overcame, and am set down with my Father on His throne"* (Revelation 3:21).

Only one man in this modern age was appointed—"set" in the Church of God. That man was Joseph W. Tkach, Sr. He had been given great trust and authority, but he betrayed Jesus Christ in the sermon he gave in Atlanta, Georgia on December 17, 1994. *"Who opposes and exalts himself above all that is called God, or that is worshiped; so that he as God <u>sits</u> in the temple of God, showing* ["Showing" in the Greek means "to show forth, to expose to view, to reveal."] *himself that he is God"* (2 Thessalonians 2:4). His actions exposed his rebellion. That sermon revealed that he had lifted himself above God by declaring that the Church no longer needed to observe God's Sabbaths. This prophecy, given by Paul, began to be fulfilled on that Sabbath day when Mr. Tkach gave that infamous sermon. *"Let no man deceive you by any means: for that day shall not come, except there come a falling away first, and that man of sin be revealed, the son of perdition;"* (2 Thessalonians 2:3). After this, a massive "falling away" from the truth followed.

The attitude and spirit of placing oneself above God is the same thing that mankind did from the very beginning. Adam and Eve began to decide for themselves what was right and wrong. They no longer looked to God as the true source of all that is right and good. God alone determines good and evil: He alone can establish law. By taking on a prerogative that is only God's, they raised themselves above God. *"And the LORD God said, Behold, the man has become as one of us, to know good and evil: and now, lest he put forth his hand, and take also of the tree of life, and eat, and live for ever: therefore the LORD God sent him forth from the garden of Eden, to till the ground from which he was taken. So He drove out the man; and He placed at the east of the garden of Eden Cherubim, and a flaming sword which turned every way, to keep the way of the tree of life"* (Genesis 3:22-24). It was from this very time and for this very reason that mankind was cut off from God—cut off from the spirit of God. From that time forward, only those that God called could come into a spiritual relationship with Him. The tree of life would no longer be offered to all mankind, but to only a few until the time of the Messiah's return.

The Man of Sin Revealed

Although Mr. Tkach showed his opposition to God by delivering a sermon contrary to sound doctrine, God had not yet revealed that he was indeed the "man of sin"—"the son of perdition." Although brethren may have wondered if he did fulfill such a prophecy, only God could declare it so. For anyone to make such a declaration apart from God's revelation would be presumptuous and taking on a prerogative that is God's alone.

There is more to Paul's prophecy. As we continue the story in 2 Thessalonians, we should begin to see more clearly why this unique event is so pivotal to end-time prophecy.

"And now you know what withholds [Greek– "restrains, holds back, detains"] *that he* [the man of sin] *might be revealed* [Greek– "to make known, to disclose what before was unknown"] *in his time. For the mystery of iniquity is already working; only he who now lets* [same Greek word– "restrains, holds back, detains"] *will do so, until he be taken out of the way. And then shall that wicked be revealed* [Greek– "to make known, to disclose what before was unknown"]*, whom the Lord shall consume with the spirit of His mouth, and shall destroy with the brightness of His coming:"* (2 Thessalonians 2:6-8).

What is being restrained, held back and detained from happening? It all refers back to what Paul was addressing from the beginning of this prophecy. *"Now we beseech you brethren, by the coming of our Lord Jesus Christ, and by our gathering together unto Him, that you be not soon shaken in mind, or be troubled, neither by spirit, nor by word, nor by letter as from us, as though the day of Christ is at hand. Let no man deceive you by any means: for that day shall not come, except there come a falling away first, and that man of sin be revealed, the son of perdition;"* (2 Thessalonians 2:1-3). Paul was not explaining that this event was delaying the return of Jesus Christ, but that the return of Jesus Christ would not begin until these things happened. The very return of Jesus Christ was being held back—detained <u>until</u> these events occurred in the Church. This did not prevent a specific timing for the coming of Jesus Christ in His Kingdom, but these things had to occur first before it would be revealed to the Church that the end-time had come and that it was now time for Christ to return.

This prophecy shows that the man of sin—that wicked—would be revealed *"whom the Lord shall consume with the spirit of His mouth, and shall destroy with the brightness of His coming."* Many who were once in fellowship in the Church of God have not been able to understand this verse because they can only see it being fulfilled in a literal, physical way. They believe this prophecy can only be fulfilled at the time of the actual coming of Jesus Christ on the very day the end-time comes to a close.

But it is this very verse that shows how God alone would reveal who the man of sin was and what this meant for the Church. Although most had neither ears to hear nor eyes to see, God did make it abundantly clear that He was the one who would reveal who the man of sin was. After Mr. Tkach betrayed the trust placed in him by giving that defiant sermon in Atlanta, the Spiritual Temple of God became defiled. An abomination of unprecedented proportions had taken place within the Church. As will be discussed later this led to massive desolation and destruction of the spiritual temple itself. Remember Jesus' words in the Olivet Prophecy? *"When you therefore shall see the abomination of desolation, spoken of by Daniel the prophet, stand in the holy place (whoso reads, let him understand:)"* (Matthew 24:15).

Exactly 40 Sabbaths (to the day and very hour) after Mr. Tkach gave that sermon, he died. This was God's own declaration. By taking his life, God revealed that Mr. Tkach was indeed the "son of perdition"—"the man of sin." By this, God also revealed that the Church and the world had entered the end-time. This was finally the time, after 6,000 years, for end-time prophecies to be fulfilled. The process had begun. It all began on the same day Mr. Tkach gave his defiled sermon, but it was God who had to reveal it.

"And then shall that wicked be <u>revealed</u> [Greek– "to make known, to disclose what before was unknown"], *whom the Lord shall consume with the spirit of His mouth, and shall destroy* [It was God Himself who took his life.] *with the <u>brightness</u>* [illumination] *of His coming:"* (2 Thessalonians 2:6-8). This prophetic fulfillment, of God destroying the man of sin, is the very event that declared—illuminated—the coming of Jesus Christ. His time had now come and was no longer being held back from view by the Church. The time had come—the end-time was here!

The number 40 is used as a declaration of the very judgment of God. Do you remember the flood that lasted for 40 days and nights because of man's rebellion? Do you remember the wandering of the children of Israel in the wilderness for 40 years because of their rebellion? The very man who had been set in authority in God's Church on earth, directly under Christ, declared the seventh-day Sabbath was no longer a sign for God's people. Is it any wonder then that God gave a judgment upon Mr. Tkach that would be accomplished exactly 40 Sabbaths—to the hour—from the Sabbath day when Mr. Tkach declared it?

The Affects of the Apostasy
In the Olivet Prophecy Jesus foretold what would happen in the Church toward the end-time. Before Mr. Armstrong's death the Church experienced scattered occurrences of spiritual tribulation. After Mr. Tkach took over the reigns of leadership, this condition continued to grow and become more prevalent in the Church. But after Mr. Tkach gave the Atlanta sermon, great spiritual tribulation came upon the entire Church. All those things that Jesus foretold would lead up to the end-time with increasing momentum were now at their worst.

Two or three years prior to this event, some ministers and brethren fled the doctrinal heresy that was beginning to work its way into the Church. Some people were informed of the doctrinal heresy in various ways before it was officially announced to the Church, so they fled to other organizations that had already left the Worldwide Church of God. Within a year of Mr. Tkach's sermon several other organizations emerged. Brethren began fleeing to them, trying to hold onto the doctrines that they had learned from the beginning of their calling into the truth. Within only two to three years, over three hundred various splinter groups had sprung up from among those who fled the heresies of the "new" Worldwide Church of God—a church organization that no longer had God's spirit working in it.

This also fulfilled other prophecies.

"When you therefore shall see the abomination of desolation, spoken of by Daniel the prophet, stand in the holy place, (whoso reads, let him understand:) then let them who are in Judea flee into the mountains:" (Matthew 24:15-16). The fleeing that took place when the physical temple was destroyed was the "physical type"—fleeing into the mountains. Now came the "spiritual type." It was time for spiritual Judea, the Church, to flee into the mountains. "Mountains" is used prophetically to mean countries and nations—governments, both small and large. When this happened to the physical temple, it was time for people to escape by fleeing into other countries other than Judea. When the "spiritual type" came upon the Church, it was time for people to escape the Worldwide Church of God because it was no longer spiritually safe to dwell there.

Yes, the time had come for brethren to flee into some of the other organizations where fragments of the previous government of God had been scattered.

This also marked a time for the fulfillment of Christ's parable of the ten virgins. This parable actually reveals a condition that would exist in the Church at the time the announcement was made that Jesus Christ was coming. This condition is that same lukewarm condition of Laodicea. By the early 1990s the Church was falling asleep. Brethren began to be shaken from their slumber and sleep just prior to Mr. Tkach's outward rebellion, but when he gave his Atlanta sermon, the Church was shaken from top to bottom. This event served as a wake-up call to the Church. This was indeed the very announcement to God's Church that Jesus Christ was now coming—no longer being held back. The end-time had come.

The prophecy in Ezekiel 5 began to be fulfilled. This prophecy, as it pertains to spiritual Israel, the Church, unfolded quickly. One-third of the Church apostatized—fell away from the truth almost immediately. In essence, one-third of the temple was demolished quickly.

Over the next few months another third of the Church simply gave up in despair and complete loss of faith. They abandoned everything. They had no understanding of how or why this could possibly happen to a Church that was God's. They had no answers and no hope—nothing left for which to fight.

But what about the last third?

There are many prophecies about this group. At this time God made known His displeasure toward His people because they were no longer holding fast spiritually. They had become spiritually lukewarm—they had not been spiritually alert. Instead, they had been slumbering and sleeping, and they had become lifted up with pride. It was time for God to chasten them. They needed to be awakened and brought to repentance.

Laodicea had to be shaken out of its sleep. God would have to humble them mightily if they were to have any hope of changing their destructive course. *"So then because you are lukewarm, and neither cold nor hot, I will spue* [vomit] *you out of my mouth"* (Rev. 3:16). God separated the Church from His presence. This description is not complimentary; it was not intended to be. God's desire was that all would awake from their sleep, repent of their lukewarm spirit, and once again seek to be zealous for His way of life. *"As many as I love, I rebuke and chasten: be zealous therefore, and repent"* (Verse 19).

This same event is described in the Olivet Prophecy when Jesus said, *"There shall not be left here one stone upon another, that shall not be thrown down"* (Matthew 24:2). Every stone was shaken from its place and cast down. The Church was scattered. It was spued out—vomited out of God's mouth—away from His presence. Only through repentance could brethren come back into a relationship with Him and thereby continue their spiritual development.

Several prophecies about the Church are spoken of in the context of being scattered. One such example of prophecy concerning the Church is in a sobering word translated as "scatter" in Daniel 12. It is a word that means to shatter, as a potter rejects a piece of pottery and casts it to the floor, where it is shattered and the pieces scattered.

Returning to the First Seal

Much of the Church's history has been covered to bring us full circle, back to where the chapter began. We need to see what happened to God's Church—prophecies that have already been fulfilled in the actual history of the Church, especially toward the end of Philadelphia and on into the era of Laodicea.

Now we need to return to the prophecy in Revelation regarding the opening of the First Seal of Revelation. *"And I saw when the Lamb opened one of the seals, and I heard, as it were the noise of thunder, one of the four living creatures saying, Come and see. And I saw, and behold, a white horse: and he who sat on him had a bow; and a crown was given unto him: and he went forth conquering, and to conquer"* (Revelation 6:1-2).

It was shown earlier that Mr. Armstrong knew that the key to understanding the seals of Revelation was contained in the Olivet Prophecy. If you know the Olivet Prophecy is about the Church, then you can begin to understand how the opening of the first six seals of Revelation is also about the Church.

The "abomination of desolation" that was about the destruction of the spiritual temple began when this seal was opened by Jesus Christ. The opening of this seal marks, reveals and actually announces the very beginning of the end-time. It reveals that a countdown has begun and Jesus Christ will soon return. It marks the beginning of great tribulation in this world. The end-time is already here. The seals of Revelation have already begun to be opened. But the world and most of the scattered Church have not noticed.

This end-time tribulation concerned the Church and therefore the world did not see it because it did not see God's Church. The Church has gone through great spiritual tribulation. Most of the seals have already been opened. The Church and the sign of those things Jesus said would come upon it have nearly been completely fulfilled. Great physical tribulation is soon to be unleashed upon the whole earth!

The first seal is about the Church. It is about a leader who was set in the temple of God with great power and authority. When the time came for this seal to be opened, he went forth to conquer—to destroy the Church—to commit the "abomination of desolation."

God brought this man's life to an end exactly 40 weeks after this seal was opened, revealing that this event did indeed mark the beginning of the coming of Jesus Christ. The end-time prophecy would now proceed forward, in exact timing, until the last event, the final revelation at the end of the Seventh Seal is fulfilled, the actual coming of Jesus Christ in the Kingdom of God.

But the world doesn't know that the countdown has begun. Not even most in the scattered Church know this. The reason why follows this first seal.

Second and Third Seal Opened

The affect of Mr. Tkach's defiled sermon opened the way for far greater destruction to follow. The floodgates had been opened to free-flowing, doctrinal perversion and wide spread, private interpretation of God's Word through human reasoning and demonic influence.

The opening of the next two seals was a direct response, and natural consequence, of the destruction unleashed from the opening of the first.

"And when He had opened the second seal, I heard the second living creature say, Come and see. And there went out another horse that was red: and power was given to him who sat thereon to take peace from the earth, and that they should kill one another: and there was given unto him a great sword" (Revelation 6:3-4).

After the first seal was opened, peace was taken from the Church. The growing unrest over the previous decade, the doctrinal battles and fighting amongst brethren and ministers who increasingly yielded to distortion of doctrine were now unleashed upon the Church in a massive onslaught, almost overnight. Ministers and brethren began to choose different sides and fight over doctrinal differences.

The opening of this second seal followed instantly behind the first. Nearly three-quarters of the ministry yielded to this new doctrinal format. They turned towards this newly embraced false way: they turned away from the truth. Many ministers fully adopted the new teachings of Mr. Tkach, while others adopted only portions of them. Nevertheless, a broad movement towards false doctrine was thrust upon the Church.

This emergence of so many false ministers led to a quicker dissemination of false doctrine and teaching. Those ministers were no longer wielding the sword of God's word, in spirit and in truth, but a false sword that served to take truth from brethren and destroy spiritual lives.

As the peace of God was taken from their midst through this process, brethren entered into the greatest time of spiritual warfare the Church had ever experienced since it began on Pentecost in 31 A.D. Multiple thousands of brethren began to lose their spiritual lives as people began to kill one another spiritually.

Yes, when false ministers were made manifest, on a spiritual plane, the result brought fighting, destruction, hatred, and death (spiritually). The sword of false ministers was false doctrine, and with that came great devastation and spiritual murder.

"And when He had opened the third seal, I heard the third living creature say, Come and see. And I looked, and lo a black horse; and he who sat on him had a pair of balances in his hand. And I heard a voice in the midst of the four living creatures say, A measure of wheat for a penny, and three measures of barley for a penny; and see that you hurt not the oil and the wine" (Revelation 6:5-6).

These two verses are well understood by most who read them as pertaining to famine. The Church has always understood that this was about a time of famine that would come upon the world at the end-time, but it was only seen as a time of physical famine. Such a time will indeed come upon all the world physically, but these verses are about the Church and spiritual famine.

These actually fulfill an Old Testament prophecy that was to occur in the end-time. *"Behold, the days come, says the Lord GOD, that I will send a famine in the land, not a famine of bread, nor a thirst for water, but of hearing the words of the LORD"* (Amos 8:11).

As false ministers and false doctrine grew in power, brethren became weak and fell victim to a growing famine. The truth of God—the Word of God that brethren need to eat and digest in order to be spiritually fed was becoming very scarce. A time of great spiritual famine had indeed come upon God's people.

The first three seals were a time of abomination and desolation within the spiritual temple of God. The destruction was unprecedented, and yet, the world didn't know. But that was about to change.

The Fourth Seal Opened

As the opening of the second and third seals was a consequence of the first, the opening of the fourth seal was a consequence of the first three being opened. Additional history will give understanding of this seal.

"And when He had opened the fourth seal, I heard the voice of the fourth living creature say, Come and see. And I looked, and behold a pale horse: and his name who sat on him was Death, and Hell [Gk.– "grave"] *followed with him. And power was given unto them over the fourth of the earth, to kill with sword, and with hunger, and with death, and with the beasts of the earth"* (Revelation 6:7-8).

The things mentioned in this seal are similar in nature to those mentioned in the first three seals. The power to conquer, the false sword that destroys life, and the hunger due to famine all worked together to take spiritual life away from brethren.

To understand, we need to pick up the story flow of what happened in the Church, along with those prophetic things that are mentioned in Ezekiel 5 that will have both a physical and spiritual fulfillment in the world. The physical fulfillment of Ezekiel 5 concerns physical destruction and great tribulation that will come on the modern-day nations of Old Testament Israel. The spiritual fulfillment upon the Church of God has nearly been fulfilled.

The first four seals of Revelation describe the first fulfillment of Ezekiel 5, which is upon the Church. *"You shall burn with fire a third part in the midst of the city, when the days of the siege are fulfilled: and you shall take a third part and strike about it with a sword: and a third part you shall scatter in the wind: and I will draw out a sword after them"* (Ezekiel 5:2).

This describes what transpired, in the environs of the Church, once the first seal was opened. Very early in the process approximately one-third of the Church simply gave up and quit. They were spiritually defeated. Another third became swayed by false doctrine (the false sword), and they were spiritually destroyed. But there was another third that fled to the mountains (Matthew 24:16)—to various organizations made up of those who were scattered from the Worldwide Church of God. As God said to Laodicea, He would spue or vomit the Church out of His mouth. Ezekiel tells us that one-third was to be scattered in the wind.

But more is said concerning this last third. God says, *"I will draw out a sword after them."* The first two-thirds was destroyed spiritually. The last third was scattered—for a great purpose. The Laodicea Era of the Church became so spiritually weak (in a deep sleep) that even when these end-time events came, they did not fully awaken the Church. People were being given the opportunity (through separation) to escape from the destructive power that was working in the Worldwide Church organization. Now, they could repent.

Everyone had been vomited out of God's mouth, but only those who had escaped (fled from Worldwide) had any potential, through repentance, to become "hot" spiritually—on fire for God's way—zealous to God. Laodicea was only "lukewarm." God was correcting it. God offered Laodicea repentance and the opportunity to return to a relationship with Him. There was no other way they could return to God. Repentance was the only means.

Many of that last third started the process of repentance, but within a short time many began drifting off to sleep, once more—becoming spiritually lukewarm. This is the ongoing battle for Laodicea. Repentance for most was never complete because they would not receive the truth concerning their own spiritual condition. As a result, some organizations began to drift toward the same condition of Worldwide through the acceptance and teaching of false doctrine.

Other organizations focused on doing the same "work" that they were accustomed to doing during Philadelphia—those same things Mr. Armstrong had done. They did not accept that the work of Philadelphia had ended. God had completed His work for that era through Mr. Armstrong. As a result, the focus became one of rebuilding "the work" of Philadelphia rather than addressing what was actually confronting the Church in Laodicea.

Most brethren returned to a semblance of the past, appeasing themselves by going through the motions and efforts of days gone by. This pacified most so that they would not have to deal with the truth concerning a battle that was still upon them. The presence of too much pride prevented them from admitting the truth. Only when one admits the truth can one then repent of what is false.

Within only a few years, <u>nearly half</u> of those scattered had given in to false doctrine and could not come back into a relationship with God. The destruction on the spiritual temple continued. That last third initially survived the first wave of destruction, but the fourth seal revealed that the sword came again, with death and famine, upon those that remained.

The <u>other half</u> of that last third was primarily associated with one of the two largest organizations that emerged from Worldwide. One of those organizations used the name Living Church of God and the other used the name United Church of God. Both have worked hard to revive the "work" of the past—work that God had already completed through his end-time Elijah, Herbert W. Armstrong.

Both organizations failed to address the realities of those things that happened to the Church. God was chastening them, but they have not listened.

They have not been able to repent because they have not admitted their true spiritual condition. Most brethren and most ministers in these groups refuse to acknowledge some very basic truths. If they would only admit them, then they could be led to repentance. They have a semblance of being the Church of God, but they remain separated from returning to a true relationship with God because they have not repented. They are cut off from the Body of Christ.

They cannot accept that they are Laodicea. They believe they are Philadelphia. They see themselves as being "better" than what God says they are. They see themselves as "rich and increased with goods," instead of being spiritually blind, naked and lukewarm.

They cannot accept that all the stones of the temple have been cast down. Most of them actually believe that the Olivet Prophecy is about a physical temple and the world, not about the Church. They will not admit that they have been vomited out of God's mouth. To acknowledge such a thing requires true humility and full acceptance of what God says is true. But most of them hold to being Philadelphian—doing "the work," preaching the gospel to the world, and never having been spued out of God's mouth.

Most do not admit they are scattered, yet everyone is the product of scattering. They do not believe that the seals are being opened, let alone believe that six have already been opened. They do not believe that Herbert W. Armstrong was the end-time Elijah. They do not believe that all foundational truth was fully restored to the Church through him. They do not believe that he fulfilled Matthew 24:14—preaching the gospel into all the world for a witness to all nations. They do not believe the abomination of desolation has occurred within the Church. They do not believe that Joseph W. Tkach, Sr. was the man of sin and the son of perdition. They do not believe that end-time prophecies are nearing the end of their fulfillment.

Nearly all who were scattered have failed to believe God and His Son, Jesus Christ. They have not been fully awakened from having been spued out of God's mouth.

God declared through the fourth seal that many more within the environs of the Church would be spiritually destroyed. This was all due to their refusal to repent. But not all would be destroyed. God continued in Ezekiel 5 by saying, *"You shall take thereof a few in number, and bind them in your skirts* [A Hebrew word for "wings" that is used as an expression of protection.] *"* (Verse 3).

The Church fell asleep. It was scattered and told to awaken, but it soon began to return to the same condition. Only God can fully awaken someone who has fallen asleep spiritually, and only He could keep them awake. It was through this means that God would give special protection to a few—a group that would become a "remnant" of what had been scattered. This is what is spoken of in Ezekiel 6:8, that says, *"Yet will I leave a remnant, that you may have some who shall escape the sword among the nations, when you shall be scattered through the countries"* (Ezekiel 6:8). But this group would also go through much trial and spiritual refining. *"Then take of them again, and cast them into the midst of the fire, and burn them in the fire; for thereof shall a fire come forth into all the house of Israel"* (Ezekiel 5:4).

At this point in time, these things have not been fulfilled. God is yet to awaken brethren from sleep. Several prophecies reveal that of all that was scattered only a tithe (ten percent) of that last third would be delivered. At this very moment in time, only a tithe (ten percent) of that tithe has been given opportunity for deliverance. More will come after this book has been published. The whole tithe makes up this remnant, and many of those will be delivered after great physical tribulation bursts forth on the earth.

The first four seals of Revelation are about the Church and those things that would come upon her with great destructive power at the end-time. As the seals are opened, however, a shift begins to take place as the power of destruction being revealed begins to turn its focus away from the Church and upon this world. The first four seals reveal destructive power unleashed upon the Church. It is a great spiritual tribulation.

Devastating power has been at work to make the Church

desolate. But God will not allow this abomination of desolation to destroy the entire portion of the temple that exists now. This is part of an overall process of trying and refining the Church. A portion of the remnant will survive and be changed at the appearing of Jesus Christ. Another portion of the remnant will not be changed at that time, but will live on into the new world that is coming.

Others who have turned away from the truth and refused to repent will die. A few of them will await a final resurrection, to final judgment, but many will await a resurrection to life at the end of the thousand year reign of Jesus Christ. Then they will be able to repent of those things that they couldn't repent of during Laodicea. They will be able to live a second time in mortal bodies—repenting and continuing their spiritual growth, if they choose to do so at that time, in order to become a part of God's eternal family. These things are explained more fully in the sixth chapter.

A Transition In Time

The fifth and sixth seals unveil a change in focus from events that have been happening to the Church (spiritual Israel) to events that will begin to happen to the world, especially physical Israel—the modern-day nations of Old Testament Israel.

"And when He had opened the fifth seal, I saw under the altar the souls of them who were slain for the word of God, and for the testimony which they held: And they cried with a loud voice, saying, How long, O Lord, holy and true, do You not judge and avenge our blood on them who dwell on the earth? And white robes were given unto every one of them ; and it was said unto them, that they should rest yet for a little season, until their fellow servants also and their brethren, who should be killed as they were, should be fulfilled" (Revelation 6:9-11).

After the destruction upon the Church, from the opening of the first four seals, there is a time of reflection to acknowledge that a "little season" remains before all will be complete and the Kingdom of God will be established on the earth. Obviously, those who are dead in Christ are still dead; they do not speak. However, a long time has passed as we finally approach the end, and those still living have experienced great suffering because of the events of the first four seals, resulting in their common spiritual cry, *"How long, O Lord?"*

It is at this time that God comforts His people, those He is calling to be a part of a final remnant. He tells them that all who have suffered will be requited soon and that we are near the end of the complete fulfillment and purpose He is working out in the first phase of His plan of salvation for mankind. All who suffer and hold fast to the word of God and the testimony which they hold will be clothed in white robes.

It is after the opening of this seal that the remnant is able to focus more fully on the purpose of those things that have gone before—especially during the opening of the first four seals. It is at the opening of this seal that the remnant begins to more fully focus upon and prepare for what yet lies ahead.

The Sixth Seal

The sixth seal of Revelation marks an awesomely dramatic time for all human history. It sets the way for the conclusive events that must take place before the Kingdom of God can finally come to this earth. This seal establishes the fulfillment of a very specific work that God has been doing for the past 6,000 years. It is at this time that the calling and choosing of all who will be resurrected first into that Kingdom will have been fully determined by God.

This momentous occasion is unveiled amidst the backdrop of the revelation that the time for God's end-time wrath has now come and is about to be unleashed upon this earth. But before this final time of great trouble on earth is released, the final total of all who will be in the first resurrection is sealed. God focuses on this just before the last seal is opened. But first, God has us focus on the warning that is given that will lead into the seventh seal being opened.

"And I looked when he had opened the sixth seal, and, lo, there was a great earthquake [shaking]*; and the sun became black as sackcloth of hair, and the moon became as blood; and the stars of heaven fell unto the earth, even as a fig tree casts her untimely figs, when she is shaken of a mighty wind. And the heaven departed as a scroll when it is rolled together; and every mountain and island were moved out of their places. And the kings of the earth, and the great men, and the rich men, and the chief captains, and the mighty men, and every bondman, and every free man, hid themselves in the dens and in the rocks of the mountains; and said to the mountains and rocks, Fall on us, and hide us from the face of Him who sits on the throne, and from the wrath of the Lamb: For the great day of His wrath is come; and who shall be able to stand?"* (Revelation 6:12-17).

The opening of the sixth seal is the announcement of a transition in time, when the moment for great physical tribulation has finally come and is about to commence, as the end of a great spiritual tribulation is finally concluding as the Church is set in judgment. The end-time has finally come for all mankind, toward the end of his allotted 6,000 years of self-rule, and the foundation of this world will be shaken. Mankind is about to be brought face-to-face with an impending annihilation if God does not intervene.

This last section of Revelation 6 gives us an overview of the cataclysm that is about to follow and the result for all quarters of mankind who will, "in that final end-time after the seventh seal is opened," be seeking to hide themselves and escape this wrath.

But first, an ominous foreboding. Many people will not like what is going to be written now because great suffering and pain is connected with it.

September 11, 2001 is a date the whole world knows! Say "9/11" and everyone will think of the two towers in New York City that crashed to the earth, killing hundreds of people. That same day a jet plunged into the Pentagon. This was a prophetic event fulfilled upon the world, not the Church! This marks a transition in time for end-time prophecy to begin being fulfilled. This focus upon the world will increase and lead up to World War III.

At this point in writing, I am having a very difficult time because it grieves me deeply to say what I must. I have a job to do that God has given me. Writing this is part of it. I do not enjoy it—quite the contrary, I hurt inside because God has shown me clearly what is to come. This is difficult for other reasons as well.

Would you want the task of telling people things that are true, knowing that upon telling them, many will hate you? Some will wish me dead for saying it. This too, God has shown. But all that is minor as to why I feel so sick inside because it is not about myself that I hurt.

As I write, I am sitting on the balcony of the inside section of the Gaylord Opryland Hotel in Nashville, Tennessee. I am in the Cascade area of this huge complex. This area is under a large, glass-domed roof with lush vegetation, a man-made waterfall, flowing streams, and walkways everywhere. It is peaceful and very beautiful. People of all ages walk through it. On this particular day hundreds of young children are present. They are honor students about ages 11 and 12 from the surrounding schools. It is for these children and millions like them throughout America that I mourn.

In only a short time from now most of them will die. The 9/11 tragedy was a forewarning of it all—of what is coming. There is no good news in what is about to come, but there is good news behind it all—the gospel of God's coming Kingdom. It is on the coming of that Kingdom that you must focus. What God says is about to come to pass will come, and soon.

September 11 changed the world. Many know that is true, but they do not comprehend the magnitude of it. The result of the heinous acts of demonic minds on that day will lead to World War

III. These events, the response from the United States (Manasseh) and the response from his brother, the United Kingdom (Ephraim) are the very things that have forever (in this final age) changed attitudes and alliances among nations. The Muslim world, the Middle East, Europe, and Asia have been affected. This day shook the world, and it shook the course of this world—all prophesied to happen!

The United States of America over the last century has been the recipient of the greatest wealth and power bestowed on any nation in all the earth's history. It has been the recipient of promises God gave to Abraham, Isaac and Jacob. This prosperity is the result of fulfilled promises that were to occur exactly as God gave them, at the end of the age of mankind—at the end of 6,000 years of man's self-rule. Everything this nation possesses came from God, but as with the Church in Laodicea, America has become lifted up with pride, "rich and increased with goods"—spoiled. All nations are witness to this truth. It is the primary reason why so many hate us.

This country, one of the tribes of Old Testament Israel, is going to be humbled by God. It will happen before World War III begins. Tribulation will come on this country and the other scattered nations of Old Testament Israel.

The things that symbolize the greatness of our nation (wealth, power, government) were struck a great symbolic blow on that dark September day. The financial center of this great nation—a nation that I love so deeply—was struck with a near fatal blow. It was so very close! It could have crippled the entire nation economically, and the world. As it was, markets had to close for a time in order to regroup.

Two towers, standing so tall, were brought to rubble. This is a foreboding and a forewarning of what will soon follow. All that is "lifted up" in this nation will be brought down. This nation will be the first to fall. It will serve symbolically for the downfall of all nations before Jesus Christ comes in the Kingdom of God.

Washington, D.C. will not escape. The entirety of this government and its military will be brought low—to an end.

That which will be unleashed upon this nation and other modern-day nations of Old Testament Israel will begin as soon as the seventh seal is opened. You are incapable of fully believing all these things now, but soon—when it begins—you will be able to more fully understand and believe. At that time you will have the choice of whether or not you will repent and seek God's forgiveness, favor and help to live His way of life and to be delivered into His new world that will be ruled by His Son.

Yes, on that day, 9/11, every nation and country, large and small (prophetic mountains and islands), was moved by what happened. They were startled and sobered. It was a prelude to that time which is about to come. Yes, the time for God's great wrath is about to unfold. Who will be able to stand? That is the announcement of this sixth seal!

As the two towers fell from the sky, the eerie sight of a cloud rolled open and over New York. From inside it all, the sky became black as the sun disappeared. The affect of dust in the air causes the moon and stars to turn reddish in color. All these things are forebodings of what will soon come in massive ways over large portions of the earth.

The opening of the sixth seal is a forewarning of what will follow over all the earth once the next seal is opened.

We are in the end-time. We are far into it. You should be sobered to the core of your being to understand that the end-time prophecies that have been sealed from man's understanding for centuries have now been unveiled. Six of the seven seals listed in Revelation have already been opened.

The Long Work of Pentecost
The sixth seal not only gives an overview of what is about to come upon this world, as a transition is about to take place from a focus

on the Church to a focus on this world, but it also reveals the completion of a process that entails a work of God that has covered this span of 6,000 years. It is during the time span between the sixth and seventh seals being opened that this great event is finalized.

For nearly six millennia, God has called people to repentance from their own ways to the development of holy, righteous character. This has been the work of Pentecost, most of which has been done during the past 2,000 years within the Church. Firstfruits have been called by God to be in His Kingdom which will come when Jesus Christ returns as King of kings. God has worked for a long time to come to this moment for the opening of this sixth seal when this process will be finalized and all those who will make up His Kingdom will be sealed.

The seventh seal cannot be opened until this process is complete. Angels are actually held back from unleashing their phase of end-time devastation until all who are to be in the first resurrection have been made ready, chosen of God and sealed.

"And after these things I saw four angels standing on the four corners of the earth, holding the four winds of the earth, that the wind should not blow on the earth, nor on the sea, nor on any tree. And I saw another angel ascending from the east, having the seal of the living God: and he cried with a loud voice to the four angels, to whom it was given to hurt the earth and the sea saying, Hurt not the earth, neither the sea, nor the trees, till we have sealed the servants of our God in their foreheads" (Revelation 7:1-3).

These four angels, who are being withheld from releasing devastation over the earth, are the first four angels who will sound their trumpets after the seventh seal is opened. This will mark the beginning of the final three and a half years of great "physical" tribulation.

The first four angels of the seventh seal are held back from unleashing the beginning of physical tribulation upon this world until God has completed the final determination of all who will be in the first resurrection. All who are dead in Christ have already been determined and are in the count of Pentecost—firstfruits who will be in the first resurrection. Their destiny has already been sealed and now the destiny of those who are yet alive and who will have been chosen by God to be part with them is about to be sealed.

Those who return with Jesus Christ, as part of His Kingdom, make up the work of Pentecost—those who will be part of the temple that God has been building for 6,000 years. Because God is the Builder, that structure is very exact! God made the blueprints and has shaped every stone. These stones are exact in number—not too many and not too few, and they will fit into the temple exactly as He has fashioned them. The ability to accomplish such a feat is a glory to the awesome greatness of God and His power to perform it. This temple is exact in every detail, just as God predetermined it before the foundation of the world. *"According as He has chosen us* [speaking to the Church] *in Him before the foundation of the world, that we should be holy and without blame before Him in love: having predestinated* [Gk.– a "predetermined" plan] *us unto the adoption of children by Jesus Christ to Himself, according to the good pleasure of His will, to the praise of the glory of His grace, wherein He has made us accepted in the beloved"* (Ephesians 1:4-6).

The opening of the sixth seal reveals a time for awesome fulfillment in the Work of God over the past 6,000 years. All who will become part of His family, from the first harvest of all mankind, will have been determined and sealed before final tribulation comes on this world. But before these firstfruits can enter into that Family, the world must first go through a time of trouble such as it has never encountered throughout all human history.

Just as we must count an exact number of days to know when to observe Pentecost, there is an exact number of firstfruits that make up the work of Pentecost (this observance is explained more fully in Chapter 6). God is perfect in all His ways and what He builds is exact! God has been building a spiritual temple over the past 6,000 years. That temple is comprised of all who will be the firstfruits in His family when His Kingdom comes to this earth.

"And I heard the number of them who were sealed: and there were sealed one hundred and forty-four thousand of all the tribes of the children of Israel" (Revelation 7:4).

This number of 144,000 is exact and complete in perfection according to God's will. Only these will be resurrected as part of the Family of God at the time of Jesus Christ's return. The number twelve for perfection is used as God describes these firstfruits as being 12,000 each of the twelve tribes of Israel. This is spiritual Israel—not the physical tribes of Israel.

Although some of this was discussed earlier, more will be added now since these things are spoken of in Revelation and in the opening of this seal.

144,000 Returning With Christ

It is important that we fully understand the clearest account that speaks of the 144,000. *"And I looked, and, lo, a Lamb stood on the Mount Zion, and with him an hundred and forty-four thousand, having his Father's name written in their foreheads. And I heard a voice from heaven, as the voice of many waters, and as the voice of a great thunder: and I heard the voice of harpers harping with their harps: And they sung as it were a new song before the throne, and before the four living creatures, and the elders: and no man could learn that song but the hundred and forty-four thousand, which were redeemed from the earth. These are they which were not defiled with women; for they are virgins. These are they which follow the Lamb wheresoever He goes. These were redeemed from among men, being the firstfruits unto God and to the Lamb. And in their mouth was found no guile: for they are without fault before the throne of God"* (Revelation 14:1-5).

The account is clear. The number is exact! These are called firstfruits who have been redeemed from among mankind. The process is complete. These are all who have been redeemed from mankind over the past 6,000 years.

In reality, both accounts of the 144,000 (Revelation 7 and 14) are one and the same. At the point in time of Revelation 7:4, that number has not yet been fully achieved, but it is about to be. When we arrive on the scene in Revelation 14, that number is complete, and they are now with Jesus Christ, having been resurrected.

This group in Revelation 7 is not about a specific number of physical Israelites who are going to receive physical protection from the end-time tribulation. Also, it is not about a specific number in the Church who are going to be protected.

After the twelve tribes are listed, notice what is said. *"After this I looked, and, lo, a great multitude, which no man could number, of all nations, and kindreds, and people, and tongues, stood before the throne, and before the Lamb, clothed with white robes, and palms in their hands;"* (Revelation 7:9).

This is not some new mysterious group. This is not a group of Gentiles or the Laodicean Church that is going to be delivered out of great tribulation in the end-time, as some still believe. This verse is simply projecting ahead in time and showing the outcome of the 144,000 that were earlier sealed in verse 3.

No man could "number" these (Greek word "arithmeo"). The point being made is that only God knows the number, since it was God who brought this number together. We have no means of knowing how many God redeemed from each millennia, but He told us the total (verse 4).

Yet this multitude clearly stands in the same place as those mentioned in Revelation 14—those redeemed from among mankind. These are the same because they are clothed in white and have *"washed their robes, and made them white in the blood of the Lamb"* (Revelation 7:14).

The question is even asked about who this multitude is. *"And one of the elders answered, saying unto me, Who are these who are arrayed in white robes? And where did they come from? And I said unto him, Sir, you know. And he said to me, These are they who come out of great tribulation, and have washed their robes, and made them white in the blood of the Lamb. Therefore are they before the throne of God, and serve Him day and night in the temple: And He who sits on the throne shall dwell among them"* (Revelation 7:13-15).

This group makes up the temple of God. The following verses clearly show that they have been changed from mortal to immortal. They are now spirit—in the spiritual family of God. They did not arrive there easily. All who are called and begotten into the spiritual Family of God must go through intensive refining, trial and testing in order to be molded and fashioned into stones for this temple.

With some of the final instruction that Jesus Christ gave the Church on Passover night He said, *"These things I have spoken unto you, that in me you might have peace. In the world you shall have tribulation: but be of good cheer; I have overcome the world"* (John 16:33).

Paul later spoke of the same thing when he said, *"Wherefore, when we could no longer forbear, we thought it good to be left in Athens alone; and sent Timothy, our brother and minister of God, and our fellow laborer in the gospel of Christ, to establish you, and to comfort you concerning your faith: that no man should be moved by these afflictions [same Greek word for "tribulation"]; for yourselves know that we are appointed there unto. For verily, when we were with you, we told you before that we should suffer tribulation; even as it came to pass, and you know"* (1 Thes.3:1-4).

Tribulation and suffering is not new to God's people. It is part of their calling. That is why the example of fire and the refining of gold and silver is so meaningful. It takes much fire to try brethren in order for them to be transformed—to mold and fashion holy righteous character within them. As Peter said, *"That the trial of your faith, being much more precious than of gold that perishes, though it be tried with fire, might be found unto praise and honor and glory at the appearing of Jesus Christ:"* (1 Peter 1:7).

So when we are told, concerning this great multitude, that *"these are they who come out of great tribulation,"* we need to understand that all who are able to become a part of the Family of God in the first resurrection must go through much tribulation in the world. That is the process whereby one can be transformed. So those being spoken of as coming out of great tribulation are not restricted to only those who come out of the end-time physical tribulation that comes on the whole world. All 144,000 have had to come through great tribulation in life in order to be among those in the first resurrection.

Yes, before the seventh seal is opened and the end-time physical tribulation is unleashed upon this earth, the work of Pentecost will be finished. All who are to be in the first resurrection will have been determined—all will have been sealed.

It should be profoundly sobering to understand that at the time this book is being written we are in the time when the sixth seal has been opened. We are at a transition in time when end-time spiritual tribulation upon the Church is about to conclude and end-time physical tribulation on this world is about to commence.

This time between the opening of the sixth and seventh seals is when the final determination of all who will be firstfruits—in the temple of God—is completed. When the sealing is complete, great destruction will come on this earth since the first four angels of the seventh seal will no longer be restrained.

Chapter 6

THE REVELATION OF GOD'S PLAN

People in every religion on earth believe they understand the truth. That is the problem. Thousands in different religions are teaching doctrines they believe to be true—doctrines that conflict partially and sometimes mightily with other religions.

We will have major religious barriers and conflicting beliefs even if we narrow the field by eliminating all religious ideas that stem from Buddhism, Confucianism, Hinduism, Taoism, and all others that have no claim to the God of Abraham. There is only one God of Abraham. But the Muslim world, Judaism and traditional Christianity all claim to be the guardians of the truest beliefs—those closest to the will of God. Yet these three groups cannot agree amongst themselves.

This religious confusion is the reason man has remained deceived as to the true purpose and plan of God. That plan has remained a mystery to the world since the days of Adam and Eve, except for those few that God has called. Since the creation of mankind God has called only a few to give understanding in order to train them—to mold and fashion them—for a future time when He would intervene to remove all ignorance, deception and confusion from all mankind.

That time has come. God is about to remove all ignorance and reveal Himself and the truth of His very purpose for mankind. He will do this to all who live on into the new world that is coming—one ruled by the Kingdom of God. The beauty of it all is that it doesn't matter whether one believes this or not; it is still going to happen exactly like it is described throughout this book.

Although religious organizations believe they know God and His ways, God's plan and purpose has remained a mystery. It has been revealed to only a few over the past 6,000 years. Now that is going to change. You may be one of those who will now be given opportunity to SEE the truths of God. You may be given the ability to understand—for the first time—what God's plan and purpose is all about, since God is going to begin a process of revealing Himself to those who are going to live on into His new world.

After the Church was established in 31 A.D., God began to reveal His truth to more people, but the Church still remained small. God was only calling some to understanding. These would undergo training, in order that those who would fully yield themselves to the process could become part of those who will help establish the Kingdom of God when Jesus Christ brings it at His return. God's truth has remained a mystery to all the rest of mankind. Notice how Paul described part of this in his letter to the Corinthians.

"But we [those in the ministry] *speak the wisdom of God in a mystery* [a mystery to the world—man cannot know the truth of God unless God reveals it]*, even the <u>hidden wisdom</u>, which God ordained before the world* [before the "age" man was put on this earth] *unto our glory* [for those He called to see His truth—those called into the Church]*: Which none of the princes of this world knew: for had they known it, they would not have crucified the Lord of glory. But as it is written, Eye has not seen, nor ear heard, neither have entered into the heart of man, the things which God has prepared for them who love Him* [quoted from Is. 64:4]*. But God has revealed them unto us* [those He called into the Church] *by His Spirit: for the Spirit searches all things, yes, the deep things of God. For what man knows the things of a man, save the spirit of*

man which is in him [..save by his own natural physical ability to reason with physical surroundings]? *even so the things of God knows no man, but the Spirit of God* [God chooses to reveal His truth to whomever He will. Only by His spirit working in individuals will they be able to truly SEE what is true.]. *Now we have received, not the spirit of the world, but the spirit which is of God; that we might know the things that are freely given to us of God"* (1 Corinthians 2:7-12).

Paul told them that the truth of God and His way of life have remained a mystery to all the world except to those that God gave His spirit because only in that way can someone actually understand what is spiritual. Man is physical and can only deal with the physical reality around him unless God gives him the help he lacks—His spirit.

That is what God is now beginning to do on this earth. For the first four thousand years of man, only a very few had been given understanding and were worked with by God, being prepared for a future time when they would be able to serve Him in the Kingdom of God, when it comes. Then after the ministry, death and resurrection of Jesus Christ, God began to work with larger numbers of people who were called into His Church by Him. But the Church was still very small in size. It is interesting to note at this point a very basic truth that people have not understood, especially those in traditional Christianity.

Many in traditional Christianity believe that a person can be convinced to become converted and "give their heart to the Lord." This is the reason why so many groups proselytize. They believe that through their efforts they can get some to "turn to Christ." They believe they can help bring them to conversion. But God does not work like that. Notice what Jesus Christ said about those who were able to come to Him.

"No one can come to me, except the Father who has sent me draw him: and I will raise him up at the last day" (John 6:44).

People do not understand this verse. Jesus Christ is telling us that no one can, on their own ability or through any kind of coercion, reasoning or preaching, come to Jesus Christ unless God the Father personally draws them (calls them) by His spirit. And God has not done that except to a few who have been called to be in the Kingdom of God—to reign with Jesus Christ when He comes. Those God calls will make up the 144,000 who will return with Christ. God the Father does the calling!

Then Jesus went on to say that He would raise up on the last day those whom the Father would give to Him. That is the time we are rapidly approaching. We are in the end-time. On the last day of the great tribulation, the 144,000 will be resurrected and return to earth with Christ.

All of this has remained a mystery to mankind. But now it is going to be revealed to the whole world. It is God's time to do so. This chapter focuses on God's plan and purpose for mankind and how He will accomplish it.

Although we live at the end of 6,000 years of man's self-rule, a time when the world will experience the worst times of trouble and tribulation ever, it is also the time when the most exciting things ever given to mankind are about to come to pass. You live at the most momentous time of all human history! The time that follows this great tribulation will be the most exciting and most fulfilling ever in the history of man. It is beyond our ability to grasp. A world of true peace, happiness and prosperity for all is about to come.

THE SEVENTH-DAY SABBATH

God is going to begin opening the minds of all mankind as He humbles this world through a great tribulation. The tribulation will be brought to a close by the return of Jesus Christ as King of kings over all nations.

God will begin to introduce His truth, plan and purpose for mankind to a small percentage of the earth's population that will come through this great tribulation. As God establishes His Kingdom on this earth, His truth will no longer remain a mystery to man. Man has been deceived by Satan for 6,000 years, but that is about to come to an end.

The framework of God's plan is revealed by a very basic truth. That truth is about God's Sabbath! The overview of that plan is contained in the weekly Sabbath; the specifics of that plan are contained in the annual Sabbaths.

Although the Jewish people have understood when the weekly Sabbath was to be kept, they have not understood it or kept it as God intends. Jesus Christ condemned their hypocrisy and foolish application of the law, telling them that they made the way of God a burden to others, rather than a joy, as God intended. Jewish leaders continually found fault with Jesus Christ in matters pertaining to the Sabbath day because they simply did not understand it! They still don't understand it.

Yes, Satan has deceived mankind concerning the Sabbath. The Arab people, primarily descended from Ishmael, Abraham's son, believe they are to worship God on Friday. The Jewish people, also descended from Abraham, have known the correct day for the Sabbath, but they have failed to understand it. They have made it a burden.

Most professing Christians observe the first day of the week (Sunday) to worship God. As covered earlier, they have followed the way of the worship of Baal from Old Testament times. They call it worshiping God and Jesus Christ, but it still is worshiping that old sun god.

So the plan of God, revealed through the seventh-day Sabbath, remains a mystery to man.

All are in error. All have been deceived! Now is the time for people to begin to come to repentance and learn what is true! When

God reveals His truth concerning the Sabbath day, people must choose whether or not they will repent of going their own way. Most people perpetuate the religious beliefs they learned from their parents. Thus, deception is passed on from generation to generation. When <u>you</u> learn what is true, will <u>you</u> repent and begin to obey God? Your life depends upon it. The lives of your family and loved ones may rest upon the decision <u>you</u> make.

If you have any desire to live through the great tribulation and on into that new world that is coming, then you will have no other choice but to repent and turn to obedience to God. That process begins with keeping the seventh-day Sabbath! Disobeying God now will only postpone facing the same issue again—at the end of the 1,000-year reign of Jesus Christ. At that time you will be resurrected back to physical life a <u>second</u> time for the very purpose of choosing whether you will obey God or not. The choice is yours. No one else can decide for you. This will be explained more fully later in this chapter.

Whether now or later, you must begin with the Sabbath. If you are unwilling to receive this basic truth from God, then you are unwilling to humble yourself and admit that you have been deceived and that you have been wrong. That is one of the hardest things for anyone to do—admit being wrong. The pride in human nature makes this an almost impossible task. But with God, all things are possible. That is the very reason God is going to humble the world. When left to ourselves, we only continue to deny Him and fail to repent. Unless you are willing to repent, you cannot hope to receive God's favor to live through the great tribulation and on into His new world.

The weekly Sabbath is on the seventh day of the week. It has been since the days of Adam and Eve. Even as the week was established, at creation week, to be seven days, so was God's plan for mankind set to encompass 7,000 years. The first six days were set aside for man to do his own work, but the seventh day was

God's time—the Sabbath. Man has had 6,000 years to live his own way, but like the seventh day, the last 1,000 years belong to God! It is God's time!

Few believe the story about God delivering Noah into a new world. We live at a time when people will find it even harder to believe that God is about to deliver mankind into a new world where the Kingdom of God will rule all nations. Yet, that is exactly what is rapidly approaching!

The Sabbath, From the Beginning

Let's learn about the Sabbath. To do so, we need to begin where it started. *"Thus the heavens and the earth were finished, and all the host of them. And on the seventh day God ended His work which He had made; and He rested on the seventh day from all His work which He had made. And God <u>blessed the seventh day</u>, and sanctified it: because that in it He had rested from all His work which God created and made"* (Genesis 2:1-3).

It should be clear to anyone that God set apart the seventh day by personally sanctifying it. God didn't do that for any other day of the week. To be sanctified means to be set apart for holy use and purpose. God didn't set apart the sixth day (Friday) or the first day (Sunday) for holy use and purpose. God's purpose from the beginning was to set apart the seventh day for all time, as a Sabbath for mankind.

Notice further what God said about the very establishment of recordable time. *"And God said, Let there be lights in the firmament of the heaven to divide the day from the night; and let them be for <u>signs</u>* [the "marking" of time], *and for <u>seasons</u>* [Heb.– "appointed times"], *and for days, and years:"* (Genesis 1:14).

The Hebrew word for "seasons" means "appointed times," much like we speak today of appointments. Time is exact. God made the keeping of time a calculable factor of life. We can establish and set specific moments in time for any purpose we choose. From the very beginning of creation week God established specific times that He would personally set with mankind to be appointments that we should keep with Him. The weekly Sabbath is one such appointment that never changes. Every seventh day mankind should keep this appointment with God!

God magnifies this in the book of Leviticus. *"And the LORD spoke unto Moses, saying, Speak unto the children of Israel, and say unto them, Concerning the feasts [Heb.—"appointed times"] of the LORD, which you shall proclaim to be holy convocations [Heb.—"commanded assemblies"], even these are my feasts [Heb.—"appointed times"]. Six days shall work be done: but the seventh day is the Sabbath of rest, an holy convocation [Heb.—"commanded assembly"]; you shall do no work therein: it is the Sabbath of the LORD in all your dwellings. These are the feasts [appointed times] of the LORD, even holy convocations [commanded assemblies], which you shall proclaim in their seasons [Heb.— "appointed times"]. In the fourteenth day of the first month at even is the LORD'S Passover. And on the fifteenth day [an annual Holy Day—annual Sabbath] of the same month is the Feast [This word in the Hebrew does mean "feast."] of Unleavened Bread unto the LORD: seven days you must eat unleavened bread"* (Leviticus 23:1-6).

Traditional Christianity has tried to do away with this command concerning the seventh-day Sabbath. They find no fault with nine of the ten commandments, but they have tried to "do away with" the fourth commandment that says *"Remember the Sabbath day, to keep it holy"* (Exodus 20:8). Either they have sought to do away with the command of the Sabbath or they say the Sabbath is now Sunday. A few verses later it says, *"For in six days the Lord made heaven and the earth, the sea, and all that in them is, and rested the seventh day: wherefore the Lord blessed the Sabbath day, and hallowed it"* (Exodus 20:11). Yet man has tried to set apart other days for holy use and purpose. But God said that observing the seventh-day Sabbath is a perpetual covenant! (Exodus 31:15-17).

The Levitical system, with its ceremonies and sacrifices, was changed through Jesus Christ from what is commonly referred to as Old Testament times to New Testament times. Through that time period, however, the law of God contained in the Ten Commandments was never changed.

The apostles and New Testament church observed the seventh-day Sabbath and annual Sabbaths. The apostle Paul, some thirty years after the death of Jesus Christ, taught God's people the importance of observing the Sabbath.

"For He spoke in a certain place of the seventh day on this wise, And God did rest the seventh day from all His works" (Hebrews 4:4). Paul explained that Israel had refused to hear God's instruction and was incapable of doing so because they lacked the faith that is made possible only by receiving God's spirit. Paul showed that a specific day was set aside for people to hear God's voice—His instruction. *"Again, He limits a certain day* [God "designated" or "limited" a specific day—sanctified the seventh day.]*, saying in David, Today, after so long a time; as it is said, Today if you will hear His voice, harden not your hearts"* (Vs. 7).

Paul further explained that, for the Church, *"There remains therefore a rest* [Greek word— "Sabbatismos"—a keeping of the Sabbath] *for the people of God. For he who has entered into His rest* [into God's weekly seventh-day Sabbath rest]*, he also has ceased from his own works* [ceased from his own carnal ways by seeking to live God's ways]*, as God did from His* [in like manner, as God rested from the beginning, on the seventh day] *"* (Vs. 9-10).

The Sabbaths of God (weekly and annual) are an identification—a sign—of God's people because only His people know them and keep them in spirit and in truth as He commands.

"And hallow my Sabbaths; and they will be a sign between me and you, that you may know that I am the Lord your God" (Ez. 20:20). You must begin with the Sabbath if you want to know God.

PASSOVER

The First Annual Observance

The weekly Sabbath reveals God's 7,000 year plan for mankind. The first 6,000 years belong to man. But God will reign over man during this last 1,000 year period.

God's plan is more fully revealed through the annual observances He gave as "appointed times" for us to keep with Him. This first annual observance is not an annual Sabbath, but it is to be observed first each year before the annual Sabbaths. That observance is Passover. God's plan of salvation begins with this day. Without receiving the Passover, mankind cannot enter into a relationship with God. Receiving the Passover allows mankind to begin the process of salvation that will produce the blessings God wants for him.

The awesome importance of the precise timing of Passover is covered near the end of chapter seven. The importance of that timing is the primary means by which one can begin to know the true Messiah and those things that are false. It is by this same means that you can identify false teachers, false religions and any organization that condones false teachings. It should be noted that at this time Judaism observes Passover one day late. The actual date for Passover on the Roman calendar is in error. That will be explained more fully later.

Leviticus 23 lists all of God's appointed times. The annual observances begin with Passover. *"In the fourteenth day of the first month at even is the LORD's Passover"* (Leviticus 23:5).

Many are familiar with the story of the exodus out of Egypt. It was at this time that God gave the Passover observance to the Israelites. *"And the LORD spoke unto Moses and Aaron in the land of Egypt, saying, This month shall be unto you the beginning of months* [it begins in the spring]*: it shall be the first month of the year to you. Speak you unto all the congregation of Israel, saying, In the tenth day of this month they shall take to them every man a*

lamb, according to the house of their fathers, a lamb for an house:..
Your lamb shall be <u>without blemish,</u> a male of the first year: you
shall take it out from the sheep, or from the goats: " (Ex. 12:1-5).

This lamb without blemish was symbolic of Jesus Christ who
was without sin. The apostle Peter explained this to the Church by
saying, *"Forasmuch as you know that you were not redeemed with*
corruptible things, as silver and gold, from your vain conduct
received by tradition from your fathers; but with the precious blood
of Christ, as of a lamb without spot" (1 Pet. 1:18-19).

The account in Exodus continues. *"And they shall <u>take of the</u>*
<u>blood</u>, and strike it on the two side posts and on the upper door post
of the houses, wherein they shall eat it" (Exodus 12:7).

"For I will pass through the land of Egypt this night, and will
smite all the firstborn in the land of Egypt, both man and beast; and
against all the gods of Egypt I will execute judgment: I am the
LORD. And the <u>blood</u> shall be to you for a token upon the houses
where ye are: and when I see the blood, I will <u>pass over</u> you and the
plague shall not be upon you to destroy you, when I smite the land
of Egypt" (Verses 12-13). This pictures what Jesus Christ would
fulfill for mankind. He is our Passover and by His blood we can be
saved from the penalty of sin, which is eternal death—a final
judgment for all time. *"For the wages of sin is death; but the gift of*
God is eternal life through Jesus Christ our Lord" (Romans 6:23).
The penalty for sins that are not forgiven is death—eternal
judgment—eternal death.

Jesus Christ, the Son of God, the Lamb of God, was God's
Passover sacrifice given to mankind whereby we can be saved from
death. Death passes over us. This is where we must begin in God's
plan of salvation. It begins with Jesus Christ. All of us face the
death penalty for our sins until we accept the sacrifice of Christ to
remove them. Only the blood of Christ, in our stead, can remove
that penalty. This is God's Passover sacrifice for us.

"Wherefore, as by one man sin entered into the world, and death

by sin; and so death passed upon all men, for that all have sinned: " (Romans 5:12).

The Passover is the beginning of God's plan of salvation. We must be forgiven of our sins in order to enter into a relationship with God the Father. Only upon repentance and baptism can we begin the process of being delivered from the pull of our own selfish human nature and the power of Satan that holds man in darkness and deception. This is God's plan of deliverance from spiritual Egypt. *"Who has delivered us from the power of darkness, and has translated us into the kingdom of His dear Son: In whom we have redemption through His blood, even the forgiveness of sins: "* (Colossians 1:13-14).

God's Church observes this annual memorial in the very same way Christ did on Passover night with His disciples after He had His last supper with them.

The apostle Paul gave instructions concerning this observance. *"For I have received from the Lord that which also I delivered unto you* [how to observe Passover], *That the Lord Jesus the same night* [the Passover night] *in which He was betrayed took bread: and when He had given thanks, He broke it, and said, Take, eat: this is my body, which is broken for you: this do in remembrance of me* [each year at Passover time]. *After the same manner also He took the cup, after supper, saying, This cup is the new covenant in my blood: This do you, as often as you drink it, in remembrance of me. For as often as you eat this bread, and drink this cup, you do show the Lord's death till He come "* (1 Cor. 11:23-26).

In this instruction to the Church (the spiritual Israel of God) Jesus Christ instituted the symbols for Passover on the same night the Passover lamb was killed, roasted and eaten. On the night of the fourteenth day of the first month the Israelites were to observe this annual occasion by killing the lamb and eating it. Now the Church of God is to partake annually of the symbols of eating the flesh and drinking the blood of the Lamb of God. The flesh is symbolized by eating a piece of unleavened bread; the blood is symbolized by drinking a small amount of wine.

As explained earlier, God gave man the means for dividing one day from another by beginning a new day at the very moment the sun sets on the previous day. The night time portion of the observance of Passover is at the beginning of that day. The activities that were to follow during the daylight portion of that same Passover day were also fulfilled in Jesus Christ.

When Israel kept the Passover, the killing of the lamb that their families were to eat is described in scripture as "the sacrifice of the LORD'S Passover." Both the eating of the lamb by the Israelites on the night of the fourteenth and, later, the Church's observance of partaking of the symbols of the bread and wine are symbolic of God giving His Son to be sacrificed for mankind. It also pictures the Messiah's own agreement to give His life as that sacrifice. God the Father and Jesus Christ willingly gave this sacrifice to mankind, and it was therefore truly "the sacrifice of the LORD'S Passover."

However, the actual time Christ died was in the mid-afternoon of Passover day. This too fulfilled activities the Israelites were busy carrying out during that same period of time on Passover. During the afternoon portion of Passover, the Israelites were preparing for the first day of the Feast of Unleavened Bread that would follow after sunset on Passover. The actual killing of the sacrificial animals and their preparation for the feast to follow took place throughout the afternoon of the Passover day. But the feasting and the actual offerings upon the altar could not begin until after sunset. Those animals that were killed during the afternoon of Passover, in preparation of the first day of the Feast of Unleavened Bread, are referred to in scripture as the "Passover offerings." So when scripture spoke of "killing the Passover," it included those things symbolized by the "LORD'S Passover" that was killed and eaten on the night of the fourteenth and also the symbolism contained in the killing of those animals on the afternoon of the Passover that were to be feasted upon and offered up to God after sunset.

The entirety of Passover in both the night and day time portions has great meaning in all the symbolism that Jesus Christ actually fulfilled in His life and death.

The Annual Sabbaths—Annual Holy Days

THE FEAST OF UNLEAVENED BREAD

Once we have received the Passover sacrifice of Jesus Christ to pay the penalty for our sins, we can proceed with the plan of God. The next area of focus is the meaning of the observance of the Feast of Unleavened Bread.

The first day and the seventh day of the Feast of Unleavened Bread are annual Sabbaths, annual Holy Days. The first annual Sabbath, which is the first day of Unleavened Bread, begins immediately after sunset on Passover day.

"And on the fifteenth day of the same month is the Feast of Unleavened Bread unto the LORD: seven days you must eat unleavened bread. In the first day you shall have an holy convocation [as the weekly Sabbath, this day is also a "commanded assembly"]*: you shall do no servile work therein* [it is a Sabbath day]*. But you shall offer an offering made by fire unto the LORD seven days: in the seventh day is an holy convocation* [Heb.—"commanded assembly"]*: you shall do no servile work therein"* (Leviticus 23:6-8).

This entire period of "appointed time" is one week in length. During this week we are to eat unleavened bread. We are to have no leavening in our homes during this period of time and we are to refrain from eating bakery products, such as breads and cakes that contain leavening agents.

The symbolism, in this observance, is that leaven puffs up just like pride puffs up. Leaven is symbolic of sin. It is an expression of pride against the laws of God. We live as we please rather than express God's will in our lives. Eating unleavened bread symbolizes our desire to obey God and eat of His way of life, the spiritual unleavened bread of life.

This symbolism is also about Jesus Christ who was without sin—unleavened. The Church pictures this on Passover night when unleavened bread is eaten as a symbol of Christ's broken body. Jesus described much of this process in the Book of John. Now, with this fundamental understanding of the observance of Passover and the Feast of Unleavened Bread, consider how revealing the following scriptures truly are.

"Then said they unto Him, What shall we do, that we might work the works of God? Jesus answered and said unto them, This is the work of God, that ye believe on Him whom He has sent. They said therefore unto Him, What sign do you show then, that we may see, and believe you? what do you work? Our fathers did eat manna in the desert; as it is written, He gave them bread from heaven to eat. Then Jesus said unto them, Verily, verily, I say unto you, Moses gave you not that bread from heaven; but my Father gives you the true bread from heaven. For the bread of God is He which comes down from heaven, and gives life unto the world. Then said they unto Him, Lord, evermore give us this bread. And Jesus said unto them, I am the bread of life: he that comes to me shall never hunger; and he that believes on me shall never thirst. But I said unto you, That you also have seen me, and believe not. All that the Father gives me shall come to me; and him that comes to me I will in no wise cast out. For I came down from heaven, not to do my own will, but the will of Him that sent me" (John 6:28-38).

"The Jews then murmured at Him, because He said, I am the bread which came down from heaven. And they said, Is not this Jesus, the son of Joseph, whose father and mother we know? how

is it then that He says, I came down from heaven? Jesus therefore answered and said unto them, Murmur not among yourselves. No man can come to me, except the Father which has sent me draw him: and I will raise him up at the last day" (John 6:41-44).

"I am that bread of life. Your fathers did eat manna in the wilderness, and are dead. This is the bread which comes down from heaven, that a man may eat thereof, and not die. <u>I am the living bread</u> which came down from heaven: if any man <u>eat of this bread</u>, he shall live for ever: and the bread that I will give <u>is my flesh</u>, which I will give for the life of the world. The Jews therefore strove among themselves, saying, How can this man give us his flesh to eat? Then Jesus said unto them, Verily, verily, I say unto you, Except you <u>eat the flesh</u> of the Son of man, and <u>drink His blood</u>, you have no life in you" (John 6:48-53).

Jesus Christ explained that if someone did not receive the Passover (*"eat the flesh of the Son of Man and drink His blood"*) they could not have the life of God dwelling in them (*"you have no life in you"*) through the power of His spirit. They were yet in sin until this could be a reality in their life. One must first receive the Passover in order to come out of sin and live God's way of life—become unleavened.

After we are baptized and our sins are forgiven we are to begin changing our lives. Contrary to the teaching of traditional Christianity, we are not to remain the way we are by simply accepting grace, but we are to change by becoming a new <u>creature</u> (Greek– "creation") in God. We are not to continue living the same way we did before baptism, however, we will have that same nature in us which we will have to resist all our lives.

Paul corrected the Corinthians in a matter that involved two people in their midst who were flaunting their disobedience before the Church. The Church was preparing to observe the Passover season and the Feast of Unleavened Bread, so Paul used this occasion to show them their error.

"Your glorying is not good. Know you not that a little leaven leavens the whole lump? [Their sin of condoning disobedience to God was like leaven. It would spread throughout the Church, if not corrected.] *Purge out therefore the old leaven, that you may be a new lump* [They were to get rid of the sin and live a new way of life.]*, as you are unleavened* [They were not fully rid of sin in their lives. Humans will always find leaven (sin), but we are to get rid of it when it is revealed to us. This is speaking of the fact that they were observing the Feast of Unleavened Bread and had removed leavening from their homes for this period of time—"as you are unleavened."]*. For even Christ our Passover is sacrificed for us: Therefore let us keep the feast* [Paul told them how they were to keep the Feast of Unleavened Bread and that the lessons from it should carry on into their everyday lives.]*, not with old leaven, neither with the leaven of malice and wickedness; but with the unleavened bread of sincerity and truth* [...with the absence of sin, living true obedience before God in His way of life]*"* (1 Corinthians 5:6-8).

Although those in traditional Christianity teach that the laws of the Old Testament are done away, it should be obvious that they are not because the early Church of the New Testament kept the weekly seventh-day Sabbath and Paul's instructions to the Corinthians clearly show that the Church observed the annual Sabbaths as well. Obedience to God in these matters was just a way of life for the Church. Different accounts throughout scripture reflect that truth. The New Testament is not written in the same way as the Old Testament when Israel was given the law of God. The New Testament time is simply a witness of how the Church sought to live by the law of God. It is not written to convince people of the validity of the law of God; that fact is simply taken for granted.

The Feast of Unleavened Bread teaches us that after forgiveness of sin through Christ we are to begin a journey out of spiritual Egypt—out of sin and the bondage it holds over our lives. We are to begin a process of change with a new way of living. When scripture speaks of being converted, it means we are to change from our old ways of carnal human nature to the new way of righteousness in God's way of life.

Churches in this world fail to tell this truth. Instead, they teach that we are under grace by the sacrifice of Christ and that the law has been done away. They believe grace means being free from the law of God.

"What shall we say then? Shall we continue in sin, that grace may abound? [Paul is asking... if the law is done away through grace, then should we sin even more so that God's grace might be even greater in our lives?] *God forbid. How shall we, that are dead to sin, live any longer therein? Know you not, that so many of us as were baptized* [Greek– "fully immersed in water"] *into Jesus Christ were baptized into His death? Therefore we are buried with Him by baptism into death: that like as Christ was raised up from the dead by the glory of the Father, even so we also should walk in newness of life. For if we have been planted together in the likeness of His death, we shall be also in the likeness of His resurrection: Knowing this, that our old man is crucified with Him, that the body of sin might be destroyed* [Gk.– "done away with"], *that henceforth we should not serve sin"* (Romans 6:1-6).

It isn't the law of God that is <u>done away</u>, but it is the old man of sin that is <u>to be done away</u>. We are to come out of the watery grave of baptism and begin living a new life as a new creature (Greek– "creation") in God, just as Paul told the Ephesians *"...that you put off concerning your former conduct the old man, which is corrupt according to the deceitful lusts; And be renewed in the spirit of your mind, And that you put on the new man, which after God is created in righteousness and true holiness"* (Eph. 4:22-24).

Coming out of spiritual Egypt, becoming unleavened in our lives, is a life-long battle. As Paul explained in Romans 7, there is a constant battle against the carnal human mind that is in us, but this phase of God's plan shows us the beginning of a process of being freed from bondage as we enter into a war of fighting against sin. We have to fight against our human nature and strive to live by God's true way of righteousness. It is through this process, this struggle, that holy righteous character can be developed within us.

Just as God commands us to put leavening out of our homes, to eat only unleavened bread during the seven days of the Feast of Unleavened Bread, He also tells us to put leavening (sin) out of our lives and eat only of the true unleavened bread of life which comes in and through Jesus Christ.

PENTECOST

The next step in God's plan of salvation is pictured by Pentecost. Pentecost in the Greek means to "count fifty." The date for keeping this appointed time with God can only be known if we understand and observe the Passover and Feast of Unleavened Bread. God very specifically tells us when to begin counting, from within a period of time inside the Feast of Unleavened Bread, so we can know when to convene before Him on this third annual Sabbath.

God's plan proceeds forward in an orderly and sound progression with each annual observance revealing more about the process by which man is able to receive salvation and become part of His spiritual Family. Let's begin learning about Pentecost in Leviticus where all of God's "appointed times" are listed.

"Speak unto the children of Israel, and say unto them, When you are come into the land which I give unto you, and shall reap the harvest thereof, then you shall bring a sheaf of the firstfruits [the Hebrew simply means the "first" or "beginning"] *of your harvest unto the priest: And he shall wave the sheaf before the LORD, to be accepted for you: on the day after the Sabbath the priest shall wave it"* (Leviticus 23:10-11).

The period of time being spoken of in these verses is the Passover season, specifically during the Feast of Unleavened Bread. The smaller, early harvest in Israel began in the spring time. But the larger, fall harvest, which is also pictured symbolically in God's plan of salvation, will be covered later in another annual Sabbath.

In Israel, many spring crops are ready to be harvested before Passover. Israel is being given very specific instructions regarding the ceremonies concerning this early harvest that they were to observe during the Feast of Unleavened Bread.

"And you shall eat neither bread, nor parched grain, nor green ears, until the selfsame day that you have brought an offering unto your God: it shall be a statute forever throughout your generations in all your dwellings" (Verse 14). As part of this instruction, the Israelites were told to bring a sheaf of the first—of the beginning—of this harvest. It was to be used in a ceremony that would take place during the Feast of Unleavened Bread. Although harvesting could begin before this day, they could not eat any of the new harvest until this ceremony was observed. The things symbolized by this entire process are awesomely revealing.

This sheaf was to be waved before God as an offering during this ceremony that was always held on the first day of the week during the Feast of Unleavened Bread. The "wave sheaf offering" was symbolic of Jesus Christ. Christ was to be presented to God to be "accepted" for us just as He fulfilled this symbolism when He was received of the Father after His resurrection.

We have already covered the fact that Jesus Christ was resurrected from the dead at the end of the seventh-day Sabbath. However, Christ did not <u>ascend</u> to God until later on the first day of the week. Notice the story... Mary had come to the tomb in the early morning of the first day of the week during the Feast of Unleavened Bread. Mary wondered where Jesus had been taken; she did not know that he had been resurrected from the dead.

"But Mary stood outside at the tomb weeping: and as she wept,

she stooped down, and looked into the tomb, And saw two angels in white sitting, the one at the head, and the other at the feet, where the body of Jesus had lain. And they say unto her, Woman, why do you weep? She said unto them, Because they have taken away my Lord, and I know not where they have laid Him. And when she had said this, she turned herself back, and saw Jesus standing, and knew not that it was Jesus. Jesus said unto her, Woman, why do you weep? whom do you seek? She, supposing Him to be the gardener, said unto Him, Sir, if you have carried Him away, tell me where thou have laid Him, and I will take Him away. Jesus said unto her, Mary. She turned herself, and said unto Him, Rabboni; which is to say, Master. Jesus said unto her, <u>Touch me not</u>; for I am not yet ascended to my Father: but go to my brethren, and say unto them, I ascend unto my Father, and your Father; and to my God, and your God. Mary Magdalene came and told the disciples that she had seen the Lord, and that He had spoken these things unto her. Then the same day at evening [This was as the sun was nearing the time of going down, toward the end of the first day of the week, just before the second day began.], *being the first day of the week* [...still the first day of the week], *when the doors were shut where the disciples were assembled for fear of the Jews, came Jesus and stood in the midst, and said unto them, Peace be unto you"* (Jn. 20:11-19).

Between these two periods of time, between the time of speaking to Mary in the morning and this time in the late afternoon, Christ had ascended to the Father. This fulfilled the symbolism of the wave sheaf being waved before God on the first day of the week during the Feast of Unleavened Bread—being lifted up before God to be "accepted" for us.

It is clear that His being received of God was accomplished after Mary had spoken to Him because He would not let Mary touch Him. But later that afternoon Jesus gave His disciples permission to touch Him when He appeared to them.

"And as they spoke these things, Jesus Himself stood in the

midst of them, and said unto them, Peace be unto you. But they were terrified and frightened, and supposed that they had seen a spirit. And He said unto them, Why are you troubled? And why do such thoughts arise in your hearts? Behold my hands and my feet, that it is I myself: handle me, and see; for a spirit has not flesh and bones, as you see me have" (Luke 24:36-39).

Jesus Christ fulfilled perfectly all of the symbolism contained in the Passover observance, and He perfectly fulfilled the symbolism of the "wave sheaf" offering that was presented to God on the first day of the week during the Feast of Unleavened Bread.

Now we can continue with the instructions on how to count Pentecost, as it is given in Leviticus.

"And you shall count unto you from the day after the Sabbath, from the day that you brought <u>the sheaf of the wave offering</u>; seven Sabbaths shall be complete: [The "sheaf of the wave offering," which represented Jesus Christ, was a specific part of the ceremonies that were to be carried out during the Feast of Unleavened Bread. Therefore, this first day of the week always fell <u>inside</u> these days of observance.] *Even unto the day after the seventh Sabbath shall you <u>number fifty days</u>; and you shall offer a new meat offering unto the LORD"* (Leviticus 23:15-16).

Again, God is very specific as to the timing of this annual Sabbath. This annual Holy Day of Pentecost was to be counted from a specific day (the first day of the week) within the observance of the Feast of Unleavened Bread. Seven weekly Sabbaths, from this day, was forty-nine days. Adding one more day, making it a total of fifty days, would bring us to another period of time on the first day of the week. Pentecost always falls on the first day of the week (Sunday on the Roman Calendar), but that day must always be counted from the first day of the week (Sunday), <u>during</u> the Feast of Unleavened Bread.

The instruction for Pentecost now begins in Leviticus. *"You shall bring out of your habitations two wave loaves of two-tenths deals: they shall be of fine flour; they shall be baked with leaven;* *they are the firstfruits unto the LORD"* (Leviticus 23:17). *"And the priest shall wave them with the bread of the firstfruits for a wave offering before the LORD, with the two lambs: they shall be holy to the LORD for the priest. And you shall proclaim on the selfsame day, that it may be an holy convocation unto you: you shall do no servile work therein: it shall be a statute forever in all your dwellings throughout your generations"* (Vs. 20-21). On this day of Pentecost the Israelites were to observe this ceremony. It is about those who will be firstfruits in the Kingdom of God.

God has a plan of salvation whereby mankind is offered the blessing of becoming a part of His Family—to live in the God Family for all eternity as spirit beings. This Holy Day pictures those God calls early in His plan to become part of His Family first. As the early spring harvest is referred to in scripture as the "firstfruits of the land," so are these, the firstfruits of God's plan, to become a part of His Family earlier than the majority of mankind. The much greater fall harvest of the land pictures salvation for the far larger remainder of mankind represented in the last two annual Sabbaths.

These firstfruits are symbolized in the ceremony of the two wave loaves. As the "wave sheaf offering" picturing Jesus Christ is waved to be accepted by God, during the Feast of Unleavened Bread, so are the two "wave loaves" to be waved in an offering to be accepted by God. These firstfruits are pictured as being accepted by God and will become part of the God Family when they are given eternal life.

There is also symbolism in the fact that these wave loaves are mixed with leaven. Jesus Christ is always pictured as "unleavened"—being without sin. But these, although accepted by God, are pictured as being leavened—having been mixed with sin.

These wave loaves picture the 144,000 that God has called and chosen out of all mankind in the first 6,000 years of man on earth. They are resurrected to eternal life as spirit beings in the God

Family—in the Kingdom of God—when Jesus Christ returns. Notice how they are described in Revelation.

"And I looked, and, lo, a Lamb stood on the Mount Zion, and with Him one hundred and forty-four thousand, having His Father's name written in their foreheads. And I heard a voice from heaven, as the voice of many waters, and as the voice of great thunder: and I heard the voice of harpers with their harps: And they sang as it were a new song before the throne, before the four living creatures, and the elders: and no man could learn that song but the hundred and forty-four thousand <u>who were redeemed</u> from the earth. These are they who were not defiled with women; for they are virgins [speaking of that which is spiritual]. *These are they who follow the Lamb wheresoever He goes. <u>These were redeemed</u> from among men, <u>being firstfruits</u> unto God and to the Lamb"* (Rev. 14:1-4).

These firstfruits are redeemed from among mankind during the first 6,000 years. They were brought out of sin—forgiven of sin—were clean before God through Jesus Christ. This 144,000 referred to as "firstfruits" in Revelation 14:4 are the same ones spoken of that have been "redeemed to God" by the blood of Christ (Revelation 5:9) as well as those that *"have washed their robes, and made them white in the blood of the Lamb"* (Revelation 7:14).

Even as these two loaves are made from a very small amount of the grain of this "firstfruits of the land," so are the 144,000 very small compared to all the billions of people that have lived during this same 6,000-year period of time.

As people come to better understand the plan of God revealed through His Sabbaths, they can begin to understand why so few are spoken of in the Old Testament as having a genuine relationship with God. The Old Testament period covers the first 4,000 years of man up to the time of Christ's first coming as the Passover Lamb of God. This same understanding will also help you see why the Church is spoken of as His little flock over the past 2,000 years. The Church has never been a large organization on earth because

God's plan involves redeeming only 144,000 from this 6,000-year period of time.

The story flow of Unleavened Bread and Pentecost in Leviticus 23 is directly tied together. Both involve the early harvest referred to as "the firstfruits of the land." Jesus Christ is the first of the firstfruits of God's harvest; the 144,000 are pictured as the rest of the "firstfruits of the land."

There is much more to the meaning of Pentecost, but you have been given a basic understanding of those who are called firstfruits.

The story of Pentecost is a powerful one. God brought the children of Israel out of Egypt and took them through the wilderness to Mt. Sinai where, on the day of Pentecost, He gave them His law in the form of the Ten Commandments. However, the whole history of the Israelites is that they could not keep the law. Carnal human beings, of and by themselves, are incapable of keeping the righteousness of God's law. Even to this day, the tribe of Israel known as Judah, generally referred to as the Jewish people, is the epitome of this story. The very best that man can do, on his own ability, is reflected in the life of the Jewish people. None of the other tribes of Israel held to the law of God like the tribe of Judah. All the others rebelled against God, long before Judah.

While man's best example of adherence to God's laws is found in the Jewish people, Christ found himself being attacked by these same people. This revealed that although they had an appearance of holding to the law of the God of the Old Testament, they did not understand Him, His ways, or even the law itself. If they had, then they would have recognized Jesus Christ as the Messiah. In their blindness, the Jewish people refused the teaching and instruction that came to them from the Son of God.

The witness in their lives and in the lives of all the Israelites is that mankind, of and by himself, is incapable of living by the ways and laws of God. Pentecost reveals what is lacking in their lives—why they have not understood the teachings of the Old

Testament—and why they did not recognize the Messiah when he came and spoke to them nearly 2,000 years ago.

The book of Acts reveals more about the importance of Pentecost in the plan of God. After Jesus Christ died and was resurrected He appeared to the disciples. This is that story in the opening of the book of Acts.

"The former account have I made, O Theophilus, of all that Jesus began both to do and teach, until the day in which He was taken up, after He through the Holy Spirit had given command-ments unto the apostles whom He had chosen: to whom also He showed Himself alive after His passion by many infallible proofs, being seen of them forty days, and speaking of the things pertaining to the Kingdom of God" (Acts 1:1-3). The gospel—good news—that Jesus Christ taught the disciples was about the Kingdom of God. We'll focus more on that as we continue with God's plan.

"And, being assembled together with them, commanded them that they should not depart from Jerusalem, but wait for the promise of the Father, which, He said, you have heard of me. For John truly baptized with water; but you shall be baptized with the Holy Spirit not many days from now. When they therefore had come together, they asked of Him, saying, Lord, will You at this time restore again the kingdom to Israel?" (vs. 4-6). The disciples did not understand that Jesus Christ came the first time to fulfill Passover and that it would be nearly 2,000 years before the Kingdom of God would come. They thought he might fulfill prophecy by bringing that Kingdom to them at that very time.

"And He said unto them, It is not for you to know the times or the seasons, which the Father has put in His own power. But you shall receive power, after that the Holy Spirit is coming upon you: and you shall be witness unto me both in Jerusalem, and in all Judea, and in Samaria, and unto the uttermost part of the earth" (vs. 7-8).

The coming of the Kingdom of God to this earth was not for their time, but it is for our time—now! It is only a very short time away because God has been revealing that the seals of Revelation have already begun to be opened. The sobering reality is that six have already been opened, and only one remains to be opened at the time of writing this book. As this last seal is opened, God's two end-time witnesses will come on the scene, and the first four angels will blow their trumpets announcing the beginning of great end-time destruction. These events mark the beginning of the three and one half years of great physical tribulation.

But concerning the day of Pentecost, Jesus was making it very clear to the disciples that they were to stay in Jerusalem until they received the promise of God's spirit. More of this account and the pouring out of God's spirit upon the disciples can be read in Acts 2. Many people who witnessed this great event on the day of Pentecost became convicted of the words they heard, so much so that they asked what they needed to do next. *"Then Peter said unto them, Repent, and be baptized every one of you in the name of Jesus Christ for the remission of sins, and you shall receive the gift of the Holy Spirit"* (Acts 2:38).

Although the law of God was given to the Israelites on the day of Pentecost, God revealed to mankind that His way of life cannot be lived through human effort alone, but mankind must also have the power of His spirit living in them. That is what was lacking in the children of Israel. It is still lacking in the lives of all who dwell on the earth except for those in the true Church of God whom the Father has called to understand His truth. God's word and way of life is a matter of the spirit, and one must receive that spirit in order to understand the true will of God. Otherwise, man is limited to his own human reasoning to read God's words and come up with his own ideas and beliefs about God and Jesus Christ. That is why there are so many religions on this earth—all conflicting with one another in their teachings. There is only one true Church and one truth—one way of life that comes from God.

Again, mankind is not able to come out of sin on his own. He cannot obey God by coming out of sin, as Unleavened bread pictures, unless God's spirit dwells in him. It is only by acceptance of Jesus Christ, as our Passover, that we can be forgiven of our sins. As the process of repentance and forgiveness takes place, God is there with the help of His spirit to make salvation possible.

The Book of Acts continues by showing that after baptism we receive the "laying on of hands" through God's ministry, and if we have repented, then we are begotten of God's spirit. It is the actual impregnation of the spirit of God that begets us. This is on a spiritual plane, but it is revealed by the "physical type" of human begettal. At the time a sperm cell impregnates the human egg, a life is begotten. It is not yet born into the world, but it grows in embryo until time for actual birth into the world.

This process, whereby humans are begotten of God's spirit, is likened to the human process. After we are begotten of God's spirit, we begin to grow—spiritually in embryo. As we continue in spiritual growth by conquering and overcoming the way of our selfish human nature, we continue to mature until the time we can be born into God's Family—into the very Kingdom of God. Traditional Christianity does not understand what it means to be "born again."

The expression "born again" is seen by most to mean a kind of "religious experience" leading to the acceptance of Jesus Christ. Though such people often do experience an emotional change accompanied by a life-changing focus, it is not what God reveals to be true.

Nicodemus, who was recognized as a great religious leader of his time, came to Jesus and asked Him about the Kingdom of God. But Nicodemus could not understand what he heard. Jesus had told him, *"Verily, verily, I say unto you, Except a man be born again, he cannot see the kingdom of God"* (John 3:3). Nicodemus could only think physically and asked, *"How can a man be born when he is old? Can he enter a second time into his mother's womb and be born?"* (Verse 4). Notice Jesus' response:

"Jesus answered, Verily, verily, I say unto you, except a man be born of water and of the Spirit, he cannot enter into the kingdom of God. That which is born of the flesh is flesh; and that which is born of the Spirit is spirit" (John 3:5-6).

The actual physical type of human birth is also the type of a spiritual birth. Jesus made it very clear. He said that which is born physically can only be produced by something physical. In human life when a physical sperm cell impregnates a physical egg, a physical embryo is produced. It is all physical. The physical process of an embryo growing in a mother's womb produces a child at birth.

God has given man a human spirit that makes us different from animals. It gives us individuality. We are not pre-programed to respond to nature as God made the animal kingdom. With this "spirit essence" in the human mind we have the God-like capacity of thought, creativity and memory. This ability makes us individually unique. We have freedom of choice; we are free moral agents.

God cannot create perfect righteous character in others; it can only be accomplished as a matter of free choice. Otherwise, we would have to be programmed to respond "robotically" in matters of morality to live perfectly in accordance with God's law. But God wants us to choose on our own; we must choose between our own selfish ways or the ways of God. Again, the opportunity to choose comes in God's own time. Before this time comes to man—before God is able to give this opportunity to man—the witness of man is that he will always reject God! So in God's perfect timing He will give man the best opportunity possible to be able to receive Him and His way of life.

Paul shared this knowledge of the human mind with the Corinthians. Paul explained that those in the Church could understand the mysteries of God. These "mysteries" cannot be understood without God's spirit and, therefore, His ways remain hidden.

"But God has revealed them unto us by His Spirit [One must be drawn by God's Spirit and then impregnated by that same power.]*: for the Spirit searches all things, yes, the deep things of God* [Only when God begins to draw people, by His Spirit, can they begin to understand Him.]. *For what man knows the things of a man, save the spirit of the man which is in him? Even so the things of God knows no man, but the Spirit of God* [One must receive God's Spirit to know the spiritual things of God. That is why Nicodemus could not understand. He was not being drawn by God's Spirit.]. *Now we have received* [speaking to the Church]*, not the spirit of the world, but the Spirit which is of God* [The Spirit is the power of God. It is not a "being" as traditional Christianity teaches. The teaching of a trinity is false! There is no being called the spirit.]*; that we might know the things that are freely given to us of God* [God alone has to give it. No one can understand it by physical human capacity alone.]. *Which things also we speak, not in words which man's wisdom teaches* [physical human intellect, through physical limitations, from the spirit in man]*, but which the Holy Spirit teaches; comparing spiritual things with spiritual. But the natural man* [physical human being] *receives not the things of the Spirit of God: for they are foolishness unto him; neither can he know them, because they are spiritually discerned"* (1 Corinthians 2:10-14).

This is the reason man has continually rejected God and His ways. The pride in selfish human reasoning rejects the truth of God. Instead, man has formulated his own religious ideas and concepts of God that are more to his liking. The witness of mankind over 6,000 years is that he rejects God. That is why many people will hate what is written in this book. They cannot get past their own pride! That is also the reason why this world must be humbled before Jesus Christ comes as King of kings.

If you are understanding these things, then there is only one way that is possible! God is giving you that opportunity now. You are being drawn by God's Spirit. If that is the case, then the choice is yours. Will you accept what is true? You may yet have to go through more humbling in the great tribulation. The longer people reject God, the less likely they will be to receive His help and favor to live through those things that are coming.

God is going to begin to call the whole world! Most will not humble themselves to receive the Kingdom of God that is coming.

Let's return to the story flow of Pentecost. The physical process for human birth can only produce that which is physical, and the same is true of spiritual birth. A human being must be begotten of God's spirit. This is the impregnation of God's spirit with the "human spirit" God gave mankind. After the baptism of "water" (baptism in the Greek means immersion) one comes up out of this symbolic watery grave to walk in newness of life. It is immediately after baptism that the "laying on of hands" is performed by the ministry and the impregnation of God's Holy Spirit begets us.

Once begotten of God's Holy Spirit you begin to grow spiritually, but only in embryo within the Church. We must live in a "physical body" that is impregnated with God's Holy Spirit. We begin living a life of conquering the flesh—the pulls of human nature—thereby developing holy, righteous character. This process eventually allows us to be "born" into the Kingdom of God—the God Family—as spirit beings, fully "born of the spirit."

Jesus Christ explained to Nicodemus that, *"that which is born of the flesh is flesh."* He was explaining that flesh (that which is physical) can only produce something that is flesh. Human physical begettal leads only to human physical birth. But He went on to explain: *"that which is born of the Spirit is spirit."* Only when you are impregnated with the Holy Spirit of God can you, through time, be born into—enter—the Kingdom of God.

It is through this process that all of the firstfruits will enter the

Kingdom of God. When Jesus Christ returns, they will be resurrected into spirit life, as spirit beings, composed of spirit in God's Family.

Pentecost pictures the "means" by which a person can understand and live God's ways. Through spiritual maturity and time you can be changed from mortal to immortal—from physical to spiritual—born into God's spiritual Family. Pentecost pictures the firstfruits of God's Family, those who will be resurrected first, out of all mankind, at the end of the first 6,000 years of man on earth. But all those who follow will also go through the same process of being drawn by and then begotten of His Holy Spirit which can lead to their being born into the very God Family.

FEAST OF TRUMPETS

God's annual Sabbaths continue to reveal more about the plan of God. Now we come to the fourth annual Holy Day. This day is known in Judaism as Rosh Hashanah, and the correct timing of its observance is generally listed on the Roman Calendar in September or early October. This annual Sabbath coincides with those things that will occur at the end of the 6,000 years God has allotted to mankind.

"And the LORD spoke unto Moses, saying, Speak unto the children of Israel, saying, In the seventh month, in the first day of the month, shall you have a Sabbath, a memorial of blowing of trumpets, an holy convocation" (Lev. 23:23-24).

The Feast of Trumpets reveals an exciting time because it concerns the second-coming of Jesus Christ, not as a lamb, but as a King who will rule on the earth. This is the time you live in now! This world, after 6,000 years of man's rule, is about to undergo a dramatic change. It will be ruled by the Kingdom of God with Jesus Christ as King of kings. As trumpets are so often used to herald a king, so it is with the coming of Jesus Christ as King of kings.

Paul talks about Trumpets in his first letter to the Thessalonians.

"But I would not have you to be ignorant, brethren [Paul is addressing this to the Church, to those who are called to be among the 144,000.], *concerning them who are asleep* [Paul is speaking of those who were called and died in the faith over the past 6,000 years.], *that you sorrow not, even as others who have no hope. For if we believe that Jesus died and rose again, even so those also who sleep in Jesus will God bring with Him* [They will be resurrected, to return with Jesus Christ, when He comes.]. *For this we say unto you by the word of the Lord, that we who are alive and remain unto the coming of the Lord* [Those in the Church who have the spirit of God dwelling in them—called to be a firstfruit.] *shall not precede those who are asleep. For the Lord Himself shall descend from heaven with a shout, with the voice of the archangel, and with the trump of God: and the dead in Christ shall rise first: Then we who are alive* [Those few called to be firstfruits, who are still alive in the Church, at the time of His coming.] *and remain shall be caught up together with them in the clouds, to meet the Lord in the air: and so shall we ever be with the Lord"* (1 Thessalonians 4:13-17).

Paul described this same event to the Corinthian church. *"In a moment, in the twinkling of an eye, at the last trump: for the trumpet shall sound, and the dead shall be raised incorruptible, and we shall be changed"* (1 Corinthians 15:52). Paul explained this same phase of God's plan that will take place when the last trumpet—the seventh trumpet—is sounded, as described in the Book of Revelation. When this trumpet is blown the 144,000 are resurrected. Those who are dead are resurrected first, then immediately following that, those who are yet alive, who are part of the count of 144,000, are changed and return with Jesus Christ on the same day.

This is the day that all the firstfruits will be resurrected. Nearly all of the firstfruits are dead, but they will be resurrected then to immortal life. Those few firstfruits, who are alive at this time, will be changed from mortal to immortal spirit beings to become a part of the God Family—the Kingdom of God.

All the firstfruits called over the past 6,000 years will be resurrected on the day the last trumpet sounds, the seventh trumpet of the seventh seal. *"And the seventh angel sounded; and there were great voices in heaven, saying, The kingdoms of this world are become the kingdoms of our Lord, and of his Christ; and He shall reign for ever and ever"* (Revelation 11:15). This is the day when Jesus Christ will come to rule all nations on this earth. Even more is revealed in the events of this day.

The actual fulfillment of the Feast of Trumpets occurs on the very last day of the three and one half years of great tribulation that is now about to come on this earth. This is a day that is also described as the great day of God's wrath on mankind. As previously described in this book, a ten-nation power-block will rise up in Europe when the fifth trumpet of the seventh seal is blown. Seven trumpets are blown in the seventh seal. The last trumpet is blown on the last day of great tribulation.

The fifth trumpet is described as the time for the "first woe" upon mankind. It is the time when a final European power begins World War III. Multiple millions on the earth will be destroyed by this great army. In response to this, another great military power in the far east is awakened. It numbers two hundred million—mostly out of China. This is described as the "second woe." It is announced by the blowing of the sixth trumpet during this great end-time tribulation.

"One woe is past; and, behold, there come two woes more hereafter. And the sixth angel sounded, and I heard a voice from the four horns of the golden altar which is before God, saying to the sixth angel who had the trumpet, Loose the four angels who are bound at the great river Euphrates. And the four angels were loosed, who were prepared for the hour, and a day, and a month, and a year, for to kill the third part of mankind. and the number of

the army of the horsemen were two hundred million: and I heard the number of them" (Revelation 9:12-16).

This great army emerges on the scene later in the time of final great tribulation. It will destroy a third of all mankind! Hundreds of millions will die at the hand of this terrifying power. This Asiatic power that is unleashed upon the earth is in direct response to the emergence of the European power.

Then it is time for the "third woe." This is the time of the blowing of the seventh trumpet announcing the resurrection of the 144,000 and the coming of Jesus Christ as King of kings. This day is described as the day of God's great wrath. On this day seven vials are to be poured out upon the earth. These vials are the seven last plagues that will come upon those who are destroying the earth. It comes upon those who support and are part of the European military that rose up during the "first woe" as well as on those of the "second woe" who came out of the far east.

On this day, God will humble those people by bringing them down to nothing. On this day tens of millions will be put to death, even into the hundreds of millions. It is on this very day that the prophesied Battle of Armageddon occurs. This is the "third woe," when the seven vials of the seven last plagues are poured out.

"The second woe is past; and, behold, the third woe comes quickly. And the seventh angel sounded; and there were great voices in heaven, saying, The kingdoms of this world have become the kingdoms of our Lord, and of His Christ; and He shall reign forever and ever" (Revelation 11:14-15). At this time it is announced that all the kingdoms of this world are now become the kingdoms of Jesus Christ. He will rule all kingdoms of the earth. Many nations have already been humbled by this time, but on this last day the rest of all the nations on the face of the earth will be brought low.

The European and Asiatic powers are angry. By this time, nuclear weapons have already caused much destruction on earth.

Realizing this, as well as the possibility of annihilation, these two armies come together in the region of Megiddo for a head-on, face-to-face confrontation—the Battle of Armageddon.

"And the nations were angry, and your wrath is come [the time for God's great wrath in the form of the seven last plagues], *and the time of the dead, that they should be judged, and that you should give reward to your servants the prophets, and to the saints* [the same day the 144,000 are resurrected], *and those who fear your name, small and great; and should destroy those* [those Europeans and peoples of the far east] *who destroy the earth"* (Rev. 11:18).

The seven last plagues are poured out upon the peoples of these very nations who continue to war and to destroy the earth. *"And I saw another sign in heaven, great and marvelous, seven angels having the seven last plagues; for in them is filled up the wrath of God"* (Revelation 15:1). *"And I heard a great voice out of the temple saying to the seven angels, Go your ways, and pour out the vials of the wrath of God upon the earth"* (Revelation 16:1).

After tens of millions have lost their lives among the nations of these end-time military powers and after all the vials have been poured out, Jesus Christ returns. These very powers that have come together to fight each other are stopped by what they see happening in the heavens on this day—God makes it clear that the coming of Jesus Christ will be seen in the heavens in our atmosphere. These two military machines are already receiving reports of millions being killed, by great plagues, in their own nations.

They have not believed God's two end-time witnesses, therefore they will not believe that Jesus Christ is coming. Who can know the thinking of these people at such a time? Perhaps this is an invasion from another world. It is understandable how they might think such a thing because what they will see is far more massive and magnificent than Hollywood's production of the movie *Independence Day*. God reveals that these armies actually stop and unite, with one mind, to fight against what they see coming. This is the final battle—the Battle of Armageddon.

Toward the end of this day, Jesus Christ finally comes out of the heavens of the earth's atmosphere. His coming is great, and it is powerful—He comes to make war against those armies gathered together in Megiddo.

"And I saw heaven opened, and behold a white horse; and He who sat upon him was called Faithful and True, and in righteousness He does judge and <u>make war</u>. His eyes were as a flame of fire, and on His head were many crowns; and He had a name written, that no man knew, but He Himself. And He was clothed with a vesture dipped in blood: and His name is called The Word of God [It is Jesus Christ.]. *And <u>the armies</u> which were in heaven followed Him upon white horses, clothed in fine linen, white and clean* [the 144,000 who return with Him]. *And out of His mouth goes a sharp sword, that with it He should smite the nations: and He shall rule them with a rod of iron: and He treads the winepress of the fierceness and <u>wrath of Almighty God</u>. And He has on His robe and on His thigh a name written, KING OF KINGS, AND LORD OF LORDS. And I saw an angel standing in the sun; and he cried with a loud voice, saying to all the fowls that fly in the midst of heaven, Come and gather yourselves together unto the supper of the great God; That you may eat the flesh of kings, and the flesh of captains, and the flesh of mighty men, and the flesh of horses, and of them that sit on them, and the flesh of all men, both free and bond, both small and great. And I saw the beast, and the kings of the earth, and their armies, gathered together* [...gathered in Megiddo] *to make war against Him who sat on the horse, and against his army. And the beast was taken, and with him the false prophet* [...a great false religious leader through whom Satan works to deceive the masses] *that worked miracles before him, with which he deceived them that had received the mark of the beast, and them that worshiped his image. These both were cast alive into a lake of fire burning with brimstone. And the remnant were slain with the*

sword of Him who sat upon the horse, which sword proceeded out of His mouth: and all the fowls were filled with their flesh" (Revelation 19:11-21).

All those gathered together to fight against Jesus Christ as He returns are destroyed quickly.

On this great day all the kingdoms of this earth are delivered over to Jesus Christ, who has come to be King of kings over all the earth.

The Feast of Trumpets (an annual Sabbath) marks the very last day of the 6,000-year period of man's self-rule on earth. It is the very beginning of God's Kingdom ruling on earth. It begins the last 1,000 years of God's 7,000-year plan of salvation for man. This is God's time; it is symbolized by the weekly seventh-day Sabbath. The end of the sixth day begins God's Sabbath. The end of 6,000 years marks the beginning of God's Kingdom ruling over mankind and showing mankind the way into His Kingdom.

This day, with the resurrection of the 144,000 firstfruits, marks the end of God's plan for the fulfillment of the early spring harvest. Now it is time to begin the later harvest, pictured by the very large fall harvest.

The return of Jesus Christ will bring an end to all wars. Man has tried to accomplish this very thing, but he has failed miserably. The very statue in the United Nations garden that depicts man's goal of ending all war derives its inspiration from a prophecy that will, instead, be fulfilled through Jesus Christ. *"And He shall judge among the nations, and shall rebuke many people: and they shall beat their swords into plowshares, and their spears into pruning hooks: nation shall not lift up sword against nation, neither shall they learn war any more"* (Isaiah 2:4).

THE DAY OF ATONEMENT

The fifth annual Sabbath is the Day of Atonement. Judaism calls this time Yom Kippur. The correct day for this observance is generally recorded on the Roman Calendar by that same name.

"And the LORD spoke to Moses, saying, Also on the tenth day of this seventh month there shall be a Day of Atonement: it shall be an <u>holy convocation</u> [Commanded assembly] *unto you; and you shall <u>afflict your souls</u>* [accomplished by a total fast from food and drink]*, and offer an offering made by fire unto the LORD. And you shall do no work in that same day: for it is a <u>Day of Atonement</u>, to make an atonement for you before the LORD your God. For any person who shall not be afflicted in that same day, he shall be cut off from among his people. And any person who does any work on that same day, the same person will I destroy from among his people. You shall do no manner of work: it shall be a statute forever throughout your generations in all your dwellings. It shall be unto you a Sabbath of rest* [annual Sabbath]*, and you shall afflict your souls: in the ninth day of the month at even* [beginning from sundown of the ninth day]*, from even unto even* [observed until sundown of the next day]*, shall you celebrate your Sabbath"* (Leviticus 23:26-32).

This annual Sabbath pictures the entire process covered from Passover to Trumpets. Much of that process will have been fulfilled when Christ returns and Satan has been removed from the presence of mankind.

This day pictures the atoning process—the process whereby everyone can be reconciled to God. The firstfruits of God, after Trumpets has been fulfilled, are now fully atoned—reconciled—to God. The entire process (revealed through Passover, Unleavened Bread, Pentecost, and Trumpets) shows how the firstfruits were able to be born into God's Family—becoming part of the Kingdom of God.

Although the complete process has been accomplished in the

firstfruits, billions remain who are yet to be atoned—reconciled—to God. Every human being must still go through the same process as those called in the first 6,000 years. The Day of Atonement pictures that entire process. Everyone must come into unity and oneness—must be at one with God. Being reconciled to God the Father by the blood of Jesus Christ begins with Passover. We must repent, come out of spiritual Egypt (sin), be baptized, and receive the impregnation of God's spirit. As we grow spiritually and overcome our nature, God can begin to transform (Romans 12:1-2) the very way we think and bring us into unity and harmony with His one true way of life. After someone has successfully gone through this entire process, they will be able to be made fully at one with God by a change from mortal to immortal, from physical to spiritual, into the Kingdom of God.

The Kingdom of God is the Family of God. It will be composed of spirit beings who were once physical. They will be at one with God for all eternity.

Although this day pictures the entire process of reconciliation, of being fully atoned to God, it also pictures the fulfillment of another great event that pictures man's complete removal from the presence of sin and complete atonement to God. When the Kingdom of God comes to this earth, everyone on the face of the earth will be able to enter into this process of atonement to God, as opposed to only a few during the first 6,000 years.

When God's Kingdom comes, man will have been delivered from his own destructive ways. Now Jesus Christ will rule over all the earth with the 144,000 that were resurrected at His coming. The ways of God will govern the course of mankind. Justice will be swift. The knowledge of God will fill the earth. True peace will be brought to the earth. People will learn to live in peace and harmony with others. There will be only one religion on earth. There will be only one government ruling the earth. Everyone will keep the seventh-day Sabbath and the annual Holy Days. Great harmony, peace and genuine love will fill the lives of families, communities and businesses—all relationships.

False religions, politics, lobbyists, and corporate greed will not exist. The way of competition will be replaced by the way of cooperation geared toward benefitting all. Large insurance corporations and massive medical research will not be needed. People will not need the scores of hospitals and trauma units we have now.

But even with all these awesome improvements for mankind, one great obstacle still stands in the way of total peace and harmony. That obstacle is Satan and his demons (angels who rebelled with him). The Day of Atonement also pictures the removal of Satan and his demons from the presence of mankind.

Lucifer was one of the archangels of God. He and a third of the angelic realm were given the responsibility of caring for the earth. The government of God on the earth was administered through this great archangel. His story is one of pride and rebellion toward God. Isaiah 14:12-14 and Ezekiel 28:12-17 give a general outline of this being, yet much more of the story is contained in fragmented areas throughout scripture.

God has not revealed the duration of timing of these various events. However, the evidence in our immediate solar system as well as the earth itself reveal a great deal when combined with the true accounts of scripture. Millions of years ago God created the universe and our earth. But, again, God has nowhere revealed the exact timing or the order of these events.

God created the angelic realm. God is spirit and the beings He created are spirit. Nothing existed except the spirit world. The limited capacity of the human mind can deal with the physical world around us, but our ability to grasp a spirit world is limited to physical concepts. God revealed that He did create a physical universe which included this earth. It is recorded that the angels rejoiced in God's physical creation. God revealed to the angelic realm portions of His plan to expand His own Family through human beings. The Book of Hebrews reveals that the angelic realm—the angelic kingdom—was created to minister, in time, to those who would live physical lives and eventually be born into God's very Family.

At some point in time Lucifer began to desire more for himself. He did not agree with God's plans or the purpose for the physical creation. He rebelled against God, and nearly a third of the angelic realm rebelled with him. As a result, a great angelic war was fought; it extended into the physical creation. God declared that the original creation was made perfect and beautiful. Life was on the earth, but it was not the life that would exist when man would eventually be created. The earth had early forms of life on the land, in the sky and in the sea. Some of the bones of these creatures can be seen in museums. As a boy growing up in western Kansas, I visited areas near our home where oceans once were. Prehistoric shark teeth could be found there. Only a few miles away, some even found bones of prehistoric land animals in the higher elevations. Large areas of beach front property actually existed in Kansas at one time.

What happened? Scientists try to give their "intellectual" interpretations of these matters, but the simple reality is that every-thing was <u>swiftly</u> <u>destroyed</u> at the time of Lucifer's rebellion. All life on earth was destroyed suddenly. That was millions of years ago. The story in Genesis is speaking of man's creation along with appropriate plant and animal life to complement man. It is not the actual creation of the earth itself—that happened millions of years before man's creation.

"In <u>the</u> [There is no definite article in Hebrew. It should read, "in a beginning..."] *beginning God created the heaven and the earth* [In a beginning, God did create the earth and the entire universe—millions upon millions of years ago. There was no evolution, but simply an enormous amount of time.]. *And the earth*

was [Hebrew—"became." It is the same verb as the account in Gen. 19:26 that says Lot's wife "became" salt.] *without form, and void; and darkness was upon the face of the deep. And the Spirit of God moved upon the face of the waters"* (Genesis 1:1-2).

In this account, the earth already existed. It had come to be in a state of waste and disorder. Darkness shrouded the entire earth. The waters already existed. Then, God began to work on the entire earth—to bring back life. The entire picture here was one of chaos. God renewed the face of the earth as described in Psalms. Yes, the earth is millions of years old, but man has only been here 6,000 years.

When this rebellion took place, God changed Lucifer's name to Satan, and those angels who followed him became known as demons. God left them on this earth. Their presence and influence on mankind would serve as part of God's plan to reveal the destructiveness and evil of all that resists His righteous ways.

When Lucifer rebelled, the government of God on earth had ceased. It is now, in our time, that the government of God is going to once again be restored over all the earth. Jesus Christ will usher in the Kingdom of God—the government of God over the earth.

Yes, this Day of Atonement also pictures the removal of Satan and his demons from the presence of God and man. They will no longer be able to influence and deceive mankind, except for a very short time at the very end of the 1,000-year reign of the Kingdom of God over mankind. At that time, this Day of Atonement will have even more fulfillment when Satan and the demons are once again removed, and this time—for all time—for all eternity. Some of this story is contained in Revelation 20.

"And I saw an angel come down from heaven, having the key of the bottomless pit [Greek—"a place of restraint"] *and a great chain in his hand. And he laid hold on the dragon, that old serpent, who is the Devil, and Satan, and bound him for a thousand years* [This occurs at the return of Jesus Christ.]*, and cast him into the*

bottomless pit, and shut him up, and set a seal upon him, that he should deceive the nations no more, till the thousand years should be fulfilled: and after that he must be loosed for a little season" (Revelation 20:1-3).

"And when the thousand years are expired, Satan shall be loosed out of his prison, and shall go out to deceive the nations which are in the four quarters of the earth, Gog and Magog, to gather them together to battle: the number of whom is as the sand of the sea. And they went up on the breadth of the earth, and compassed the camp of the saints about, and the beloved city: and fire came down from God out of heaven, and devoured them. And the devil who deceived them was cast into the lake of fire and brimstone, where the beast and the false prophet are ["were earlier cast"], *and they* [Satan and the demons] *shall be tormented day and night forever and ever"* (Revelation 20:7-10).

This last verse is the reason so many believe there is a place of "hell fire" where "bad" people go to be eternally tormented by demons. Satan has succeeded in deceiving people into believing in a fiendish kind of punishment that awaits them for not pleasing God. Yet it is Satan who will be suffering for all eternity, once he and the demons are removed eternally from the presence of man and God's creation. Satan and the demons will have no part in God's future, and that will be torment to these beings for the wrong choices they made so many millions of years ago.

This annual Sabbath wonderfully pictures this world being fully atoned to God.

THE FEAST OF TABERNACLES

This period of time has great meaning, but we will only cover a condensed version of this holy day season. Leviticus 23 continues with the annual holy days and describes a final observance that lasts for eight days. The first seven days is called the Feast of

Tabernacles with the first day being an annual Sabbath. This period of seven days is followed by an eighth-day observance, which is also an annual Sabbath, the last day in the revelation of the plan of God. It is called the Last Great Day.

This Feast of Tabernacles pictures the time when the Kingdom of God will come to rule mankind for a 1,000 years. Much has already been said about the coming Messiah and His reign on the earth. This festive season is about to be ushered in on this earth. It will come as soon as we come through the final end-time tribulation.

As we have already covered, the weekly Sabbath pictures the last 1,000 years in the 7,000-year plan of God. The Feast of Tabernacles focuses mostly on this same period of time. In this final 1,000 years, everyone will live under one government on the earth. The government of God, the Kingdom of God, will rule all nations during that time.

Revelation 20 speaks about this time, which begins immediately after the return of Jesus Christ as King of kings (covered in Revelation 19). It is a time when Satan will no longer have power to deceive the nations any more (except for a short time at the end of that 1,000 years).

"And I saw an angel come down from heaven, having the key of the bottomless pit and a great chain in his hand. And he laid hold on the dragon, that old serpent, who is the Devil, and Satan, and bound him for a thousand years [Part of Atonement.]*, and cast him into the <u>bottomless pit</u>* [abyss—a place of restraint] *, and shut him up, and set a seal upon him, that he should deceive the nations no more, till <u>the thousand years</u> should be fulfilled: and after that he must be loosed for a little season. And I saw thrones, and they sat upon them, and judgment was given unto <u>them</u>* [the firstfruits of Pentecost—the 144,000]*: and I saw the souls of them that were <u>beheaded</u>* [Greek—"cut off" from the world, through their calling] *for the witness of Jesus, and for the word of God, and who had not*

worshiped the beast, neither his image, neither had received his mark upon their foreheads, or in their hands [The mark or sign of the Church is the Sabbath, and it reveals what we believe (forehead), when we will work, and when we will not work (hands). The mark of the beast is revealed by Sunday observance.]*; and they* [firstfruits] *lived and reigned with Christ a thousand years"* (Revelation 20:1-4).

This scripture describes the time of the rule of the Kingdom of God on earth over mankind for 1,000 years. It speaks of Jesus Christ and the 144,000 who will reign with Him. Those who are resurrected to reign with Jesus Christ are in the first great resurrection—picturing the early harvest in God's plan of salvation. The beginning of the 1,000 years pictures the beginning of a much greater harvest in God's plan of salvation. Billions will begin the process of becoming a part of the Kingdom of God—eventually being born into the very Family of God—just as the first 144,000 were. This process will be available to everyone for a thousand years and then for one-hundred years (explained in the last annual Sabbath).

"But the rest of the dead lived not again until the thousand years were finished. This is the first resurrection" (Revelation 20:5). The first resurrection refers to the firstfruits who have been resurrected first in God's plan of salvation. Those in the first resurrection, the 144,000, are the only people at this point in time who have been resurrected. All the other billions who have died up until this time, over the past 6,000 years, will remain dead until after the thousand-year reign of the Kingdom of God on earth is fulfilled. The story of these people is revealed in the meaning of the last annual Sabbath.

"Blessed and holy is he who has part in the first resurrection: on such the second death has no power, but they shall be priests of God and of Christ, and shall reign with Him a thousand years" (Revelation 20:6). The 144,000 who are in the first resurrection are now spirit beings in the God Family. They are now immortal spirit

beings who can never die. They will indeed reign with Jesus Christ during this time.

Finally, peace is ushered in on the earth under one worldwide government. Everyone who has come through the great end-time tribulation and all who are born thereafter will have opportunity to know and understand the true ways of God. They will have the blessing of living under His righteous rule and favor. This brief description of the meaning of the Feast of Tabernacles brings us to the very last day in God's great plan for mankind.

THE LAST GREAT DAY

This additional day (eighth day) following the Feast of Tabernacles is traditionally referred to as the Last Great Day. It is the seventh and last <u>annual</u> <u>Sabbath</u>. It is an exciting revelation in the plan of God. As the early spring harvest of firstfruits is pictured in Pentecost, so is the larger fall harvest pictured in the Feast of Tabernacles and the Last Great Day.

The Last Great Day pictures a time of great judgment that <u>follows</u> the 7,000 year portion of God's plan. It is a <u>judgment period</u> that covers a time span of 100 years. No one will be born during this time. The process of human begettal and birth came to an end after 7,000 years.

Let's return to a verse we covered in the story of the Feast of Tabernacles. Most people read over it, never understanding what God is revealing in His great purpose. During the past 1,000 years the entirety of humanity was given the opportunity to receive the true ways of God. Jesus Christ ruled righteously in a worldwide government. Satan and the demons were removed from the presence of man. But all who lived and died, <u>before</u> the 1,000 year reign of Christ, never had such an opportunity. Now, it is time for a <u>second</u> human life for those people.

"But the rest of the dead lived not again until the thousand years

were finished" (Rev. 20:5). Who are "the rest of the dead?" Previously we explained the first resurrection of the 144,000 which occurred at the end of the 6,000-year period, but what happened to all the billions who lived and died but were not resurrected? The Last Great Day is about them!

The "rest of the dead" is the vast majority of mankind who lived and died to this point in time. This means billions of people. These people never knew God. The time has now come for them to be resurrected to a <u>second</u> physical life! Now read the following verse. *"Blessed and holy is he that has part in the first resurrection: on such the second death has no power"* (Revelation 20:6). The firstfruits have already been given immortal life. They are spirit beings in the God Family. They can never die <u>again</u>!

During all this time, no one has been in heaven (except Jesus Christ) or in a place of eternal torment. People have simply been dead; they returned to dust. But God has the power to give physical life again—a second time.

"And I saw a great white throne [time for the great white throne judgment—the last great day of mankind], *and Him who sat on it, from whose face the earth and the heaven fled away; and there was found no place for them. And I saw the dead, small and great, stand before God* [All who have ever lived and died will be resurrected at this time—those forgotten in time and those remembered by history.]; *and the books were opened* [The books of the Bible are now opened for all to be able to understand—by God's spirit]: *and another book was opened, which is the book of life: and the dead were judged out of those things which were written in the books, according to their works.* [It is now a time for judgment. A time for their minds to be opened to the truth. A time to be given a calling by God to enter into a relationship with Him. At this time all those resurrected must choose whether or not they will walk in the ways of God.] *And the sea gave up the dead which were in it; and death and <u>hell</u>* [Greek—"the grave"] *delivered up the dead which were in*

them: and they were judged every man according to their works. [And at the end of that 100 years....] *And death and <u>hell</u>* [Greek—"the grave"] *were cast into the lake of fire. This is the second death. And whosoever was not found written in the book of life was cast into the lake of fire"* (Rev. 20:11-15).

During this 100-year period everyone will have the opportunity to choose and live God's way of life. They can become part of the Family of God—the Kingdom of God—born as spirit beings, just as the 144,000 were. Those who refuse will die a <u>second time</u>—death for all eternity. God's judgment on those who do not want to be part of His Family is not eternal torment. It is a <u>punishment</u> that will last for all eternity. It is death—never to be resurrected to life again—an eternal punishment.

It is during this last 100 years that billions will be resurrected. Those who have lived and died, young and old alike, will be given life again in physical human bodies that are filled with vibrant health—whole and complete. Then they can choose to become a part of God's eternal Family. That is the story of the Last Great Day!

Chapter 7

THE TRUE MESSIAH

Religion and politics can stir up great emotion and passion in people. Putting someone in office, whether religious or political, can involve spending a great deal of money, time and energy. Yet people in nations throughout the world engage in such activities, year after year.

Of course, the basic desire of such activity is to select leaders who will help solve our problems and provide us with greater prosperity. People want deliverance from their troubles; they want life to be easier. They want peace and safety, but unfortunately, man can't deliver! It is an age old struggle!

No government can solve a nation's problems—not a democracy, not a monarchy, not a dictatorship. Man cannot solve his problems!

In the 60s, my high school science class was shown a most graphic film about starving children around the world. The film addressed the need for science and technology to help provide solutions to such growing problems. Each member of the class was to write a report on the film giving potential solutions.

As a teenage boy, I was rather shocked by the realities of the world around me, especially concerning the seemingly impossible challenges that the future would force upon mankind.

Although I was still somewhat naive, it was obvious to me that science could not solve all of our problems. It seemed to me that the greatest task that lay ahead would be that of government. So, I wrote about the need for a centralized world government. But even as a young teen, I knew that the United Nations did not hold the answers—not in its current form. It would have to be much stronger. It was evident to me that the location of the United Nations created a great obstacle—prejudice and jealousy. The answer in my mind was a single world government. Perhaps it could be a worldwide democracy with its central government located in some other part of the world, but it would also need a strong military to enforce order.

But even so, man cannot produce genuine peace and unity. Perhaps God was giving me a taste, at that young age, of the futility of man's ability to govern himself.

This is exactly what God is showing mankind. Man cannot rule himself. Carnal, selfish human nature makes it impossible. That is the witness God has been giving mankind for the past 6,000 years—man is incapable of ruling himself. World history proves it!

Even this nation, the United States, prosperous and mighty as we are, has not been able to successfully rule itself. It cannot solve its own problems, and certainly not the problems of other nations, but it keeps trying to do so. For the United States to believe it can bring any measure of lasting peace to other nations (the Middle East, the Koreas, or even Europe) is the height of arrogance. America's arrogance is a great problem in our relationships with other countries. They clearly see the arrogance that we cannot see. We simply believe our way is best. But of course, others think the same way. Yet America radiates this arrogance more strongly than other nations do.

Although this nation has been blessed by God with great wealth, many are unemployed, suffering from sickness and disease, and living in poverty. Yet people choose to look the other way if it doesn't affect them directly.

These things remind me of a story—whether true or not, I don't know. It was about a preacher who addressed his congregation with what was reported to be one of the shortest sermons ever. He began by saying, "I have only three points to give you today." He continued, "Number one is that there are over 400,000 homeless people in this country, and number two is that most of you don't give a damn!" He then concluded by saying, "And number three is that most of you are more concerned that I used the word 'damn' than you are concerned that there are over 400,000 people homeless in this country." Then he sat down.

That is the attitude of most, simply not caring. Many things are simply easy to ignore while the attitude of hypocrisy and haughtiness prevails.

The hypocrisy of this country is overwhelming. It oozes from the media, politics, courts, special interest groups, and corporations. If something crosses the eye of the media that can be "sensationalized," then others often give attention to it—all too often to get attention themselves. But the real problems of our nation, those that are deep-rooted and ongoing—lacking in sensationalism—tend to be ignored. Numerous social ills are just too unpopular to be addressed. The reasons are complacency, hypocrisy and pride.

The care of the elderly, especially in nursing homes, in a nation that is so prosperous is deplorable. Yes, some people try to address these issues, but they do so in frustration. Their efforts are like putting a band-aid on a severed artery. It isn't a "popular" cause.

And crime? With all our wealth and might, we can't seem to build prisons fast enough, and even as we do, the judicial system finds ways to put criminals back on the streets after having served only a small portion of their sentences.

The number of homicides in virtually any large American city alone will be greater annually than that of many countries of the world. How well do we govern ourselves?

Every day we hear of the senseless murder of another innocent person. Random killing happens frequently. Do you hear any great outcry because of this kind of behavior right under our noses? No!

But some do decry the loss of life of U.S. soldiers and others in the name of war. And their murders are indeed a senseless tragedy. Yet, this is another testimony to the kind of hypocrisy that looms over this nation.

Another example is the senseless loss of life on our highways. Oftentimes these tragedies are the result of alcohol or drugs or both. And punishment for these offenses amounts to a slap on the wrist. But, we wink an eye and turn our heads at such things.

How much attention is really given to matters of safe driving? Some would say, "A lot." But far more could be done and should be done to save lives on highways alone. Where is the media coverage of the tragic loss of a loved one due to a careless auto accident? What is being done about it? Where are the organized marches that decry such tragedy in our nation? Where are the fund drives to support the families who have lost their bread winners? Where are the corporations, movie stars and athletes who are raising funds to educate and care for the children who survived these accidents when the parents didn't survive?

In 2002, over 17,000 people lost their lives in auto accidents involving alcohol. That's several times more than those who lost their lives in 9/11. During the entire Vietnam war, 58,000 U.S. soldiers lost their lives. There was a thunderous outcry and tremendous social upheaval in this country over that war. But where is the outcry over the loss of life from alcohol-related auto accidents that number a far greater loss of life each year than that of the yearly loss of life by U.S. soldiers in the Vietnam war? Where are the memorials for all the young, innocent lives lost by auto accidents? Where is the outrage? It certainly doesn't exist nationally.

We have even greater loss of life each year due to medical errors. Just last year, statistics show that 98,000 people lost their lives to such error. Again, where is the media? Where is the outrage? We are a nation of hypocrites, lost in our own selfish little worlds.

This hypocrisy and perverseness of will of such a wealthy

people is exemplified by the example of millions that wear ribbons, donate millions, demand millions more, and march in large rallies so that research can be found to end a disease that is killing millions worldwide. This disease is primarily spread through perverted lifestyles, but people dare not condemn such things as the primary cause for the spread of such a disease. The illegal use of drugs (sharing needles), the perverseness of unnatural sex, and the unfaithfulness of mates are all to blame. But self-righteous people prefer a drug that will solve their problem so they can continue to live their unnatural and perverted lifestyles. Who dares to say anything against them? And who dares to bring God into the picture? ...Rest assured, God is about to bring Himself into the picture! All such perversions are about to be erased from the earth!

The smugness of society reeks! Haughtiness and hypocrisy have filled the earth! Some religious people condemn homosexuality, but they wink an eye as they wallow in adultery and other perversions. They, too, are guilty. With their infidelities they cause deep-rooted pain and suffering in the lives of those nearest them. Adultery is as destructive to families as homosexuality, and sometimes more so. Some will hate me for simply pointing out these truths.

People are consumed with political correctness today. That, in itself, is filled with incredible hypocrisy. One almost needs to carry a dictionary of politically correct terms so as not to offend—so as to allow people to more easily ignore what they choose.

Yes, man is incapable of ruling himself. And given a little more time, he would end up annihilating himself. In actuality, that is exactly what man is about to do, but God will stop it and bring His government to this earth. It is His government that will save and deliver mankind.

So again, people go to great lengths in selecting their leaders and make a big production of the entire process. But people have always rejected the only One who can lead them in the way that will produce what they want.

Since man will not make a big production of the only One who
is qualified to lead them, God will make a big production instead.
He says that the whole world will see His coming. They will see it
as clearly as they can see the moon by night and the sun by day. He
will come with the glory, honor and power of God—not man.

The True Messiah

But who is this new world leader that is about to come to this earth?
Only a few thousand in all the earth's history have truly known
about Him or actually known Him. As was stated at the beginning
of this book, those of Judaism have always believed they knew the
truth about the Messiah, yet they rejected Him when he came the
first time. Those of traditional Christianity have always believed
that they have known about Him, and many have believed they also
knew Him. But none of these have known the true Messiah.

The Sabbath and Holy Days of God reveal God's plan for
mankind. Those were covered in the previous chapter. However,
man has rejected those days as well as what they teach. Because of
this, man has not been able to come to know the true Messiah and
what He is truly like. Those days actually reveal the true Messiah.
But people in this world, especially religious leaders, have clouded
their own minds and the minds of others either by promoting their
own mistaken ideas or by perpetuating the erroneous ideas of others
about who He is and what He is like.

The remainder of this chapter is dedicated to the true
Messiah—the genuine Christ. It is about those things that will
enable you to identify Him and truly come to know Him.

Everyone would do well to begin getting to know the true
Messiah because He is about to become your ruler—your King. The
paradox in all this is quite profound. If you do begin to repent of
your ways and receive God's ways and truth into your life, then you
may receive His favor and live on into that new world. Even if you
reject the true Messiah now and die, after 1,000 years you will be

resurrected back to life a <u>second</u> time. At such time you will again have to address whether or not you will receive the truth. The Messiah will be reigning for that thousand years and for all time beyond. So either you choose to come to know Him now or you will face those same choices at a later time. When all is said and done, you must choose God's way or your only choice is death for all eternity.

God's plan for mankind centers around the Messiah—the Christ, and it all begins with the observance of Passover. The following verses were quoted about Passover in the previous chapter, but we need to be reminded of them again and build upon them.

"And the LORD spoke unto Moses, saying, Speak unto the children of Israel, and say unto them, Concerning the <u>feasts</u> [This Hebrew word is not the same word for "feasts" as the words that are used later to describe feasts, as in verse 6. This word means "appointed times." These are times appointed by God. They are "appointments" that man is to keep with God—times when we are to come before Him and meet with Him.] *of the LORD, which you shall proclaim to be <u>holy convocations</u>* [Hebrew—"commanded assemblies"], *even these are my <u>feasts</u>* [Hebrew—"appointed times"]. *Six days shall work be done: but the seventh day is the Sabbath of rest, an <u>holy convocation</u>* ["commanded assembly"]; *you shall do no work therein: it is the Sabbath of the LORD in all your dwellings. These are the <u>feasts</u>* ["appointed times"] *of the LORD, even <u>holy convocations</u>* ["commanded assemblies"], *which you shall proclaim in their <u>seasons</u>* [Hebrew— "appointed times"]. *In the fourteenth day of the first month at even is the LORD'S Passover. And on the fifteenth day* [an annual Holy Day—annual Sabbath] *of the same month is the <u>Feast</u>* [This word in the Hebrew does mean "feast."] *of Unleavened Bread unto the LORD: seven days you must eat unleavened bread"* (Leviticus 23:1-6).

God revealed the observances that mankind is to keep as well as the times that He appointed them to be kept. This law is eternal; it can never change. It has not been changed, and even so, it would be contrary to God's own way to do so. Yet those in traditional Christianity teach that these laws were done away in Christ. Nothing could be further from the truth! These days actually "reveal" Christ—the Messiah. It is by their rejection of these days that they not only have failed to know the Messiah and the truth of God, but they have followed a false Christ and taught a false Christ.

The Christ of Traditional Christianity

The Christ of traditional Christianity is nothing like the Christ of scripture. The very first annual observance, which traditional Christianity rejects, is the one that leads us to know who He is and to actually know Him. It is the Passover. Yet traditional Christianity does not observe the Passover. Instead, they observe a different time around this same season of the year; it is called Easter.

The Bible nowhere mentions such an observance. If Easter was suppose to replace the Passover or be substituted for the Passover, then surely the disciples would have made some mention of it in scripture. Surely something of this magnitude would be recorded in the Bible.

As noted earlier, the King James Bible is a translation that uses the word "Easter." *"And when he had apprehended him, he put him in prison, and delivered him to four quaternions of soldiers to keep him; intending after Easter to bring him forth to the people"* (Acts 12:4). The word translated as "Easter" is not the Greek word for Easter. The actual Greek word is "pascha." It is the same word as the English word for Passover. Nearly all other translations render this word correctly as "Passover," just as the New King James Version does.

History clearly shows that the early Church of God and other emerging groups who called themselves "Christian" kept the Passover up until the early 300s A.D.

It was the Catholic Church that adopted the observance of Easter. This church stopped keeping the Passover. They replaced it with the observance of Easter at the Nicene Council of 325 A.D. The Catholic Church, in its quest to add gentile converts to their numbers and to appease the Roman Empire of their time, adopted some of the practices of gentiles and merged them with some of the stories from scripture concerning the death of Jesus Christ. This is a prime example of the age old conflict of religion and politics

A goddess of fertility in the gentile world was mixed with the story of the virgin Mary and her son. This is the same false religion God condemned in the Old Testament. You would be wise to look up some of the names of these gods in an encyclopedia. It is quite revealing.

This goddess is referred to as the "queen of heaven" or "Ashtoreth" in scripture. Notice some of these verses and their context. Idols depicted her as a mother holding her infant son who was generally known as Tammuz.

"Behold, you trust in lying words that cannot profit. Will you steal, murder, commit adultery, swear falsely, burn incense to Baal, and walk after other gods whom you know not...?" (Jeremiah 7:8-9). *"The children gather wood, the fathers kindle the fire, and the women knead their dough, to make cakes to the queen of heaven, and to pour out drink offerings unto other gods, that they may provoke me to anger"* (Verse 18).

"For it came to pass, when Solomon was old, that his wives turned away his heart after other gods: and his heart was not perfect with the LORD his God, as was the heart of David his father. For Solomon went after Ashtoreth the goddess of the Zidonians, and after Milcom the abomination of the Ammonites" (1 Kings 11:4-5).

The worship of this goddess spread throughout the world, even among the tribes of Israel. History clearly records the names by which this goddess became known. Look up Ashtoreth in any Bible dictionary or encyclopedia. She was the principal female deity of the Phoenicians that was worshipped in war and fertility. She was also know as "Ishtar" by the Assyrians and "Astarte" by the Greeks and Romans. Easter is simply the same English word for Astarte or Ishtar.

So the Catholic Church adopted from the Roman world those gentile beliefs that they believed could be merged with scripture. This led to religious confusion and false teachings in regard to scripture and the true Christ.

A false teaching about Easter is the subject of a prophecy in Ezekiel. Traditional Christianity claims that Jesus was resurrected on Easter morning, after having died on "Good Friday." The falsity of this teaching has already been addressed. Yet, the mother church (Catholic) of traditional Christianity pushed this concept of an Easter morning resurrection because they wanted to give credibility to Sunday as a day of worship. These things were pursued in order to merge a gentile world, with its false religion, with a new form of religion known as Christianity. However, this new pseudo-religion was nothing like that of the followers of Christ, in the true Church of God.

"And he brought me into the inner court of the LORD'S house, and, behold, at the door of the temple of the LORD, between the porch and the altar, were about five and twenty men, with their backs toward the temple of the LORD, and their faces toward the east; and they worshiped the <u>sun</u> toward the east" (Ezekiel 8:16). This prophecy shows that man has turned his back on God—His ways and the truth of His word. Instead, man has turned to Easter and the observance of sunrise services, supposedly in honor of Jesus Christ. But, in reality, they are honoring Baal, the sun god, who was the supreme male god of the Phoenicians, <u>the son of Ashtoreth.</u> The symbol of the mother and child was being worshiped long before the time of Jesus Christ.

The Jesus Christ of traditional Christianity is not the true Christ of the Bible. The true Jesus Christ and the truth He taught are nothing like the teachings of traditional Christianity. For anyone to begin to truly know the true Christ, the true Messiah, they will need to learn what is true and abandon what is false. Candidly, everything about traditional Christianity is false! They teach a different Christ than scripture. Although they may quote His words, they twist them into perverted false doctrines.

Example! One of the first things Jesus taught was, *"Think not that I am come to destroy the law, or the prophets: I am not come to destroy, but to fulfill"* (Matthew 5:17). Yet traditional Christianity teaches that He did away with the law. It perverts what was meant by "fulfilling" the law. He fulfills the meaning in Passover. He will yet fulfill the meaning in the Feast of Trumpets. He will begin fulfilling much of the meaning in the seventh-day weekly Sabbath when He comes in the Kingdom of God to reign on this earth during the <u>seventh,</u> one-thousand year period of man on earth. The weekly Sabbath pictures God's time that will last a full day after the first six days are past—man's time to do his work and seek his pleasure. The seventh day is God's time when man is to rest from his work and seek Him. In like manner, Jesus Christ is coming in God's Kingdom to reign and fill the earth with God's ways—God's work—once man's allotted 6,000 years of self-rule have ended.

But traditional Christianity has clouded the way to knowing the true Jesus Christ—the true Messiah. The example of the law is only the beginning of a very long story about teachings that have been twisted, distorted and misrepresented.

When Protestant Christianity began to grow, after breaking from the Catholic Church and rejecting some of her teachings on government and faith, it failed to reject the major building blocks of the Catholic faith. Instead, it continued to embrace numerous false teachings about a different Jesus.

The teachings of a false Jesus Christ center around false

doctrines He supposedly fulfilled—instead of the law and the prophets of scripture. These false teachings include a resurrection on Easter. He wasn't resurrected on Easter! These false teachings say He fulfilled the payment of death, for all mankind, by dying on "Good Friday." He didn't die on a Friday! Sunday observance is based on the supposition that Christ was resurrected on Sunday morning. He wasn't resurrected on Sunday morning—not anytime on Sunday! The Jesus of traditional Christianity supposedly fulfills the meaning and teaching surrounding the Christmas season—the time for the "mass of Christ." Yet Jesus Christ was not born in the winter. Scripture clearly shows that Christ was born in the early fall.

On and on it goes! The lies, the fables, the paganism and continual twisting of stories from scripture seem to give people warm fuzzy feelings about "their" Jesus who will accept you just as you are. Hogwash! These things are putrid lies that have kept mankind from seeing Jesus Christ as He truly is! These are among the reasons why God is going to chasten this nation. America has been the breeding ground for promoting these false teachings through "freedom of religion." This "freedom" allowed false doctrines to thrive far more than they had for centuries under that one great false church. No wonder people are thoroughly confounded as to what is true!

Are you beginning to feel a little ill? Are you beginning to see the corruption of man toward His God? Either you are feeling ill toward me for saying these things or you are feeling ill because you know these things are true. You may become angry at the messenger, but you can be assured that God is getting ready to humble you, one way or the other.

Those who will not be humbled will die! That is God's word! God will humble this world very soon, whether you like it or not, then His Kingdom will come. If you are among those who die, then you will miss seeing that new world. You will not see the coming of the true Jesus Christ. You will not even know that you are dead!

THE PROPHESIED END-TIME   253

Your next waking moment will be in a resurrection at the end of that 1,000 year reign of Jesus Christ. And God declares that in that day, you will know that you have been dead for a thousand years because you refused His true word. So, no matter how you look at it, you will still be brought face to face with the truth—very soon! What a shame that so many will not listen to God—to His servant who has been given the responsibility of saying these things—all because of pride and self-righteousness. Strong words, but true!

The Only Sign of the True Messiah

Jesus Christ gave only one sign that would prove that He was the Messiah. We have touched upon this, but let's delve a little more deeply into it. Some in traditional Christianity have blatantly refused that sign. They hold to another identifying sign that proves they worship a false Jesus.

"Then certain of the scribes and of the Pharisees answered, saying, Master, we want to see a sign from you. But He answered and said unto them, An evil and adulterous generation seeks after a sign; and there shall no sign be given to it, but the sign of the prophet Jonah. For as Jonah was three days and three nights in the belly of the great fish; so shall the Son of man be three days and three nights in the heart of the earth'" (Matthew 12:38-40).

Jesus said that only one sign would be given to prove who He was. That sign was that He would be in the heart of the earth—in the tomb—for three days and three nights. It is hard for scholars to squeeze that time period into the time between Friday near sundown and Sunday morning when they say He was resurrected. A day is counted scripturally from sundown to sundown. It is not from midnight to midnight, as we do today.

But some scholars try to explain how Jesus could have said three days and three nights, but He really meant a day and a half. They resist the truth, even when they know they are wrong. But most people in traditional Christianity are ignorant of these matters because they are not taught the truth. On the contrary, preachers stay away from subjects like this one.

So the false Christ of traditional Christianity was resurrected in a day and a half from the time He was put in the tomb. The story is really quite basic when people have only a little understanding of certain scriptures regarding the seventh-day Sabbath and the annual Holy Days.

Let's look at the sequence of events that surrounded the death and resurrection of Jesus Christ.

"When the even was come [This is the time we would call late afternoon. It was not yet sundown, for at sundown a new day would begin and that new day would be a Sabbath. Jesus would have to be put in the tomb before sundown and the beginning of the Sabbath.], *there came a rich man of Arimathea, named Joseph, who also himself was Jesus' disciple: He went to Pilate, and begged for the body of Jesus. Then Pilate commanded the body to be delivered. And when Joseph had taken the body, he wrapped it in a clean linen cloth, and laid it in his own new tomb, which he had hewn out in the rock: and he rolled a great stone to the door of the tomb, and departed"* (Matthew 27:57-61).

Notice the parallel account and what is said in Luke.

"And, behold, there was a man named Joseph, a council member; and he was a good, and a just: (The same had not consented to the counsel and deed of them;) he was of Arimathea, a city of the Jew: who also himself waited for the kingdom of God. This man went unto Pilate, and begged for the body of Jesus. And he took it down, and wrapped it in linen, and laid it in a tomb that was hewn in stone, wherein never man before was laid. And that day was the preparation, and the Sabbath drew near" (Luke 23:50-54). So Joseph, very clearly, was preparing the body of Jesus for burial in his own tomb, before the Sabbath, which would begin at sundown. But this was no ordinary Sabbath. It <u>was not</u> the seventh-day Sabbath, as those in traditional Christianity suppose, and for

that reason, they believe that Joseph put Jesus in the tomb on Friday.

An account in the Book of John shows what kind of Sabbath this was.

"The Jews therefore, because it was the preparation [not a Friday, in preparation for the weekly Sabbath], *that the bodies should not remain upon the cross on the Sabbath day (for that Sabbath was an High Day), besought Pilate that their legs might be broken, and that they might be taken away. Then came the soldiers, and broke the legs of the first, and of the other who was crucified with Him. But when they came to Jesus, and saw that He was dead already, they broke not His legs:"* (John 19:31-33). This Sabbath was an annual High Day—an annual Sabbath. It was the first day of Unleavened Bread, and it is the day that follows the Passover day (the day in which Jesus Christ died).

Notice again the timing of God's appointed times for mankind in Leviticus that we looked at earlier. *"These are the feasts* ["appointed times"] *of the LORD, even holy convocations* ["commanded assemblies"], *which you shall proclaim in their seasons* ["appointed times"]. *In the fourteenth day of the first month at even is the LORD'S Passover. And on the fifteenth day* [an annual Holy Day—annual Sabbath] *of the same month is the Feast of Unleavened Bread unto the LORD: seven days you must eat unleavened bread. In the first day you shall have an holy convocation* [as the weekly Sabbath, this day is also a "commanded assembly"]*: you shall do no servile work therein* [it is a Sabbath day]*"* (Leviticus 23:4-7).

The Passover was on the 14th day of the first month of God's Holy Calendar. This was the 14th of Abib. This is the same day Jesus Christ died. He died in mid-afternoon on the Passover day. Passover is also a preparation day, just like Friday is the preparation day for the weekly Sabbath. The 14th can occur on different days of the week. In the year Jesus Christ died, the Passover was on a

Wednesday. That Wednesday was a preparation day for the annual High Day—the annual Sabbath—the first day of the Feast of Unleavened Bread.

Jesus Christ died late on Wednesday, in mid-afternoon. Because the first day of Unleavened Bread (an annual Sabbath—a High Day) was fast approaching, Joseph of Arimathea went to Pilate to receive permission to take Jesus down and bury him in his own tomb. He was able to bury Jesus just before sunset, just before the annual Sabbath began. Three days and three nights take us through all night Wednesday and most all day Thursday (1 full day), all night Thursday and most all day Friday (2 full days), all night Friday and most of the day Saturday (3 full days). This weekly seventh-day Sabbath began at sunset on Friday. Toward the end of the Sabbath day, before sunset Saturday, exactly three days and three nights from the time Joseph laid Jesus in the tomb, the true Jesus Christ was resurrected.

Since the Sabbath (weekly) was almost ended and the night-time portion of Sunday was approaching, the women decided to wait until the following morning to go to the tomb. They waited until the breaking of light Sunday morning to come to the tomb with the spices they had prepared to place with the body of Jesus Christ. But obviously He had already risen before they arrived. He was resurrected just before sunset of the weekly Sabbath—very late Saturday afternoon before sunset.

"In the end of the <u>Sabbath</u> [This word is plural in the Greek. It is "Sabbaths." The annual Sabbath was now past and the weekly Sabbath was now past.], *as it began to dawn toward the first day of the week,* [early Sunday morning], *came Mary Magdalene and the other Mary to see the tomb. And, behold, there was a great earthquake: for the angel of the Lord descended from heaven, and came and rolled back the stone from the door, and sat upon it. His countenance was like lightning, and his clothing white as snow: And for fear of him the guards did shake, and became as dead men.*

And the angel answered and said unto the women, Fear you not: for I know that you seek Jesus, who was crucified. He is not here: for He is risen, as He said. Come, see the place where the Lord lay" (Matthew 28:1-6).

The angel removed the stone from the tomb's entrance in order to show the women that Jesus Christ was not there. He had already been resurrected, just before sunset the previous day. The truth is so very plain. But most people hate nearly everything the true Christ taught. People today are no different than those Jewish leaders who wanted Jesus put to death. The religious leaders of today don't want this Jesus either.

The Powerful Truth of the Passover

The Passover is a powerful truth. It cuts through all false doctrine to reveal every false religion, false teacher and false believer. If the Passover is observed and obeyed as God commands, then you can come to know the true Messiah. But, if people continue to insist on holding onto anything other than the truth concerning this day, then they cannot know Christ or His Father!

This should be evident in the material we just covered. The very truths surrounding the timing and observance of the Passover day are the very things that prove that Jesus Christ is indeed the true Passover of all mankind—that He is the true Messiah.

Since traditional Christianity has held to the false observance of Easter, they have remained totally ignorant of the true Christ, the true Messiah and the truth of God.

Even the Jews have abandoned the Passover. They don't observe it at the correct time or in the correct way. Instead of keeping Passover when they should, they observe the Seder, the eating of the lamb, after the Passover day, at the beginning (after sundown) of the first day of the Feast of Unleavened Bread. Judaism rejected Jesus Christ as the true Messiah, and this in turn led to their rejection of the Passover day. Is it any wonder the world does not believe God, much less believe that the true Messiah is about to come to this earth as King of kings and Lord of lords? If people knew Him, they would know His coming is imminent!

Even God's Church began to lose the Passover! This is one of the main reasons that people began to be cut off from God's presence—from the power of His spirit working in their lives. It was through false teachings and beliefs concerning the observance of Passover that the minds of many ministers and brethren became polluted, and thereby, they became false.

Traditional Christianity believes that, after death, people will go to heaven to be with Christ, but the Catholics seem more concerned with going to heaven to be with Mary. But Mary, the mother of Jesus Christ, is still in her grave (dead) awaiting the resurrection.

Many people, in the Church that was scattered, are fast asleep spiritually because they have turned away from truth concerning Passover or they condone those who have. Either way, they have cut themselves off from God.

The Passover is the beginning of revelation in the plan of God. It is the first annual observance that God commands His people to keep. Our Passover is the first in all things. When people turn from faithful observance of all that is fulfilled in the meaning of this day—they turn away from knowing Jesus Christ and His Father.

"Who is the image of the invisible God, the firstborn of every creature: For <u>by</u> [Greek–"<u>in</u>"] *Him were all things created, that are in heaven, and that are in earth, visible and invisible, whether they be thrones, or dominions, or principalities, or powers: all things were created <u>by</u>* [Greek–"<u>in</u>"] *Him, and for Him: And He is before all things, and <u>by</u>* [Greek–"<u>in</u>"] *Him all things consist. And He is the head of the body, the church: who is the beginning, the firstborn from the dead; that <u>in</u>* [same Greek word–"in"] *all things He might have the preeminence. For it pleased the Father that <u>in</u>* [same Greek word–"in"] *Him should all fulness dwell; And, having made peace <u>through</u>* [correct Greek word–"through"] *the blood of His*

cross, by [same Greek word–"through"] *Him to reconcile all things unto Himself; by* [same Greek word–"through"] *Him, I say, whether they be things in earth, or things in heaven"* (Colossians 1:15-20).

God reveals through Paul that all things in His creation are centered "in" and "through" Jesus Christ. In all things Jesus Christ is to have the preeminence! Can you see why the Passover is the first observance in God's plan? Everything begins with Christ.

In the mid-to-late 1970s (in the Philadelphia Era), several evangelists and pastors in the Church, as well as teachers at Ambassador College, began to teach false doctrine concerning the Passover. As a result, the Church experienced great upheaval.

After Mr. Tkach replaced Mr. Armstrong in the leadership of the Worldwide Church of God, it was not long before he began to promote this false doctrine through others. It was approximately 1988 that this false teaching was surreptitiously sent out in a study format to the Church leadership. Supposedly this was done in order to better understand why modern-day Judaism observes the Passover on the beginning of the 15th of Abib, rather than on the 14th as God commands. They concluded that the Jewish observance was proper since later observances in the Old Testament show the Passover had been changed and was being kept on the 15th. That was not true! Passover was always observed on the 14th. This distorted reasoning from these Church leaders led them to conclude that Jesus had kept the Passover a day early (although the Jews of His day observed the 14th as He did) and that we should follow His example and do the same, especially since Paul clearly said it was to be observed at the same time Jesus kept it.

This false teaching led many in the Church to deny the true Messiah, the same as those in traditional Christianity. Traditional Christianity, through the rejection of knowledge of the Passover, rejected the only sign Jesus gave that He was the true Messiah. They rejected the observance of Passover by accepting Easter and a Sunday morning resurrection, and therein, the justification for changing the seventh-day Sabbath to the first day of the week. They chose rather to observe the Day of the Sun, the day Baal was worshiped.

Those in the Church, who began to teach false doctrine about the Passover, were changing the deep meaning of those things that identify the true Messiah. They began to reject the very thing that reveals how Jesus Christ faithfully fulfilled all that God the Father had given Him to accomplish. Jesus Christ fulfilled Passover exactly how and when God said—revealing that He was indeed the Messiah.

Traditional Christianity and those in the Church who perverted and polluted the deep meaning of Passover are equally guilty of perpetuating falsehoods that picture Jesus Christ in rebellion to His Father. He is pictured as someone who came along and changed His Father's law and did not fulfill the law and the prophets as God said the Messiah would do.

We must observe the things of God in the way God commands. Judaism and traditional Christianity have turned from God's truth about Passover. Many in the Church that was scattered have watered-down the truth about Passover. This is the primary reason that none of them know we are in the end-time. They do not know that six of the seven seals of Revelation have been opened, and neither do they know that the seventh (last) seal will be opened soon. For these reasons, the remainder of this chapter is dedicated to telling the truth concerning Passover. The proof of Passover and the truth about Passover identify the true Messiah. Everything else is false. If anyone believes anything else—they are false!

PASSOVER

This part of the chapter is not intended for the average reader. If you haven't read about the Passover in chapter 6, then you will have a more difficult time understanding things covered here. If you haven't read the previous chapter covering Passover, then it is recommended that you do so first and then return to this.

This last section is a far deeper study into the timing of Passover. It is geared more towards those who are familiar with Bible research, word studies, contextual translation, and Bible history. It is geared more so to former members of God's Church who have become confused or deceived over this subject. It is also geared towards those in Judaism because they have been subtly deceived by "their rabbis."

The timing of events surrounding Passover have often created controversy within the Church of God. It has also been controversial in Judaism, but that was several hundred years ago. For the Church, most of the debate centered around a single word, in English versions of the Bible, that easily misrepresented the actual meaning. In Judaism, the debate centered around the same basic Hebrew word, with its various forms of usage. However, this was not the result of a misunderstanding of the word. It was a flagrant change to a different meaning of the various forms of the word.

This entire story centers around the method God gave mankind for dividing one day from another. In our day, that division comes exactly at 12:00 midnight. But God showed man that <u>sunset</u> divided one day from the next. Great controversy has existed in Judaism over this issue. Mankind simply has not accepted God's simple instruction concerning division of time.

Some in the Church of God have had the same problem as that of Judaism because they accepted the false teaching of Judaism. They learned the truth at the beginning of their calling, but later, they turned from it. The truth they learned came from the apostle God raised up to restore truth in the Church, the end-time Elijah, Herbert W. Armstrong. (For those Jewish readers, the end-time Elijah was of the tribe of Judah. Mr. Armstrong's lineage can be traced back to King David.)

When those Church members abandoned the truth about Passover, they cut themselves off from God and His spirit. They were no longer a part of the Church of God.

Translating more than one Greek or Hebrew word into a single English word is quite common. It happens with words like love, hell and heaven. Usually, with a little digging, you can find the different meanings. Look up the word *hell* and you will find it comes from three different Greek words: hades, gehenna, and tartaroo.

Many incorrect assumptions can be made when people put their own interpretation into an English word they read in the Bible. Take the word *hell* for example. Most people in traditional Christianity will have some pretty gruesome pictures pop into their minds when they think of this word. They see agonizing torment that goes on forever. Yet, the one Greek work "hades," which means the same as its counterpart in the Hebrew word "sheol," simply means a pit or hole in the ground. It most commonly refers to a grave—a place for the dead. It is simply a place to put a dead body. It is not a place of eternal torment. There is no such place! But people have pictured God as a fiendish being who puts people in this awful place forever because they disobeyed Him.

The word "tartaroo" is another Greek word for *hell*. It simply means a place of restraint, like a jail. The word "gehenna" is about a specific location that refers to a place of final punishment. It is sometimes referred to as "gehenna" fire ("hell fire" in English). This is a place where bodies are thrown and burned up, like cremation. This is not a place of continual torture by flames, but a place of final judgment, where a dead body is burned. These bodies have no life and will never live again because this is a final judgement that will last for all eternity. It is an eternal punishment with no possibility of life again. It is permanent death.

Usage of words like *hell* are fairly easy to prove and understand. But this problem isn't so easily solved in the Passover controversy.

The word *even* or *evening* is the focal point of confusion on this subject. The Hebrew in this case becomes more difficult than usual. When you look up *even* or *evening* in a trusty Strong's Concordance, you will see the Hebrew Reference Number 6153 for *ereb*. But this is very misleading. Most people using Strong's would think that the same Hebrew word was being used each time they found #6153. That's the problem! It isn't! It has different forms, and structure of usage, in Hebrew.

The fact that different forms of the same Hebrew word give vastly different meanings is only one problem. Even when people are aware of the different words, their personal interpretation still clouds the meaning. This is what has happened in modern-day Judaism. When embracing a false belief, people will generally force their own definitions into scripture in order to give their belief validity. You should, however, let the Bible interpret itself in all such cases.

As we address these matters, we will not focus on analysis of various arguments and interpretations. We will focus, instead, on Biblical interpretations. As you see the truth made plain by God's own word, you will more easily recognize why others have stumbled. You need to clear your mind of preconceived ideas and examine honestly and openly some of the words and scriptures that clarify the timing of events surrounding the Passover.

Sundown *(ereb)*

The best place to begin is at the beginning. In Genesis, God showed man how to divide time. God's ways are simple, but the intellectualism of man has confounded that simplicity. *"And God called the light Day, and the darkness He called Night. And the evening (ereb) and the morning were the first day"* (Genesis 1:5). The expression "the evening and morning were the first day" simply means one full day as counted from sundown to sundown.

God makes plain what He wants to be obvious to us. He said the light was day and the darkness was night. Then He introduced a direct, but simple, division of time for a complete day. God said, "And the <u>*evening*</u> (ereb) and the morning were the first day." This expression may seem a little strange, when used in English, because we don't think of the English words for evening and morning as being a complete day. But we must let God define time for us. As we will come to see, He becomes even more specific when He defines Holy time.

What divides these two periods of time in Genesis 1:5? The sun does! The two periods of time (night and day) occur when the sun is down and when the sun is up. When the sun is up—any portion of it—it is day. As long as we can see any portion of the sun, it is day. When the sun is down—when no portion of it can be seen because it has moved below the horizon—it is night, or in this case, *ereb*. When the sun goes through one complete cycle, having been down and up, we have a complete day. The <u>evening</u> *(ereb)* and the morning were the first day. We don't have to concern ourselves with nebulous periods of time that are ever changing when light is still in the sky, but the sun has gone down and disappeared from sight. The sun, the source of light, is the dividing factor between the light of day and *ereb,* when the sun is down.

The Hebrew word *ereb* simply means the sun is down—out of view—no part of it can be seen. *Ereb* can be any point (moment) of time during this period when the sun is down, or it can be the entire time the sun is down. This is much like using the English word *night*. *Night* can be at the beginning of a period of darkness or at some point during that time, as long as it's dark or the sun is down. As with *night*, you couldn't say it was *ereb* at any point while the sun was still up.

Until & After

When you understand *ereb,* as any period when the sun is down, you can proceed to other combinations used in Hebrew. First, let's look at *awd ereb*. It simply means "until" *ereb* or until sundown. This is a period of time that leads up to even (*ereb*), at the moment the sun is down.

"The soul which has touched any such shall be unclean <u>until</u> <u>even</u> (awd ereb), *and shall not eat of the holy things, unless he wash his flesh with water. And <u>when the sun is down</u>, he shall be clean, and shall afterward eat of the holy things; because it is his food"* (Leviticus 22:6-7). This scripture, like Genesis, defines *ereb*. Why? Verse 7 makes it clear that the condition of being clean or unclean changes <u>once the sun is down</u>. A person was considered unclean *until even* (awd ereb). They were unclean during the day, as long as the sun was shining, but not until the sun was down (*awd ereb*) were they clean. This is describing a very specific division of time. It follows the Genesis timing for passage from one day into another. It wasn't *until* a new day began that this person was considered clean. God uses very clear language to make His instructions precise.

Another example is *ma ereb* which simply means "from" *ereb* or literally "from the very moment of ereb." This word simply means "*from*" sundown, "from" that very moment that the sun can no longer be seen. We will return to this word to see how it is used in a single verse in Leviticus. In that example, three different forms of *ereb* are recorded in Strong's as a single Hebrew word.

At Sundown *(ba ereb)*

The word *ba ereb* causes people difficulty when they try to stretch its meaning beyond the one definition God gives. If you try to force your own interpretations and doctrine into scripture, then any word can become confusing. Consider what religious teachers have done with the word *hell* that we covered earlier. Once you understand the correct usage of these terms by letting scripture interpret itself, then the confusion and foolishness of adversarial arguments is revealed.

God's word is beautifully written. It is awe inspiring to witness its simplicity. So it is with the use of the term "at" *ereb*. Instead of becoming entangled in the complicated arguments surrounding this word, let's look again at the plain language of some very basic scriptures.

The following scriptures are explicit because they concern the observance of Holy time. *"And in the fourteenth day of the first month is the Passover of the Lord. And in the fifteenth day of this month is the feast: seven days shall unleavened bread be eaten"* (Numbers 28:16-17). Leviticus 23 shows that the 15th day of the month is the first day of Unleavened Bread, an annual Sabbath, as is the seventh day of Unleavened Bread. *"And on the fifteenth day of the same month is the Feast of Unleavened Bread unto the Lord: seven days you must eat unleavened bread. In the first day you shall have an holy convocation: you shall do no servile work therein. But you shall offer an offering made by fire unto the LORD seven days: in the seventh day is an holy convocation: you shall do no servile work therein"* (Leviticus 23:6-8). Unleavened bread was to be eaten for those seven days. It is a clear scripture, but even here, some like to argue.

The usage of even (*ereb*) has caused much confusion among those who use only an English translation because it is much different than others in the usage of "even." Yet the usage here is quite simple and serves to be incredibly specific in describing time. *In the first month, on the fourteenth day of the month at even* (ba ereb), *you shall eat unleavened bread, until the one and twentieth day of the month at even* (ba ereb)" (Exodus 12:18). Many read this verse as though it is saying that the first day of the Feast of Unleavened Bread (an annual Sabbath) was to begin on the 14th day of the first month. That is not what it says, but it may seem so if you use only a translation that uses different forms of the Hebrew word "ereb" as one and the same English word.

If this verse were saying that the first annual Sabbath of this feast was to begin on the 14th, then it would contradict other scriptures that clearly say Passover was to be on the 14th and the first day of the feast was to be on the 15th. God's word always agrees and never contradicts.

So what is *ba ereb* in this verse? The very use of the word, coupled with other explicit instruction regarding this observance, gives the clear scriptural definition. What is the only use of this word that would ever allow it to fit such precise instruction? When you have the answer, you will know the scriptural interpretation.

"At" should clarify this is a specific period of time. It is "at" sundown. As we saw in Genesis, *ereb* occurs only when the sun is down. *Ereb* cannot be used to refer to any period while the sun is "going down." When it is "down," the sun divides a specific period of time from when it is "up."

Exodus 12 does not say the period for eating unleavened bread was to be from the 14th through the 21st. That would be more than seven days. Instead, it spells out the only way this word can be used. Are we to begin eating unleavened bread sometime in the late afternoon on the 14th? No. A specific seven day period is being described. If this were some period beginning from a point in mid-to-late afternoon, on the 14th, then it would have to end at the exact same point in mid-to-late afternoon on the 21st, before the days of Unleavened Bread are over. "At" *ereb* can have only one meaning, and still fit into this verse, in order to cover a full seven-day period of time. God said in Leviticus 23 that the first day of Unleavened Bread was to be observed *on* the 15th day of the month. The seventh day from the 15th is the 21st. That is the last day—the seventh day of Unleavened Bread, and it is an annual Sabbath just like the 1st day that falls on the 15th.

"At" *ereb* can only be a specific moment, at the end of one day, while "going into" another day. In this case, it is from the end of the 14th "to" the moment of the beginning of the 15th. It is from the time of the 14th to the time of the 15th, specifically "at" the point the sun has gone completely down. While we can see any portion of the sun, it is day, and it is still the 14th. When light can no longer be seen coming directly from the sun, it is night or *ereb*. God gave us plain, simple instructions. We don't have to be scholars to understand.

Our society passes from one day into another "<u>at</u>" precisely 12:00 midnight. God divided time by showing us that we pass from one day into another precisely "<u>at</u>" the point the sun is down. Exodus 12 shows us that the beginning of Unleavened Bread is "<u>at</u>" a specific point in time at the end of the 14th and the beginning of another day, the 15th. It also ends precisely "<u>at</u>" the end of the 21st, when the sun is down and the 22nd begins. God divides time very clearly.

The *ba ereb* of any day is the moment of sundown for that Biblical day. Sundown *(ba ereb)* cannot occur during the period known as *ereb*. Sundown *(ba ereb)* in <u>a Biblical day</u> can only be "<u>at</u>" the moment which ends the daylight portion of a day—the exact moment the sun is completely down. Sundown *(ba ereb)* cannot occur at any other time of *ereb* because the sun is already down at all other points of night.

Another beautiful area of scripture is found in Leviticus 23. Again, God is making it very clear when His holy time begins. This concerns the Day of Atonement. *"Also on the tenth day of this seventh month there shall be a Day of Atonement: it shall be an holy convocation unto you; and you shall afflict your souls, and offer an offering made by fire unto the Lord" (Leviticus 23:27).* Next we come to a precise and very specific instruction about the exact timing of Atonement. *"It shall be unto you a Sabbath of rest, and you shall afflict your souls: in the ninth day of the month <u>at</u> even* (ba ereb), *<u>from even</u>* (ma ereb) *<u>unto even</u>* (awd ereb), *shall ye celebrate your Sabbath" (Leviticus 23:32).* In this verse it is important to note the very specific use of *ereb*.

After seeing the clear use of *ba ereb* concerning the instructions for Unleavened Bread, we can easily understand the use of it for

Atonement. "In the ninth day of the month *at even* (ba ereb)" can only mean we are to begin the observance of Atonement at the precise moment that ends one day and begins the next. *Ba ereb* on the 9th day is at the very moment the 9th day ends, when the sun has "gone down" on that day. So again, God makes it clear that this is a precise time. The end of the 9th is precisely when the sun is completely down. Then, at that same precise moment, the 10th day begins.

This precise instruction for the timing of Atonement is further spelled out in the rest of the verse. "*Ma*" means "from," just as it is used here. It says "from even" (*ma ereb*) "unto even" (*awd ereb*). Atonement starts precisely at the point the sun is down on the 9th and goes "from" that point, the beginning of *ereb*, "unto" the next *ereb,* at the same point of time again. Atonement is a complete day. It is observed through the entirety of the 10th. God makes it clear that Atonement is between two specific evenings.

If people don't understand that three different Hebrew words are used in this one verse to describe evening, then all sorts of interpretations can emerge. If any one of these three words is misapplied, especially *ba ereb,* then God's instruction and precise timing will be misunderstood. That is exactly what has happened in Judaism and in much of the Church that was scattered.

When using the word *ba ereb* (at sundown) in a present or future tense context, it can only occur at the end of the daylight period for that specific day when the sun goes down. With the instruction given in Exodus 12:18, only unleavened bread was allowed to be eaten beginning at sundown (*ba ereb*) on the 14th, when the sun went down on the daytime period of the 14th which marks the beginning of a new day, the 15th.

If the context is in the past tense for a specific day, then "at sundown" (*ba ereb*) would apply to the end of the previous day. Using the example of Atonement, you could say, "You are to fast on the 9th day at sundown (*ba ereb*)." For Atonement it *could not be said*, "You fasted on the 9th day, at sundown *(ba ereb)*." The action is past. Using past tense action that has already occurred, it would be correct to say, "You fasted on the 10th day, at sundown *(ba ereb)*." The fasting occurred on the 10th day, beginning *ba ereb* (sundown) on the 9th. This will become important later and cannot be denied by context.

Deuteronomy 16

Before we continue to the last word to be examined, we need to pause and consider a particular verse (Deuteronomy16:6) that has led to some confusion over the term *ba ereb*. The misunderstanding surrounding this verse may be partly responsible for why some people think they can extend the definition for when the sun begins to go down, as modern-day Judaism teaches.

Some use Deuteronomy 16:6 to define *ba ereb*, rather than the verses we have used. We should always use the clearer context to better understand more difficult scriptures. The scriptural examples we have been using are an excellent exercise for learning how to let God's word define itself—in other words, let the Bible interpret the Bible.

"But at the place which the Lord your God shall choose to place His name in, there you shall sacrifice the Passover <u>at even</u> (ba ereb), *at the <u>going down</u>* (Strong's Concordance #935) *of the sun, at the season that thou came forth out of Egypt"* (Deuteronomy 16:6).

If you have fully grasped the meaning of *ba ereb* as being the precise moment the sun is down, then you will immediately notice why this verse could cause people problems. We will return later and answer the question as to why the word *ba ereb* is used in this verse. This verse holds some surprises, which makes God's word all the more exciting, as we dig deeper into it.

The purpose for pausing to examine this verse is to focus on the *"going down* (#935) *of the sun."* This phrase *"going down"* is easily misapplied, if you rely on English. "At even, at the going down of the sun" is used by some as a principle definition for *ba ereb*. When anyone focuses on the duration of time for the "going down" of the sun, their personal interpretations will become misleading.

How far back do we go in order to say this is the point where the sun begins to move downward? If we say that "going down" begins at the point the sun first touches the horizon, then what prevents us from moving this somewhat nebulous period all the way up to noon when the sundial shows it has begun its movement downward?

If we embrace the scriptures, which plainly interpret themselves, we will better understand this verse as well. There is another scripture that will help clarify what "going down" means. *"And it shall come to pass in that day, says the Lord God, that I will cause the sun to go down (#935) at noon, and I will darken the earth in the clear day"* (Amos 8:9). On this particular day, the sun obviously doesn't give the appearance of movement downward since it is an event to occur precisely at noon, but when God causes this event to happen (the sun to "go down"), the clear daylight becomes darkness at noontime. This example has nothing to do with a change in time from one day to the next since it does not concern the disappearance of the sun because it moved below the horizon. God causes the sun to disappear from sight at noon, thus giving the appearance of night over the earth. What is important in the use of this word, in the Hebrew, is not the "duration" of the thing, but the "result"!

The word "down" has been added to this definition in English Bibles and does not exist in the Hebrew. The word simply means "go" or "going." Therefore, in these instances, the sun does "go" from visible sight—it disappears from sight and thus darkness is the result. In Deuteronomy 16, the people were being instructed to "sacrifice the Passover" *at* the "going of the sun," *at* sun down *(ba ereb)*.

When we return to give further explanation of the verses in Deuteronomy 16, it will become clearer that "the going down of the sun," or more correctly "the going of the sun," can only be at the specific moment of *ba ereb*, precisely when the sun is down.

Between Two Evenings

We have finally come to the last word to be discussed. This word for evening is *"bane ha erebyim."* It literally means "between the two evenings" or "between the dual evenings." *"And you shall keep it up until the fourteenth day of the same month: and the whole assembly of the congregation of Israel shall kill it in the evening* (bane ha erebyim)" (Exodus 12:6).

Some of the main points of debate over the timing of Passover have come from this verse and the inability of people to agree on the two evenings to which it refers. Probably the most widely held interpretation within the Church of God has been that of one evening being at sundown and the second evening being when the twilight has gone and the dark of night has set in. This is vague because the point at which it becomes totally dark is somewhat hard to define. Of the various interpretations, the latter one has agreed more closely with Biblical instructions and timing for Passover events, which clearly were to occur only at night, but it is still incorrect.

The primary confusion over this whole matter began long ago when Judaism changed their observance of Passover from the evening of the 14th to the evening of the 15th. Controversy and conflict arose in the Church when brethren gravitated to the traditional Jewish and traditional Christian explanations for *bane ha erebyim* (between the two evenings). When any part of this interpretation is adopted, the killing of the Passover lamb is moved to the afternoon of the 14th while the eating of it is moved to the 15th. Some brethren have come to believe that it is permissible to observe the Passover late on the 14th, during the daylight hours before sundown.

Traditional Christianity seemingly chooses this period, since it coincides with the time of day Jesus Christ died. Jewish tradition holds that it was necessary to kill the Passover in the afternoon to allow enough time to complete the immense task of slaughtering the hundreds of animals required for everyone to keep the Passover. This is not true, as will be explained. Most Jewish teaching places the first of the two evenings at some time during the afternoon of the 14th. Some claim this is around 3 p.m., while others insist it can be no later than 1 p.m. These interpretations allow for killing the Passover lamb on the afternoon of the 14th and eating it on the night of the 15th.

Notice the interpretation of Exodus 12:6 by a renowned Jewish scholar in *The Pentateuch and Rashi's Commentary* on page 102. *"At dusk--From six hours (after noon) and upward is called ben ha arbayim, when the sun declines towards the place of its setting to be darkened. And the expression ben ha arbayim appears in my sight (to refer to) those hours between the 'evening' of day, and the 'evening' of night; the 'evening' of day is at the beginning of the seventh hour [1 p.m.] from (the time that) 'the shadows of evening are stretched out,' and the 'evening' of night is at the beginning of night"*.

This reminds me of a TV commercial that features a duck that is always on the scene trying to get people to say the name of the company that runs this commercial. One commercial is staged in a barber shop where the duck is pictured leaving as he shakes his head in total bewilderment, disgust and disbelief at what he just heard. It is a humorous commercial and captures well the astonishment sometimes experienced due to the twisted, distorted and totally unsound reasoning of others. It is with that same kind of astonishment that we shake our heads at the reasoning of this Jewish scholar. Some people, in an attempt to sound scholarly, make statements that are so outrageous that others assume they must be correct.

Jewish scholars have interpreted the first evening of "between the two evenings" (*bane ha erebyim*) as being 1 p.m. in the afternoon and refer to it as the "evening" of day. That is very creative reasoning. *Ereb* can never be a time when the sun is up.

So what are the two evenings of *bane ha erebyim?* From our investigation, there is only one answer. It is plain and simple. You are left with only one conclusion. Let's look at the words we have covered.

When God gives us a special day to observe, what period of time defines that day? We have already seen several scriptures making it clear how we define that time. Could the expression "between the two evenings" be any clearer?

Notice again the clear instruction regarding Atonement. *"It shall be unto you a Sabbath of rest, and you shall afflict your souls: in the ninth day of the month at even* (ba ereb), *from even* (ma ereb) *unto even* (awd ereb), *shall you celebrate your Sabbath"* (Leviticus 23:32). As we saw earlier, Atonement begins at the moment of sundown (ba ereb) on the 9th, which is the beginning of the 10th. "From" that moment of even (ma ereb), that begins the 10th, "unto" the even (awd ereb) that ends the 10th defines the timing of Atonement most succinctly. God makes it clear that Atonement is between two specific evenings—the one that comes at the end of the 9th day and the one that ends the 10th day—between the two evenings.

Why Bane Ha Erebyim?

"And you shall keep it up until the fourteenth day of the same month: and the whole assembly of the congregation of Israel shall kill it in the evening (bane ha erebyim)*"* (Exodus 12:6). Some will reject the clear definition of *bane ha erebyim* as the two evenings that start and end a day. They will claim that such a definition for Exodus 12:6 is too broad and therefore cannot possibly have such

a meaning. Is that a justifiable reason for rejecting God's instruction? Shouldn't we rather use God's clear definitions so we might come to better understand what God's will is?

Why would God use a term like "between the two evenings" as part of the instruction for killing the Passover? Other scriptures using this same term will begin to give us a clearer understanding. We shouldn't worry that a more specific term wasn't used in this verse. The context of the story clarifies that the killing of the Passover lamb had to take place right after sundown on the 14th because there were still many things that had to occur during that same night. We will look at the timing and story flow later.

Bane ha erebyim (between the two evenings) gives ample room within that day for additional events to be accomplished and fulfilled. This is made clearer by the instruction given for taking the second Passover, which God allowed for any who where unable to keep the first. *"And the Lord spoke unto Moses in the wilderness of Sinai, in the first month of the second year after they were come out of the land of Egypt, saying, Let the children of Israel also keep the Passover at its appointed season. In the fourteenth day of this month, at even* (bane ha erebyim), *you shall keep it in its appointed season: according to all the rites of it, and according to all the ceremonies thereof, shall you keep it. And Moses spoke unto the children of Israel, that they should keep the Passover. And they kept the Passover on the fourteenth day of the first month at even* (bane ha erebyim) *in the wilderness of Sinai: according to all that the Lord commanded Moses, so did the children of Israel"* (Numbers 9:1-5).

God gave additional instruction to Moses at this time, in the second year after coming out of Egypt. These verses indicate that the Passover observance involved much more than just killing the Passover lamb *between the two evenings* (bane ha erebyim). *Between the two evenings*, during the 14th, they were to *keep it* according to all the *rites and ceremonies*, according to *all* the Lord had commanded Moses. The verses following Exodus 12:6 show that killing the Passover lambs was only one part of God's instructions for that day.

"Speak unto the children of Israel, saying, If any man of you or of your posterity shall be unclean by reason of a dead body, or be in a journey afar off, yet he shall keep the Passover unto the Lord. The fourteenth day of the second month at even (bane ha erebyim) *they shall keep it, and eat it with unleavened bread and bitter herbs. They shall leave none of it unto the morning, nor break any bone of it: according to all the ordinances of the Passover they shall keep it"* (Numbers 9:10-12). This observance of a second Passover, established for those with valid reasons for missing the first Passover, says that "between the evenings" on the 14th they were to keep it according to all the ordinances of the Passover and eat the lamb with unleavened bread and bitter herbs. In addition, they were not to leave any of it until the morning. So these verses take us up to the morning hours of the 14th.

Is "between the two evenings" intended to cover only a part of the Passover of the 14th? We see that it includes more than just the killing of the lambs. It includes the eating of the Passover lamb, as well as rites and ceremonies. Another scripture makes it plain that "between the evenings" includes the whole of the 14th. *"In the fourteenth day of the first month at even* (between the two evenings) *is the Lord's Passover"* (Leviticus 23:5). God wasn't just giving instructions to observe the first couple of hours of Passover. He was showing that we are to keep the Passover on the 14th, for one complete day, lasting "from" one sundown "until" the next. Passover, like Atonement (Leviticus 23:32) or any Sabbath or Holy Day, is to be observed between two evenings, for one complete day.

The Actual Observance of Passover

There is little room for misunderstanding when Jesus Christ took the Passover. It was on the evening portion of the 14th day of the first month. The lamb was killed that night, and they ate this last supper together. As was the custom, the fire was already prepared. It wasn't as easy to cook in those days as it is today with modern conveniences. The lamb was killed and roasted over the fire. It took some time to cook the lamb before they could all sit down together to eat the entire meal.

After the meal, Jesus Christ instituted the symbols of the wine and bread, as Paul later relates in his instruction for the observance of the annual Passover (1 Corinthians 11). Later that night they went out to the Mount of Olives, where Jesus prayed on three separate occasions to the Father. He was preparing Himself for what was to follow in the remainder of that day that would lead up to His own death at mid-afternoon.

The time at which Jesus and His disciples kept the Passover was no different than it was for the rest of the Jewish people of that time. It was later that Judaism changed the observance of Passover so that it would begin in the late afternoon of the 14th. After this change they actually ate the Passover lamb in the early evening of the 15th.

The Roman world and Judaism hated this new and growing movement that sprang forth from the teachings of Jesus. Most of the leaders of Judaism were responsible for having Jesus Christ killed. Does it seem odd then that, once again, they would try to discredit Him? They would not have him fulfilling any of the meaning contained in the nighttime observance of Passover. They changed the observance to the 15th, and as a result, in time, they became more confused about the scriptures that were written in their own language. They became more confused about the truth of God.

In order to understand a very simple story, one that is fully misunderstood by Judaism today, we need to look at some very clear instructions regarding the observance of Passover. We will begin with the first observance recorded in the Old Testament.

"Speak you unto all the congregation of Israel, saying, In the tenth day of this month they shall take to them every man a lamb, according to the house of their fathers, a lamb for an house [Each household was to prepare for the Passover by picking out a lamb that would best suit what was needed to provide a meal for that individual household. And if the household was too small for a lamb, then they could invite others, perhaps single individuals or older couples who could not eat an entire lamb on their own.]*: And if the household be too little for the lamb, let him and his neighbor next unto his house take it according to the number of the souls; every man according to his eating shall make your count for the lamb. Your lamb shall be without blemish* [This pictured the latter fulfillment by Jesus Christ, the Passover for all mankind who would be without blemish, without sin.]*, a male of the first year: you shall take it out from* <u>*the sheep*</u>*, or from* <u>*the goats*</u> [It could be either a sheep or a goat.]*: And you shall keep it up until the fourteenth day of the same month: and the whole assembly of the congregation of Israel shall kill it in the evening* [They were to keep the lamb from the tenth day up to the fourteenth day, at which time they were to kill it after sunset, after the fourteenth had begun.]*. And they shall take of the blood, and strike it on the two side posts and on the upper door post of the houses, wherein they shall eat it. And they shall eat the flesh in that night* [In that same night, after killing the lamb and taking the blood to strike on the side posts of the door, they were to cook it and eat it.]*, roast with fire, and unleavened bread; and with bitter herbs they shall eat it. Eat not of it raw, nor sodden at all with water, but roast with fire; his head with his legs, and with the purtenance thereof. And ye shall let nothing of it remain until the morning; and that which remains of it until the morning you shall burn with fire"* (Exodus 12:3-10).

Then, when the actual time came for its observance, Moses repeated the instructions and added more.

"Then Moses called for all the elders of Israel, and said unto

them, Draw out and take you a lamb according to your families, and kill the Passover [It is important to note that these families were to kill the Passover lamb themselves, then cook it and eat it. The lamb was not a sacrifice from the people to be offered up to God. Only the Levites could do that at the temple area. Instead, this Passover is called the sacrifice of the Lord's Passover. It was God's sacrifice to mankind.]. *And you shall take a bunch of hyssop, and dip it in the blood that is in the basin, and strike the lintel and the two side posts with the blood that is in the basin; and none of you shall go out at the door of his house until the morning. For the LORD will pass through to smite the Egyptians; and when He sees the blood upon the lintel, and on the two side posts, the LORD will pass over the door* [This pictures a later fulfillment when the Passover would give His own life, and through His blood (His sacrifice to mankind) sin could be forgiven and the penalty for sin (death) could be passed over.], *and will not allow the destroyer to come in unto your houses to smite you. And you shall observe this thing for an ordinance to you and to your sons for ever* [The ordinance of the Passover service is forever!]. *And it shall come to pass, when you be come to the land which the LORD will give you, according as He hath promised, that you shall keep this service. And it shall come to pass, when your children shall say unto you, What do you mean by this service? That you shall say, It is the sacrifice of the LORD'S Passover, who passed over the houses of the children of Israel in Egypt, when He smote the Egyptians, and delivered our houses. And the people bowed the head and worshiped"* (Exodus 12:21-27).

After the children of Israel had been in the wilderness forty years, they finally came to the promised land where they continued their observance of the Passover, just as God had commanded. Their entrance into the promised land is at the time of Passover. As we read about this story in Joshua, it is important to remember to distinguish between the use for the past tense of *ba ereb* and the use for present and future tense.

"And the children of Israel encamped in Gilgal, and <u>kept the Passover</u> <u>on</u> <u>the fourteenth day</u> of the month <u>at even</u> in the plains of Jericho" (Joshua 5:10). They kept (past tense) the Passover <u>on</u> the fourteenth day of the month, but it also says they kept it "at even" (*ba ereb*). Although this is somewhat awkward in English, they indeed <u>kept</u> the Passover on the fourteenth day, which obviously began "at even" of the thirteenth, not "at even" of the fourteenth <u>that</u> <u>begins</u> <u>the</u> <u>fifteenth</u> <u>day</u>, for then it could not have been "kept" (past tense) <u>on</u> the fourteenth.

Again this is quite awkward in English, but the same thing could be applied to the Sabbath day, in past tense, and every person in Judaism would understand. If it were a matter of the Sabbath, it could just as well be said that "they kept the Sabbath on the seventh day of the week <u>at even</u> (*ba ereb*). With the clear instruction God gives concerning the seventh-day Sabbath, no one would read this believing they were being told to keep the Sabbath beginning <u>at</u> <u>even</u> (*ba ereb*) of the seventh day. *Ba ereb* of the seventh day would be "at" the exact moment that <u>ends</u> the seventh day. It would identify the beginning of a new day, the first day of the week. That would mean the Sabbath should be kept on the first day of the week. Instead, every person in Judaism would understand this to mean "they kept the Sabbath" on the seventh day which started "ba ereb" of the sixth day—"at" sunset on the <u>sixth</u> day. It would be clearly understood as being past tense.

Even <u>after</u> the captivity of Judah, when children of Judah returned and began rebuilding the temple by a decree from Cyrus, records show that after the temple was finished they kept the Passover, just as God had commanded. *"And the children of the captivity kept the Passover upon the fourteenth day of the first month"* (Ezra 6:19).

The exact timing of Passover is as clear as the timing of the seventh-day Sabbath. Judaism should clearly understand this verse in Ezra about the correct timing of Passover, especially in light of the fact that they returned to rebuild the temple after their captivity.

The Sacrifice of the Passover

Followers of Judaism have become confused about the correct way to observe Passover and Unleavened Bread because they have changed the real meaning of words like "ba ereb" and "ben ha erebyim," and therefore those who follow Judaism are confused about these observances as well.

Since people get confused when they read about these events in Deuteronomy, we will take a closer look at the scriptures describing them.

"Observe the month of Abib, and keep the Passover unto the LORD your God [A simple command is given to observe the Passover and the Passover is always on the fourteenth.]: *for in the month of Abib the LORD your God brought you forth out of Egypt by night* [Anyone keeping the Passover understands that the Feast of Unleavened Bread is part of the Passover season. The sacrifice of the Passover is what Deuteronomy is addressing here because the night being spoken of in this verse is not the same night as the Passover in Exodus 12. On that night, the Israelites were not allowed to leave their homes until morning. They gathered together during the daytime portion of the fourteenth, then they left Egypt by night on the fifteenth.]. *You shall therefore sacrifice the Passover unto the LORD your God* [Remember, the Passover itself was God's sacrifice to mankind. Each family was to kill a lamb and eat it. That lamb was not a sacrifice to be offered up to God.], *of the flock and the herd* [This verse alone should clearly indicate that this is not speaking of the Passover observance of the night of the fourteenth because on that night they were only allowed to eat a lamb or (young) goat from the flock (Exodus 12:5). This specific sacrifice speaks also of the "herd"—of cattle.], *in the place which the LORD shall choose to place His name there"* (Deu. 16:1-2).

This verse, clearly speaking of a "sacrifice unto God," has been confusing to some because it specifically says to "sacrifice the Passover unto the Lord." The obvious reasons for this will be covered as we go along. This sacrifice (sacrifice unto God) is not the Lord's sacrifice that was given to the people to consume on Passover night. The Passover night sacrifice was not to be offered up to God upon the altar.

The story continues. *"You shall eat no leavened bread with it; seven days shall you eat unleavened bread therewith* [Clearly, this is speaking of the seven-day period of the Feast of Unleavened Bread—the first night of the Feast of Unleavened Bread—the night of the fifteenth.]*, even the bread of affliction; for you came forth out of the land of Egypt in haste: that you may remember the day when you came forth out of the land of Egypt all the days of your life. And there shall be no leavened bread seen with you in all your coast seven days; neither shall there any thing of the flesh, which you sacrificed the first day at even* [ba ereb, at sundown]*, remain all night until the morning"* (Deuteronomy 16:3-4).

This verse clearly states that these sacrifices, of the flock and of the herd, were just that—they were sacrifices to be offered up before God upon the altar on the first day of Unleavened Bread, just as it says, <u>at even</u>. Again, this is past tense. They offered up these sacrifices, as it says on the first day ("which you sacrificed the first day"), but they could not begin until sundown—after the 14th.

"You may not sacrifice the Passover within any of thy gates [This means it could not be sacrificed in any community where they lived—not at their homes.]*, which the LORD your God giveth thee: But at the place which the LORD your God shall choose to place His name in* [The temple site was where sacrifices were offered. They were never offered up by just anyone in Israel, but only by the Levitical priests.]*, there you shalt sacrifice the Passover at even* (ba ereb)*, at the going down* (Hebrew—"going"—after it is "gone" on the horizon—no longer visible) *of the sun, at the season that you*

came forth out of Egypt" (Deuteronomy 16:5-6). Even here, it clarifies the use of "ba ereb" when used in the past tense. Verse 4 says that nothing would remain of the flesh by morning of all that they had sacrificed (past tense) on the first day—"at even" (*ba ereb*). Since it is speaking of the first day, which is the fifteenth day of the first month, no one in Judaism would believe this was instructing them to begin offering the sacrifices on the first day—the fifteenth—"at even" (*ba ereb*). If that were the case, it would mean that the first day had ended and this would have to occur on the second day of the feast which is *ba ereb* of the first day—beginning the second. Even in this, Judaistic scholars have contradicted themselves in their own definitions because they all believe that this was occurring on the night of the fifteenth. So verse 6 clearly defines the use of the same word, when used in past tense in verse 4.

Those in Judaism and too many of those who were scattered in the Church of God confuse the observance of the Passover with the observance of the first day of the Feast of Unleavened Bread.

The Passover of the fourteenth began immediately at sundown (ending the thirteenth). Families killed the lambs, roasted them and ate them on that same night. They did this "within their gates"—at their own homes. The lamb they killed is described in scripture as the Lord's sacrifice for the children of Israel to eat.

The sacrifices of the first day of the Feast of Unleavened Bread were never to be eaten "within the gates" of their own homes. They were to be eaten "in the place that God chose to place His name," which was the area of the temple. This means that the Israelites went to the temple area, in the late daytime period of Passover day, to prepare animals for sacrifice upon the altar after sunset, at the beginning of the fifteenth day—the first day of the Feast. They were preparing sacrifices that were to be offered up to God. They could eat some of these sacrifices, but it had to be done at that location—not at their homes.

The preparation of these sacrifices to God began on the afternoon of the fourteenth, but the actual sacrifice upon the altar could not begin until after sunset on the fourteenth. Also, any feasting on these sacrifices was to be done after the fourteenth. That is why these are referred to as the Passover sacrifices. The preparation began on the Passover day, but the religious part of the ceremony and the feasting did not begin until after sunset—at the beginning of the fifteenth.

It really is simple. The distinction should be clear. The Lord's sacrifice of the Passover was given to the children of Israel to eat, but the Passover sacrifices of the herd and the flock were sacrifices the children of Israel offered up to God.

The Passover of King Josiah

This is the story of one of the greatest Passover seasons ever observed in all Israel. Two verses need to be thoroughly understood before we begin; the reason being that some people (primarily from Judaism) will have difficulty with this story because of past teachings. It is often incredibly difficult to unlearn error. The first verse and the seventeenth verse need to be remembered because they are specific and they reveal the truth of this matter.

"Moreover Josiah kept a Passover unto the LORD in Jerusalem: and they killed the Passover on the fourteenth day of the first month" (2 Chronicles 35:1). It records here that they kept the Passover, exactly as God commanded, on the fourteenth day of the first month. That is when they "killed the Passover" lambs and ate them. But this "killing of the Passover" is also dual, as we will see.

"And the children of Israel that were present kept the Passover at that time, and the Feast of Unleavened Bread seven days" (2 Chronicles 35:17). This too must be kept in mind throughout this story because it shows they understood and obeyed God. They kept the Passover at the appropriate time along with the seven days of the Feast of Unleavened Bread. Now let's read the story.

"Moreover Josiah kept a Passover unto the LORD in Jerusalem: and they <u>killed the Passover</u> on the fourteenth day of the first month [As this story shows, killing was done on the night of the fourteenth as well as on the afternoon of the fourteenth.]. *And he set the priests in their charges, and encouraged them to the service of the house of the LORD, And said unto the Levites who taught all Israel, who were holy unto the LORD, Put the holy ark in the house which Solomon the son of David king of Israel did build; it shall not be a burden upon your shoulders: serve now the LORD your God, and His people Israel, And prepare yourselves by the houses of your fathers, after your courses, according to the writing of David king of Israel, and according to the writing of Solomon his son. And stand in the holy place according to the divisions of the families of the fathers of your brethren the people, and after the division of the families of the Levites"* (2 Chronicles 35:1-5).

The Levitical priesthood was being told by Josiah that they were to be sanctified and prepared to do the work that was before them. They had a great task to accomplish in serving the people at the temple. This included all the preparation that had to be done on the afternoon of the fourteenth along with the actual offering up of sacrifices that were to take place on the annual Holy Day of the Feast of Unleavened Bread. Josiah told them to prepare themselves to serve as the priesthood, just as they were instructed to do in the writings of King David and Solomon, his son.

"So kill the Passover, and sanctify yourselves, and prepare your brethren, that they may do according to the word of the LORD by the hand of Moses" (2 Chronicles 35:6). Again, Josiah told them to kill the Passover. This was a specific instruction regarding the preparation of the work they would be doing in the role of Levites. Josiah went on to tell them to sanctify themselves and prepare their brethren, who were the Levites, to follow God's instruction for carrying out the work of the preparation of sacrifices and the actual work of offering up the sacrifices that would follow. There was

incredible work ahead for them.

"And Josiah gave to the people, of the flock, lambs and kids, all for <u>the Passover offerings</u>, for all that were present, to the number of thirty thousand, and three thousand bullocks: these were of the king's substance. And his princes gave willingly unto the people, to the priests, and to the Levites: Hilkiah and Zechariah and Jehiel, rulers of the house of God, gave unto the priests for <u>the Passover offerings</u> two thousand and six hundred small cattle, and three hundred oxen. Conaniah also, and Shemaiah and Nethaneel, his brethren, and Hashabiah and Jeiel and Jozabad, chief of the Levites, gave unto the Levites <u>for Passover offerings</u> five thousand small cattle, and five hundred oxen" (2 Chronicles 35:7-9).

How could it be any clearer? This was not about the Passover observance—the killing of the Passover and the eating of it within their homes. That was observed on the night of the fourteenth. This was about the offerings and sacrifices that would be offered up to God after sunset on the fourteenth, at the beginning of the Feast, on the night of the fifteenth.

"So the service was prepared, and the priests stood in their place, and the Levites in their courses, according to the king's commandment. And they killed the Passover, and the priests sprinkled the blood from their hands, and the Levites flayed them" (2 Chronicles 35:10-11).

So the Levites did as Josiah said. They prepared themselves and the area where their work was to be accomplished with all the instruments, tools, containers, and everything necessary for the task at hand. Then they began to kill the animals that were to be offered. They did this in the afternoon of the Passover day. They also began to cut the meat in preparation for the offerings to be offered upon the altar, along with that which would be eaten by the children of Israel on the feast day. Notice that the Levites flayed the meat—more proof that this was not the Passover observance because that meat was to be roasted whole, not cut up and put in